GROUPS UNDER STRESS

THE CENTURY PSYCHOLOGY SERIES

RICHARD M. ELLIOTT, GARDNER LINDZEY,

AND KENNETH MACCORQUODALE

EDITORS

GROUPS UNDER STRESS:

PSYCHOLOGICAL RESEARCH in SEALAB II

ROLAND RADLOFF
NAVAL MEDICAL RESEARCH INSTITUTE

ROBERT HELMREICH
THE UNIVERSITY OF TEXAS AT AUSTIN

New York
APPLETON-CENTURY-CROFTS
DIVISION OF MEREDITH CORPORATION

648-1

Library of Congress Card Number: 68-19962

PRINTED IN THE UNITED STATES OF AMERICA

E 72600

PREFACE

Our purpose in preparing this volume was two-fold. The obvious goal was to report the results of a comprehensive study of individual and group reactions to extreme physical and psychological stress. We have some confidence that the findings and analyses can add to the understanding of human behavior under stress. In addition, we hope that our experiences will assist psychologists in conducting research in other "real-life" settings. We recognize that in a discipline which produces a million pages of reports each year, no one study is likely to have much impact. However, within psychology a marked trend towards naturalistic research seems evident. If this trend continues, it is possible that the exposition of a methodological and conceptual orientation, which is the second purpose of this report, may assume the greater importance. To those of our colleagues who choose to pursue this line of investigation, we hope to offer some useful techniques and concepts. As encouragement and forewarning to those embarking on such a course, we can say with conviction that you may find, as we have, that a study of this type can be both a most rewarding and a most frustrating experience.

In a large field study, one is indebted to many people for assistance. We can thank only a few of the many by name but wish to express our gratitude to everyone connected with the SEALAB II project.

Our deepest gratitude must go to the SEALAB Aquanauts who made the study possible. Special thanks are due the two team leaders, Commander M. Scott Carpenter, USN (Teams I and II) and Master Chief Torpedoman Robert Sheats, USN. The other aquanauts were: Chief Quartermaster Robert Barth, USN; Chief Steelworker Howard L. Buckner, USN; William J. Bunton; Berry L. Cannon; Thomas A. Clarke; Torpedoman First Class Billie L. Coffman, USN; Chief Gunner's Mate Charles M. Coggeshall, USN; Torpedoman First Class Kenneth J. Conda, USN; George B. Dowling; Gunner's Mate First Class Wilbur H. Eaton, USN; Arthur O. Flechsig; Richard W. Grigg; Chief Hospital Corpsman Glen L. Iley, USN; Wallace T. Jenkins; Senior Chief Engineman Frederick J. Johler, USN; Engineman First Class John J. Lyons, USN; Boatswain's Mate First Class William D. Meeks, USN; Chief Shipfitter Lavern R. Meisky, USN; Earle A. Murray; Photographer's Mate First Class John F. Reaves, USN; Chief Photographer Jay D. Skidmore, USN; Lieutenant Robert E. Sonnenburg, MC, USN; William H. Tolbert; John M. Wells; Chief Mineman Paul A. Wells, USN.

Sincere thanks are extended to Captain George F. Bond, MC, USN (Principal Investigator and Captain Walter F. Mazzone, MSC, USN. We are particularly grateful to Captain Lewis B. Melson, USN (Project Director), Captain Ray Spencer, USN (Alternate Project Director), Mr. Henry A. O'Neal (Project Manager) and Mr. Denzil Pauli (Assistant Project Manager). We appreciate the assistance of Lieutenants Gean P. Clapper, James Bladh and Wesley Larsen, USN and Senior Chief Journalist Ronald Sweig, USN.

We are deeply indebted to Dr. James Miller (Director of the Human Performance Program), whose assistance and collaboration in all phases of the research were invaluable. Thanks are also due Dr. Hugh Bowen, Mr. Birger Anderson and Mr. Michael Greenwood.

The keystone of the research effort was the round-the-clock monitoring of underwater activity. This work was performed flawlessly by the following students: Alex Araiza, Philip Cernius, Jack Gliddon, Donald Jones, Robert Litchfield, Harry Marriner, Michael Martin, Spencer McWilliams, Richard Roper, E. Dale Trower, John H. Wineman and Robert Wozniak.

Activities in San Diego were greatly assisted by Dr. E. K. Eric Gunderson, Dr. LaVerne Johnson and the Service Schools Command of the U. S. Naval Training Center, San Diego.

We are indebted to Mr. Luigi Petrullo of the Office of Naval Research and Dr. William W. Haythorn of the Naval Medical Research Institute.

The participation of the junior author in the project was made possible through funds provided by the Office of Naval Research in Grants Nonr (G) 00012-66 and Nonr (G) 00030-66 to Barry E. Collins and Contract N00014-67-A-0126-0001, Robert L. Helmreich, Principal Investigator.

Portions of this report were submitted by Robert L. Helmreich in partial fulfillment of the requirements for the degree of Doctor of Philosophy at Yale University. The guidance and advice of the dissertation committee, Dr. Barry E. Collins, Chairman, Dr. Irving L. Janis and Dr. Fred D. Sheffield are gratefully acknowledged.

Special thanks for assistance in computer programming and analysis are extended to Mr. Roger Bakeman of the Yale Computer Center.

We appreciate assistance in coding data, preparing tables, manuscript editing and bibliography preparation by Mrs. Leona Bard, James Dehoney, Douglas Duryea, Miss Kathleen McCue and Mrs. Elizabeth Peñaranda.

The preparation of the manuscript in its various revisions was performed by Mrs. Patricia Serling, Mrs. Jere Yeomans and Mrs. Frances Ziller, and to them we are very grateful.

We wish to thank John Wiley & Sons, Inc. for permission to reprint excerpts from *The Social Psychology of Groups* by John W. Thibaut and Harold H. Kelley.

We also wish to thank the Associated Press for permission to quote from an article by Saul Pett and Jules Loh.

R. W. R.
R. L. H.

FOREWORD

This book is a major contribution to the emerging methodology for conducting research in the real world. Laboratory experiments, often designed more for control and convenience, simulations, which seldom accommodate all relevant variables and their interactions, and models, developed to reduce the effort to formulae or computer operations, can make important but nevertheless limited contributions to hypothesis formulation and testing of real world problems. Although these methods are easier to execute and more readily available, there has been an unfortunate stress upon such methods of research *about* the real world, while often neglecting research *in* the real world.

The authors have tested their skills and the available tools of psychological research in the real world environment, represented here by the hostile elements of the ocean floor. They have shown an ability to adapt a concept to measurable aspects of the situation. They have learned that "it is probably the case in most field settings that good criteria exist, naturally embedded in the program." They demonstrate the wisdom of using such criteria rather than interjecting an artifact or contriving a measurable situation.

Of special interest and value to those who will follow as this nation moves on into oceanography are the frank statements of error in preconceived ideas, instruments and situations selected *a priori* for study. In too many other such ventures, later documentation presents a false picture of smooth operation and omniscience. Science advances as much on information from false starts as from correct, fortuitous ones. Operational studies represent the give and take, and the rephrasing of questions on the spot which add more to the challenge of one's basic understanding, insights and incentive.

This is a notable guide for others inclined to do research in the real world.

Dr. Richard Trumbull
Research Director
Office of Naval Research

CONTENTS

GROUPS UNDER STRESS

CHAPTER 1

The Hole in the Ocean

Astronaut M. Scott Carpenter told newsmen after spending 30 days underwater in SEALAB II that "the ocean is a much more hostile environment than space." [1] This summary of Aquanaut Carpenter's reactions was confirmed and extended by comments of his fellow divers:

> "You know that the Pacific Ocean is a mighty big place and you got a 36 inch hole that's home. There ain't no place you can go but there. 'Cause you know you're gonna die if you go up."
>
> "I looked at the depth gauge and it was 250 feet so I knew we were going to make it."
>
> "It's hard work, it takes a long time to do simple tasks in the water. It takes a good hour to replace a (light) bulb."
>
> "I had a real good time. I enjoyed every bit of it."
>
> "You accept the fact that part of the day is going to be spent being miserable" (miserably cold).
>
> "Looking out the port holes is fantastic—great. It made you feel like you were in the sea."

[1] *Washington Post,* September 29, 1965.

"It's quite a feeling when you come up and you say 'Well nobody's been down that deep before, for that long'."

Men and groups under stress in an overwhelmingly hostile environment, reacting with realistic fear and laboring ceaselessly to realize the exhilaration of unique accomplishments, these are the reactions summarized by the aquanauts of Project SEALAB II on their return to the surface. Their behavior and its assessment during their two week sojourn 205 feet under the ocean's surface is the subject of this book.

BACKGROUND OF THE PROJECT

SEALAB II was a research and development project sponsored jointly by the Office of Naval Research and the Special Projects Office of the U.S. Navy. Its purpose was to open up the millions of square miles of submerged territory comprising the continental shelves by showing that man can live in this environment and perform useful work for extended periods without returning to the surface. Success in SEALAB would prove a major step in making this vast space available to man.

Three ten-man teams were composed of civilian and military divers, scientists and salvage specialists. The men themselves were as varied as their occupational backgrounds, ranging in age from 24 to 50, and in educational achievement from less than ninth grade to graduate degrees. The variety and number of underwater projects to be undertaken by the aquanauts was extremely ambitious. During their stay on the bottom they worked on such tasks as salvaging of a sunken jet airplane, conducting censuses of marine life, studying current, water temperature and visibility, experimenting with underwater acoustics, evaluating the effectiveness of a trained porpoise and testing a wide range of experimental equipment. In addition, the aquanauts served as subjects for both physiological and psychological research. Of primary importance, however, was simply to determine how well a man could work under water while living there.

The importance of the SEALAB project lies in man's physiological response to diving. When a diver descends breathing compressed gas, some of these gases dissolve in his blood stream. If the diver returns suddenly to the surface, the gases coming out of solution may form bubbles in joints and in the bloodstream. This formation of gas embolisms (or the "bends" in diving jargon) may result in paralysis or death. To permit dissolved gases to leave the bloodstream without forming bubbles, the diver must decompress slowly on his way to the surface. The time required to decompress increases with both depth and duration of stay underwater as more gases dissolve at greater depth (because of higher pressure) and dissolution of gases increases over time. For example, a diver spending 15 minutes at 190 feet must decompress for 17.8 minutes while the same diver spending an hour at that depth must undergo almost four hours of decompression. The limitations imposed by this requirement on underwater work are readily apparent. A diver working for any appreciable period of time at depths over 100 feet must spend long periods of time in decompression. As a result the useful work which a man can perform diving from the surface is severely limited.

Recent research on diving, however, has disclosed that during prolonged exposure to pressure at a fixed depth, a diver's tissues become completely saturated with breathing gases (Naval Research Reviews, 1965). Consequently, after saturation occurs, the required decompression time remains fixed regardless of the length of the dive. Thus, if divers can be maintained in an undersea habitat in which the internal pressure is equal to the ambient pressure of the water, they can have free access to the sea for an unlimited time with only one decompression required on final return to the surface. This capability drastically improves the ratio of working time to decompression time and makes it possible to attempt lengthy projects at considerable depth. SEALAB II sought to test these ideas by placing teams of divers underwater in a habitat pressurized to the outside pressure of sea water at 205 feet (104 pounds per square inch) from which aquanauts could have free access to the surrounding sea, decompressing only after their two week stay was complete.

Another problem which has vexed deep divers is the toxic effect of various gases under high pressure. Nitrogen, the most common gas in earth's atmosphere, is a narcotic under high pressure, causing intoxication and deterioration of mental function ("rapture of the deep"). Oxygen, too, in high concentrations may cause anemia and pulmonary edema. Therefore, most deep diving is conducted using a breathing mixture composed primarily of helium as the inert gas, with a reduced percentage of oxygen (O'Neal, Bond, Lanphear & Odum, 1965).

Several earlier projects had pioneered the concept of living and working underwater. Open water tests were preceded by several years of intensive laboratory experimentation with animals and men systematically subjected to high pressure breathing a variety of exotic gases (Bond, 1964). Then, in 1962, Capt. Jacques Yves Cousteau placed two men 33 feet underwater for a week, and in 1963 he put five men 36 feet down for a month (Cousteau, 1964). In 1964, under the direction of Capt. George F. Bond, USN, the Navy conducted Project SEALAB I in which four men lived at 193 feet for eleven days. In the same year, Edwin Link placed two men at 400 feet for 48 hours. These early experiments in underwater living were conducted under nearly ideal environmental conditions—typically in warm, clear water, providing an optimal setting for underwater work. SEALAB II, however, was deliberately placed in murky, cold water as a more rigorous test of the operational feasibility of the concept. The chosen site provided a much closer approximation of environmental conditions prevailing over the majority of the continental shelf. SEALAB II was also the first attempt to place a comparatively large group at over 200 feet for an extended period with a variety of realistic tasks to perform.

The SEALAB II habitat which was placed 205 feet beneath the surface of the Pacific Ocean was a 12′ × 57′ steel cylinder divided into a working and recreation area, a galley, and a bunk area with sleeping facilities for ten men as shown in Figure 1-1. The habitat was equipped with 11 viewing ports looking into the water. Access to the sea was through a 36″ hatch in the deck of the capsule. As the internal pressure was maintained equal to the pressure of the water outside, the hatch remained continuously open to the sea.

Electricity, breathing gases and communications were provided from the surface through an umbilical cable attached to a support vessel moored directly over the habitat. A second connection giving alternate support led from the capsule to shore based facilities. Supplies were exchanged between the surface and the habitat in pressurized containers lowered by a trolley system. The arrangement of support facilities is shown in the photograph. (See photographic insert.)

The capsule was placed one mile offshore near the Scripps Institution of Oceanography, La Jolla, California. The ambient pressure, at which the habitat was maintained, varied between 98 and 104 pounds per square inch (approximately 7 atmospheres) dependent upon the state of the tide.

Water temperature at the 200 foot depth of SEALAB ranged from 46° to 50° F. The average visibility on the bottom was 10 to 20 feet.

The breathing gas mixture with which the capsule was pressurized consisted of approximately 78% helium, 18% nitrogen and 4% oxygen.

LIVING AND WORKING IN SEALAB

Perhaps the closest parallels to life in SEALAB would be the experiences of astronauts in orbit above the earth and of men wintering over at the South Pole. In both cases, communications with the rest of the world are possible, but physical return to the normal environment is impossible except under very special circumstances out of the direct control of the individual. SEALAB aquanauts could live and work in their underwater home, but return to the

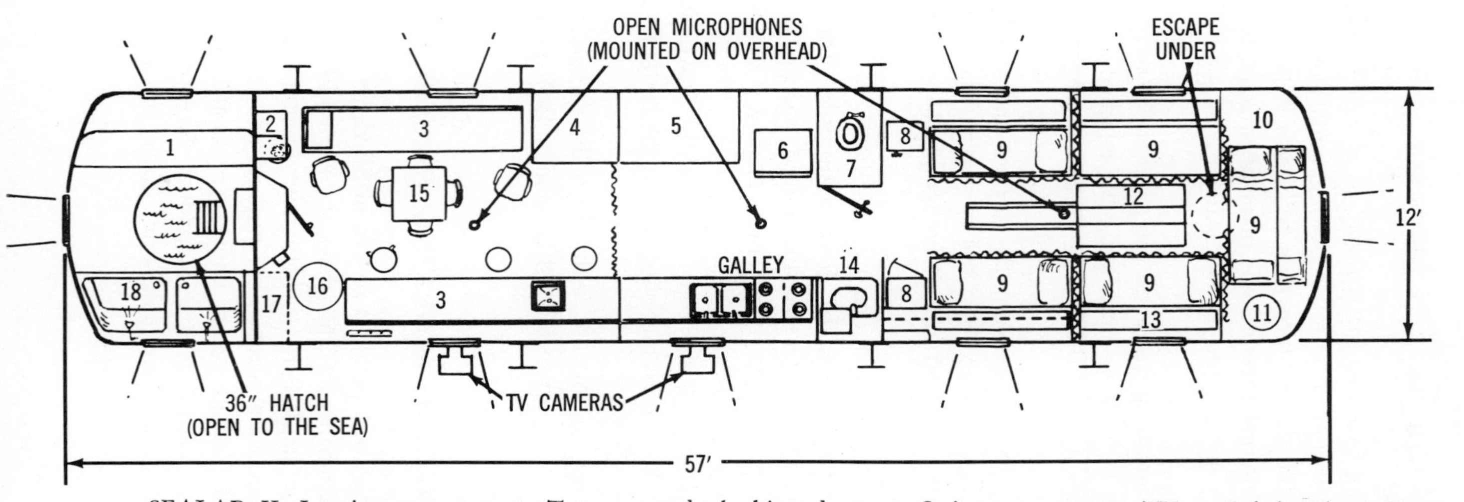

SEALAB II. Interior arrangement; Top removed—looking down. 1. Swim gear stow. 2. TV. 3. Lab bench. 4. Fan room. 5. Electric power and light. 6. Reefer. 7. Head. 8. Locker. 9. 2-Berths. 10. Stow. 11. CO_2 can. 12. Table. 13. Bench. 14. Lav. 15. Table and chairs. 16. Water heater. 17. Can stow'g. 18. Tub and shower.

surface required a trip in a portable decompression chamber operated from the surface.

Life on the bottom acquired a certain regularity with the rotation of assigned tasks. Men stood watches around the clock, ensuring that equipment and communications were in order. Watch standers were also responsible for the preparation of meals and cleanup. Diving was scheduled both for individual projects and for the transfer of equipment to and from the surface.

When not diving, a number of tasks occupied the aquanauts inside the capsule. The preparation of diving equipment was a lengthy and painstaking task—it might take up to an hour to prepare for a dive, adjusting and putting on SCUBA tanks, donning wetsuits and planning activities in the water. Numerous reports and forms had to be filled out and queries from the surface answered.

Simply existing inside the SEALAB capsule was a difficult undertaking. There was a constant danger that an object lowered from the surface might smash one of the glass ports or that a rupture of the thin-walled cylinder might occur, subjecting the aquanauts to instant drowning.

Aside from physical danger, living and working conditions inside the capsule were frustrating, uncomfortable and stressful. Life for ten men and their equipment inside a 12′ × 57′ cylinder was crowded in the extreme. There was little privacy and scant space to stow personal effects. In addition, the habitat sat unevenly on the bottom with a tilt of six degrees in two directions. As a result, drawers slid open or shut and objects toppled off counters and tables. Moving about in the capsule required walking up or down hill while leaning sideways.

The helium in the breathing mixture seriously disrupted verbal communications, as the lightness of the atmosphere gave voices a "Donald Duck" quality and made comprehension very difficult. The atmosphere also made smoking an impossibility.

A diving hatch constantly open to the water resulted in uncomfortably high humidity. Adding to this discomfort were the interactive effects of rapid heat transfer characteristic of helium atmospheres. Largely as a result of the high temperature and humidity, most aquanauts suffered from ear infections and skin rashes.

The dominating factor of life in SEALAB was, of course, the ocean outside. The sea at 200 feet is an unforgiving adversary. One of the greatest preoccupations of the aquanauts venturing out of the capsule was the knowledge that they could not escape to the surface in the event of an emergency because they were saturated with gas under 100 pounds pressure. To do so would mean certain, rapid and painful death from an explosive embolism. Many divers spoke of these dangers in interviews after returning to the surface. Perhaps their comments convey best this aspect of life at 205′.

> "There is that apprehension there and in the back of your mind you know that you've got to be careful. You know you get a chance to make *one* mistake out there and that's it. You're at 100 feet and you run out of air or something like this, and boy, you run into real trouble, you can dump your gear and head for the surface. And this is what a diver normally tends to do. The first thing you get into trouble where you need, you know you got to breathe, you dump your gear, your weights and you head for the surface 'cause you know there's air out there. But down here we couldn't head for the surface . . ."

Another aquanaut spoke of the over-all effect of diving and his reactions to the situation:

> "I think it's a function of stress—I did things in the water that didn't reflect good judgment, good forethought. It takes a long time to do things in the water and I don't know why. You don't move as fast, first of all. You get tired sooner—you get cold sooner. You can't see as well. You've got gloves that interfere with your manual dexterity. Things float away—lines get in your way—you get your gear fouled in equipment and you worry about stepping on the fish (scorpion fish)."

Scorpion fish were a real source of danger to the aquanauts. These fish lived on the bottom around the capsule in huge numbers.

Reaching a length of 18 inches, they had needle sharp, poisonous spines on their backs which could penetrate a wetsuit and cause a painful and incapacitating sting.

> "I don't like the idea of going out there and getting zapped. I was always in fear of touching the bottom. Then you could see those fish out there—like stones—like a cobblestone street. Wasn't a space of more than 4 or 5 inches from one fish to another."

There were also dangers inherent in the life-sustaining diving equipment. Divers were justifiably sceptical about it:

> "I don't feel confident about any piece of equipment that delicate. So I have a great respect for the Mark VI (the diving rig) and I am scared of it which is the thing to be."

This attitude is supported dramatically in the following account:

> "I took a lung full of air and I just didn't have any. I grabbed onto the hose and I looked toward the surface and I tried again to breathe and there just wasn't a drop of air coming out there. Well, I could see the hose floating up and I could see it was kinked but there was no way in the world I could unkink it so all I did was I rolled over, pointed my head down and straightened my legs out and I really headed for the entryway. I remembered thinking while going back 'I hope that hose don't hang up' because if that hose hung up on something I'd of never, never made it back. Well I, I laid down in my bunk that night and I thought about this. Just say I got four feet from that shark cage and it did get fouled, what would I do? I think I was pretty close to a panic stage 'cause I was hard in prayer when I did hit the entryway."

On one occasion an aquanaut's breathing bag became overinflated and started to carry him to the surface. Another diver noticed his difficulty and went to his assistance. The rescued diver reports his reactions after his close call:

> "I didn't lose confidence in the Mark VI—I lost confidence in myself. I gave serious thought to this. I just took a shower and I think

I hit the sack and got out of the way—just thought the situation over for awhile. I thought the best thing for me to do is not to try to dive any more that day—it was getting late in the day anyway—and think this thing over and try to do it again tomorrow. Talk it over with (another diver)—what he saw the problem as, etc., which we did and I was quite apprehensive about the next dive. I was quite relieved when everything went well and that dive was over."

Another diver inhaled some carbon dioxide absorbent from his diving rig:

"I had been out I guess about one half hour—we were placing some more lights. I got a lung full of something—started to cough. I did everything to cough my mouthpiece out. I had to swim back to the shark cage and came in which is a good thing I did because by the time I did I was coughing up blood with it. I was spitting—someone said 'you're spitting blood.' I said 'it can't be.' When I looked at it it was a pinkish color. It took me quite awhile to realize that I was coughing up blood. It took me a good 10 hours to stop coughing."

Visibility in the water ranged from zero to about thirty feet at best. This made the danger of becoming lost a constant and real preoccupation. One diver reports his experience of being lost:

"This was the most exciting moment, I think. When we had been following a line out and got well out of sight of the SEALAB and the line was buried . . . We were surrounded by scorpion fish . . . (We) turned around and the lights were gone and there was all of this turbidity that we had stirred up. . . . So I sank to the bottom and began feeling around for this line and couldn't find it. Eventually (we) ran into the visibility range and there was a line that we followed."

The water at 200 feet was cold as well as murky. Unlike the 72 degrees of the surface water inhabited by swimmers and surfers, the temperature around SEALAB ranged from 46° to 50° F. Coldness restricted diving performance. As one aquanaut put it:

> "The cold creeped up on you very fast. I won't say it got unbearable—it wouldn't be to the point that if any emergency arose you couldn't have stayed there. Now if somebody said 'O.K. this is important, can you stay 5 more minutes' you could have did it. But you had that feeling of wanting to get back in there. . . . I got the shakes mostly when I came into the laboratory."

Balanced against, and probably dependent upon, the risks and efforts were the rewards gained from achievement:

> "That (300 feet dive) was my highlight—personal highlight—it was a test of guts, there's no doubt about it. Damn right. It was total darkness—it couldn't have got any darker. It was a nice thing to know that I *did* have the intestinal fortitude to go out there and do it."

This, then, was the setting for a psychological study of men under stress—a novel and hostile environment where physical danger was ever-present and where even the everyday routine of living was marked by difficulty and discomfort.

The situation has obvious glamour and attraction for the usually sedentary psychologist as well as for the adventurer. But the question remains, why leave the order and precision of the laboratory for a setting which is obviously more diffuse and difficult to comprehend in its totality? In the next chapter we discuss some of the advantages and disadvantages of field and laboratory research and explain our motives for undertaking the research.

CHAPTER 2

Problems in Defining and Investigating Psychological Stress

The nature of man's reactions to extreme conditions of psychological stress has long been a major concern of psychology. The importance of the research area stems from the need to understand human behavior in such critical and recurring situations as war, natural disaster, and hazardous vocations and avocations. Such situations are defined as stressful because the individual's physical well-being and safety are threatened by environmental contingencies. This implicit definition can be extended to classify as stressful all conditions where threat of physical danger exists and is perceived, and a high degree of emotional tension is involved. Despite general agreement on this common sense definition of psychological stress, little consensus exists among social scientists concerning the formal properties of stress. In this chapter we consider the present status of the concept.

One frequently employed formulation is based on Selye's (1950) *General Adaptation Syndrome* and deals with stimuli (internal or external) which disrupt homeostasis. Menninger (1954) has used a similar construct to define psychological stress. Withey

(1956) points out that calling psychological stress an analogue of Selye's physiological construct is inappropriate because of the psychologist's inability to specify a psychological equivalent of physiological homeostasis and to deal with complications introduced by higher mental processes. Recently, greater emphasis has been placed on defining *situations* which are stressful.

Basowitz, Persky, Korchin, & Grinker (1955) advocate using the term "stress situation" to refer to stimulus conditions which are assumed to arouse an affective response of anxiety in an individual. Such a definition, however, unduly limits the area of investigation. The same stimulus situation may arouse anger directed towards others, anger directed towards the self or anxiety in persons of differing personality constellations (Funkenstein, 1957).

Janis and Leventhal (in press) propose a more general definition. According to these authors ". . . any change in the environment which typically—i.e., in the average person—induces a high degree of emotional tension and interferes with normal patterns of response" is a stressful event. In a similar definition, Scott (1949) describes the stress situation as "one in which adjustment is difficult or impossible but in which motivation is very strong."

Slotkin (1952) points out two factors, one or both of which are common to all stressful situations: (*a*) frustration, in which the external situation prevents achieving the goal toward which an ongoing activity is directed; and/or (*b*) trauma (real or anticipated) in which the situation provides stimuli which are intense enough to disrupt the performance of ongoing activities.

Holtzman and Bitterman (1956), in their review of laboratory studies of stress, have classified stressful stimuli into six classes, all of which contain one or both of Slotkin's factors. The categories are: (*a*) disruption of physiological homeostasis; (*b*) unpleasant or physically painful stimuli; (*c*) distractions, criticisms and time pressures; (*d*) real, contrived or anticipated failure; (*e*) social conflict and related procedures; and (*f*) situations threatening the individual's safety (anticipated danger).

Lazarus (1966) has made a major contribution to the field

of stress research in attempting to unify the variables and concepts subsumed under the term "stress". He considers "stress" a generic term for a whole area of problems, including stimuli which produce stress reactions, the responses to stress and the processes which intervene between stress stimuli and responses. As Lazarus points out, the stimulus situations which can elicit stress reactions are extremely varied and numerous, but responses to stress can be observed in four major classes: (1) reports of disturbed affect, (2) motor-behavioral reactions, (3) changes in the adequacy of cognitive functioning and (4) physiological changes.

Lazarus presents the concept of threat as the major intervening variable in the analysis of psychological stress. Threat is anticipatory since it involves the expectation of future harm and is dependent upon cognitions. Perception, learning, memory, judgment and thought all play roles in the cognition of threat.

The reactions to stress, as determined by the cognitions of the individual, depend to a great extent upon the particular personality involved. As Lazarus puts it, *"The important role of personality factors in producing stress reactions requires that we define stress in terms of transactions between individuals and situations, rather than of either one in isolation."*

Investigations of human reactions to stress have been of two general types, both beset with severe methodological deficiencies. The first approach consists of field studies of naturally occurring stressful events. This type of study customarily employs clinical observations during the period of threat and/or interviews of participants outside the stressful environment. An extensive literature of such research exists (cf. Bettelheim, 1943; Glass, 1953; Glover, 1942; Grinker & Spiegel, 1945; Janis, 1951, 1958; Schmideberg, 1942; Stouffer *et al.,* 1949; Wolfenstein, 1957; Disaster Research Group, 1961). This research suffers from the necessarily uncontrolled nature of the research environment and from the usual inability of investigators to make systematic observations *over time* of the behavior of individuals while they are experiencing real stress. The field setting also makes the evaluation of human performance under stress extremely difficult because objective criteria of performance are rarely available. Many cases are of sudden occurrence, thus the researcher can seldom prepare for or anticipate the collection of data.

The second general approach is to subject individuals to stress in a laboratory setting in which the environment can be rigidly controlled and measures of social behavior and performance easily collected (Berkowitz & Cottingham, 1960; Darley & Aronson, 1966; Goldstein, 1959; Grossack, 1954; Helmreich & Collins, 1967; Holtzman & Bitterman, 1956; Janis & Feshbach, 1953; Lanzetta & Roby, 1956; Lazarus & Ericksen, 1952; Leventhal & Singer, 1966; Miller & Zimbardo, 1965; Sarnoff & Zimbardo, 1961; Schachter, 1959; Zimbardo & Formica, 1963). Two characteristics inherent in the laboratory-experimental approach severely limit the generality of findings and can offset the advantages gained from controlled experimentation.

First, it is ethically impossible to induce a *level* of stress in a laboratory study comparable to that found in naturally occurring stressful situations such as combat, disasters, flying, deep sea diving, etc. Indeed, subjects rightfully believe that an experimenter will not expose them to undue risk or permit them to sustain permanent damage (Orne, 1962). Laboratory studies where a high level of psychological stress has been achieved (such as Milgram's (1963) work on obedience) have generated heated discussion about the whole question of the ethics of experimentation with human subjects (Baumrind, 1964). Similarly, field research in which stress has been experimentally manipulated (Berkun *et al.,* 1962) has encountered the same criticisms. Furthermore, it is doubtful whether differential levels of stress have been successfully induced in many such cases.

Second, prolonged stress cannot feasibly be maintained in the laboratory. It is practically impossible to keep subjects in states of high stress for extended periods to observe changes in behavior over time. Even in studies of some duration, the subjects customarily have the option of terminating the experience at will. As a result, laboratory investigations typically deal with the momentary effects of stress rather than reactions to prolonged stress. Field studies have reported that although initial exposure to stress may not lead to cognitive disorganization, physical deterioration, repression and social withdrawal, such responses may appear after extended periods of stress (Grinker & Spiegel, 1945; Sobol, 1949; Janis, 1963).

Investigators, both in field settings and in experimental laboratory research, have been concerned with the effects of stress on similar phenomena. These interests cluster in three major areas:

1. *Group behavior.* Stress affects the relationship of an individual to a primary group. Desire for affiliation and group identification have been found to increase under stress (Fritz & Marks, 1954; Grinker & Spiegel, 1945; Helmreich & Collins, 1967; Janis, 1951, 1963; Miller & Zimbardo, 1965; Schachter, 1959; Shils & Janowitz, 1948; Melita Schmideberg, 1942; Stouffer, Suchman, DeVinney & Star, 1949; Zimbardo & Formica, 1963). Increases in dependency and increased salience of group leaders have been observed frequently (Bettelheim, 1943; Glover, 1942; Grinker & Spiegel, 1945; Helmreich & Collins, 1967; Janis, 1958, 1963). Widespread increases in conformity to group norms are also reported (Grinker & Spiegel, 1945; Janis, 1951, 1963; Stouffer, *et al.,* 1949).

2. *Performance under stress.* Widely differing findings on the effectiveness of performance under high stress abound. In some cases, stress appears to facilitate, in others to impair performance, while differential effects are sometimes reported on tasks of differing complexity. In addition, no stress effects on performance are reported in some studies (Fleishman, 1958; Harrison & Purcell, 1959; Lanzetta & Roby, 1956; Lazarus & Ericksen, 1952; Murphy, 1959; Ross, Rupel & Grant, 1952; Zimny, 1956).

3. *Individual differences in reactions to stress.* Many studies report differences in tolerance for stress and behavior in stressful situations as a function of background or personality variables (Davidson, Andres & Ross, 1956; Deese, Lazarus & Keenan, 1953; Fenichel, 1945; Janis, 1958; Lazarus, Deese & Hamilton, 1954; Lucas, 1952; Schachter, 1959; Spence, Farber & Taylor, 1954).

SEALAB AS A RESEARCH SETTING

The SEALAB II project seemed to the authors to be an excellent natural laboratory for research into psychological stress—combining advantages of both the laboratory and the field. It appeared to be a setting uniquely suited to the investigation of all three of the areas discussed above. A list of the considerations which were weighed in our evaluation of the research potential may be of value to the psychologist contemplating field research on stress.

1. *Real and prolonged stress.* The divers' reports of their reactions presented in the first chapter leave little doubt as to the stressful nature of SEALAB life. The very nature of the project permitted us to anticipate with certainty the occurrence of stress reactions. Thus, the possibility that subjects would not be under real stress was not an issue. The fact that each aquanaut would spend 15 days underwater made it possible to look at trends in behavior over time rather than forcing us to limit our investigation to momentary responses.

2. *Minimal demand characteristics from psychological research.* By this we mean that the subjects did not perceive themselves as subjects in a psychological research project, but rather as participants in a project of underwater exploration and research. They were told that psychological research was simply one part of the overall study of "Man in the Sea." As one aquanaut put it during debriefing, "We were motivated to do a good job and that (the psychological testing) was part of a good job." Since continual monitoring of SEALAB activity was necessary for health and safety, additional monitoring by psychologists presumably had little effect on behavior.

3. *Relatively stable environment.* All aquanauts lived in the same environment and performed similar work. This gave us comparability over teams and men for evaluation of individual reactions to stress.

4. *Facilities for observation.* Remote TV and audio monitoring of the subjects was possible 24 hours a day. In addition,

observers and facilities for systematic collection of data over time were available.

5. *Availability of background information.* As subjects were chosen well in advance of the operation, it was possible to obtain a fairly complete battery of background information on each man prior to his participation.

6. *Adequate number of subjects.* We felt that this was perhaps a borderline issue. Three teams with a total of 28 subjects did not give us overwhelming degrees of freedom for comparisons, but the number was at least sufficient to permit systematic contrasts between individuals and subgroups.

7. *Objective criteria of performance.* One of the primary attractions in considering the study was the availability of objective performance criteria. As all participants worked at similar tasks under similar conditions, it was possible to define objective criteria and to relate these to background and situational variables. The ability to use objective criteria for evaluating the effects of psychological variables adds greatly to the power and validity of research.

8. *Data processing capability.* Facilities were available and plans were formulated to transfer all data to punch cards for computer processing. This capability made it possible to collect data on a large number of variables with a large number of observations per variable. By planning data analysis in advance, we were able to deal with a mass of data rapidly and to perform many analyses without being overwhelmed by the sheer volume of collected information.

Given these considerations, the project seemed to have great potential, and a large program of data collection was planned. This planning represented a major portion of the research effort and is discussed at length in the next chapter.

CHAPTER 3

Planning Data Collection

INTRODUCTION

SEALAB II promised to be an excellent, in many respects an unexcelled opportunity to gather data on small groups under stress. But was it? No sooner had we committed ourselves to the project than we were assailed by nagging doubts as to the wisdom of forsaking the secure and controlled environment of the laboratory for the uncertainties and the uncontrolled environment of the field. For the most part, colleagues were supportive and acquaintances were impressed by the glamour of the project. But on the other hand, there were questions such as "What if your TV fails?", "Or your audio?", "or both?" "How do you know the aquanauts will have time or will be willing to answer questionnaires?" "If they do respond, how do you know the answers will be valid in any sense of the term?" And finally, "Suppose all data collection goes off without a hitch. Twenty-eight is not a very large N and variances may be too large to reveal any meaningful trends." So there was a very real possibility of spending months in planning and ending with no data at all, or possibly worse of spending additional months of analysis only to find sparse and largely meaningless results. Such questions will doubtless plague any investigator contemplating a large field study. In essence they boil down to "Is such a study worth trying?" But our commitment was made and the question became how to reduce the risk of a fiasco. That is, how to plan data collection to maximize the chances of learning something that would make a contribution to our knowledge of men and groups under stress.

OUTLINE OF CHAPTER

This chapter has a dual purpose, as does the whole report. On the one hand it is a report of research on groups under stress. On the other hand it is a case history of a rather unusual study. We hope this type of research will become more common and that our experiences may have some transfer value. In other words, we hope that a discussion of some of our decisions and problems will help other investigators to know now what we wish we had known then.

Thus, we attempt to include more than a description of the data collected. In the following order this chapter covers:

Deciding What to Measure
Data Collected
Failures
Principles of Data Collection

DECIDING WHAT TO MEASURE

Inputs to planning data collection came from several sources. Probably most important was, of course, a review of what others had done when faced with similar situations (Grinker & Spiegel, 1945; Stouffer *et al.,* 1949; Rohrer, 1960; Lester, 1964; Gunderson and Nelson, 1966; Smith, 1966). Theoretical and methodological works in social psychology were valuable but by no means definitive in suggesting hypotheses to test or detailed methods of collecting data.[1] But generalizing from previous studies similar in nature or from broad theoretical principles and methodological discussions cannot specify measures to be gathered in a particular field study. Decisions as to what marks an observer should tally on a data form, and what that data form should look like, can be made only after a careful analysis of the situation at hand. The foregoing may be a truism to which no one will object, but putting this truism into operation can be rather tricky. All preparations must be made weeks and months in advance without knowledge of many critical details. As there is seldom an opportunity for pilot runs in the field, there is no substitute for careful planning.

Psychological research on SEALAB II had three major purposes:

1. To expand knowledge of adjustment and adaptation of groups and men to stressful environments.

2. To measure group and individual work performance of the aquanauts.

3. To collect data which would be useful in selecting and screening personnel for similar future missions.

In summary, planning of data collection was guided by a variety of considerations: first, there was the influence of previous work in similar situations (Gunderson & Nelson, 1966; Lester, 1964; Rohrer, 1960); second were the ideas gained from methodological and theoretical work in social psychology (Lindzey, 1954; Festinger and Katz, 1953; Newcomb, 1953); third, the major purposes of the study stated above; fourth, and probably most important, was an analysis of the SEALAB project, the research environment, to determine what was likely to happen which might be of significance and might provide data which would be evidence of individual and group performance, adjustment and adaptation.

[1] For example, a recent book by Webb, Campbell, Schwartz, & Sechrest (1966) would have been very useful in planning data collection for SEALAB II. Unfortunately this book was not yet available when we needed it. Fortunately, we find in retrospect that we followed many of the useful principles for data collection in the social sciences it recommends.

Fortunately one of the authors had observed briefly on Project SEALAB I, conducted in August, 1964. This project was similar to SEALAB II except that only four men were submerged for eleven days. The exposure to this study provided many useful ideas for planning data collection during SEALAB II.

DATA COLLECTED

Table 3-1 contains an outline of data collected during Project SEALAB II. We will discuss briefly the rationale for the various measures; that is, the reasons for gathering a certain type of data and the reasoning underlying the data collection process as a whole.

It should be emphasized that data collection was planned with the idea of using high speed computers for processing and analysis as the quantity of data anticipated and gathered during the project could not be handled with hand calculating equipment. Along this line, it is vital to consider the types of analyses which will be done and to organize the data so that the most appropriate analyses can be made. The availability and limitations of computer programs using the necessary statistics should be determined.

Pre-Dive Data

Pre-dive data, with the exception of sociometric ratings and the mood checklist, provided descriptive information on the individual aquanauts. One purpose guiding the selection of instruments was the goal of making some comparison between aquanauts and other groups serving in isolated and hazardous environments, specifically, men wintering over in Antarctica in the Navy's Deep Freeze stations and members of the 1963 American Mt. Everest expedition. Thus, instruments were chosen or adapted from ones which had been used on either or both of those groups. The instruments used, except for the copyrighted tests (Allport–Vernon–Lindzey, Strong and FIRO–B), appear in Appendix A.

TABLE 3-1 List of Measures, Frequency of Collection, Method of Collection and Variables Derived from Each Measure

Instrument	When Collected	Frequency	Method of Collection	Type of Instrument	Variables Derived
Personal History Booklet	Pre-Dive	1	Self-Report[a]	Adapted[b]	Demographic characteristics[c]
Attitude Inventory	Pre-Dive	1	Self-Report	Adapted	Personality Scales
Adjective Checklist	Pre-Dive	1	Self-Report	Adapted	Scales indicating characteristics desired in a friend
FIRO-B	Pre-Dive	1	Self-Report	Standard	Interpersonal Relations Attitudes
Allport–Vernon–Lindzey Scale of Values	Pre-Dive	1	Self-Report	Standard	Value scales
Strong Vocational Interest Blank	Pre-Dive	1	Self-Report	Standard	Vocational Interest Scales
Mood Adjective Checklist	Pre-Dive & During Dive	1 7 times per man	Self-Report	Adapted	a. Mood Scales Pre-Dive b. Changes in mood Pre to during c. During dive moods

[a] Self-report is information supplied by a subject about himself.
Other report is information about a man supplied by a teammate.
TV Observation is information systematically recorded from observing men in the capsule on TV.
Log Record is an official log kept for purposes other than behavior measurement.

[b] An adapted instrument is one which has been used in other studies but is not published.
A standard instrument has been published. An ad hoc instrument was devised for this study.
Copies of adapted and ad hoc instruments appear in Appendix A.

[c] Variables derived from Pre-Dive and Post-Dive self-report measures will be defined when they are used later.

(continued)

Instrument	When Collected	Frequency	Method of Collection	Type of Instrument	Variables Derived
Sociometric Choices of Leaders and Teammates	Pre-Dive & Post-Dive	1 1	Other Report	Adapted	a. Choice of Man as Peer Pre b. Choice of Man as Peer Post c. Change in Pre Post Peer Choices d. Total team peer choices Pre & Post (Cohesiveness) e. Choice of Man as Leader Pre f. Choice of Man as Leader Post g. Change in Pre Post Leader Choices h. Number of choices within team by each man Pre i. Number of choices within team by each man Post j. Changes in number of within team choices by man
Daily Activities Checklist	During Dive	Once each day	Self-Report	Ad hoc	a. Amount of sleep b. Quality of sleep c. Meal satisfaction d. Number of meals missed
Order of Arising	During	Once each day	TV Observation	Ad hoc	a. Time up in morning b. Mood on arising
Meal Recording	During Dive	Three times per day	TV Observation	Ad hoc	a. Helpfulness—who prepared and cleaned up b. Mood of group and individuals c. Order of eating

(continued)

Instrument	When Collected	Frequency	Method of Collection	Type of Instrument	Variables Derived
Location Record	During Dive	30 times per day	TV Observation	Ad hoc	a. Gregariousness b. Time in work area c. Time in galley area d. Time in bunk area e. Mood f. Activity
Activity level	During Dive	8 times per day	TV Observation	Ad hoc	Activity level
Night Watch Record	During Dive	Continuous each night	TV Observation and audio	Ad hoc	a. Times up during night b. Solitary behavior
Telephone Calls	During Dive	Continuous	Log Record	Ad hoc	Contacts outside the group
Sortie Reports	During Dive	One per day	Self-Report	Ad hoc	Number of tasks performed
Post SEALAB Questionnaire	Post Dive	1	Self-Report	Ad hoc	Scales of adjustment and adaptation
Debrief Interview	Post Dive	1	Self-Report	Ad hoc	Anecdotal Reports
Leader Ratings	Post Dive	1	Other Report	Ad hoc	Quantified Comparative Ratings of Aquanauts

This pre-dive battery of paper and pencil measures was also designed to provide information which could be correlated with indices of performance, adjustment and adaptation in SEALAB. We wanted a broad range of data measuring a variety of characteristics. We had a limited number of investigators and we were allotted a limited amount of time with the aquanauts. These latter considerations eliminated the possibility of individual tests or pre-dive interviews.

The battery of pre-dive measures included: Personal History Booklet—demographic data; Attitude Inventory—personality scales; Adjective Checklist—additional personality type data; the Allport–Vernon–Lindzey Scale of Values—data on value orientations; the Strong Vocational Interest Inventory—data on vocational preferences; and the FIRO-B—a measure of social relations orientation.

Sociometric ratings

The use of sociometric ratings for Project SEALAB II should require little explanation for social scientists. These were expected to provide sensitive indices of informal status and group cohesiveness, as well as changes in these variables. For a variety of reasons, to be indicated later, we feel that sociometric choices were among the most valuable data we gathered.

As Lindzey and Borgatta (1954) indicate, there are a variety of ways in which sociometric ratings may be made. We chose to use positive ratings only and to limit the number of choices. No doubt somewhat superior data would result if negative as well as positive ratings were used (that is, asking a man whom he would *not* prefer as a team mate as well as whom he would prefer). However, in close knit volunteer groups, such as SEALAB aquanauts, the risk of creating resistance to sociometric questions by including a request for negative ratings is probably sufficient to offset the potential gain from such measures. This opinion is shared by other investigators in the area.

Forms for sociometric questions appear in Appendix B. Aquanauts were asked to name the five men they would choose as team mates and the five men they would choose as leaders. This particular form was adapted from Lester (1964). Choices were restricted to the 28 man group scheduled to participate. On the post-dive sociometric measure they were asked to name men they would choose for a hypothetical future dive. Since choices were made from among the 28 man group, excellent indices of pre and post cohesiveness and changes in cohesiveness for each ten man team could be easily derived. In addition, a variety of measures on each man, reflecting his acceptance as a team mate and potential leader within the total group and his own team were derived from sociometric choices.

Timing the administration of the post sociometric questionnaire presented a problem. Choices were made immediately after the men came out of decompression. Thus, for Team I choices were made before they had any knowledge of the performance of Teams II or III. Team II made its post choices after observing Team I but not, of course, Team III. Team III was the only group with knowledge of the performance of all three teams when sociometric choices were made. Just what effect this timing may have had on the choices is unknown and unknowable. We could have delayed any post sociometric measurement until all three teams had completed their sojourns under the sea; however, this would have posed confounding variations due to differential memory and decay of affect. But perhaps the most important consideration determining our choice of gathering sociometric data immediately after the dive for all three teams was the principle—get your data when you can. We felt that some men might be unavailable at a later date, but all were available immediately after decompression.

During Dive Measures—Facilities and Personnel

Careful attention must be given to facilities and personnel to be used in gathering data in field studies. We discuss briefly a few salient points concerning facilities and personnel. Some of the details mentioned below are doubtless unique to this particular study, but they are representative of the type of contingencies which are likely to prevail in field research.

"Topside", or the staging vessel for SEALAB II, was located approximately one mile off shore. In many respects this would have been a good location for our operations. However, for a variety of reasons, we decided to stay on shore. Foremost among these reasons was the possibility of being "bumped" in favor of other aspects of the program. Also, there was the problem of transporting observers back and forth to the site. At one point, high seas did cause suspension of travel to the staging vessel for a two day period. A more subtle consideration was the desire to stay out of the way. While the aquanauts knew that psychologists were observing them, they did not know exactly *what* data we were gathering. Since nonsubmerged aquanauts were serving as support divers from the staging vessel, they would probably have become aware, for example, that we were keeping track of who got up first in the morning, who washed the dishes, etc., had we been right next door. Their behavior might not have been much influenced by this knowledge, but then again it might have.

A shore based station also had its drawbacks. Chief among these was the possibility of communications being cut off or severely degraded in transmission. Audio and TV coverage to shore were interrupted for two brief periods and they never were equal in quality to that available on the staging vessel. On the day a 13′ high truck tried to go under the 12′ high coaxial cable linking shore to SEALAB, we questioned ruefully our decision to be landlubbers. Another possible disadvantage of being on shore was that we were farther from the center of the operation. Thus we missed out on certain bits of data and information that it might have been useful to have. However, it is quite possible that this slight detachment from ongoing operations was an advantage rather than a disadvantage. What we mean is this: we had planned a program of systematic data collection, attempting to mesh our observations with the living and working schedule of the aquanauts. The program, however, was multipurpose, not to mention extremely hazardous; thus, there were constant interruptions and alterations in the schedule. Furthermore, on important parts of our carefully planned data collection program we got no data at all while on others the data were of uncertain quantity and quality. As a result, there was a great temptation to scrap this system at times and to measure opportunistically rather than systematically. Fortunately, as it turned out, we were able to resist most such temptations. Had we been closer to the center of operations and more aware of interfering contingencies than we were, it would have been harder to resist the temptation to abandon our original plan of systematic data collection.

The important point about selecting a site for collecting data, a base of operations, is that the physical location of the data collector in relation to other aspects of the program can have profound effects on his data collection. A proper balance must be struck between the ability to be aware of what is going on and the danger of being overwhelmed by details, between involvement and detachment. This balance is determined in large part by the centrality of the data collection base. In brief, choice of data collection site deserves careful consideration.

Our observing room was approximately 10′ × 12′, rather cramped quarters as it turned out. Significant items of equipment were two 19″ television monitors, two two-channel tape recorders, an intercom linking us to SEALAB, the staging vessel, the communications center and shore headquarters, a telephone, a filing cabinet, and several chairs. The room had plentiful shelf space, a necessary facility for the mountains of paper generated by a large study of long duration.

Observers

Observers were twelve students (2 graduate students and 10 undergraduates) recruited from the psychology departments of San

Diego area colleges and universities and selected in May[2] for a project to begin in early August. Despite the fact that applicants were warned that we could not be certain of the starting date of the project, indeed, that we could not guarantee that they would be employed at all, there were a large number of highly qualified applicants.

One of the large unknowns in planning the study was just how much we could expect of naive observers who would necessarily have to be trained on the job for tasks requiring meticulous attention to detail, intense concentration and ready adaptability. Our concerns were unfounded. All details of data collection were handled superbly under very trying circumstances.

Schedules

Observer schedules followed the work day schedule of the aquanauts. Reveille was scheduled at 0700. Two observers worked together on a six hour shift from 0700 to 1300. Another two man team monitored from 1300 to 1900. At 1900, diving operations were normally concluded for the day and the evening meal was nearly finished. We had one man observing from 1900 to 0100 and one man on the graveyard shift from 0100 to 0700. This schedule was maintained continuously for 43 days with the exception of a two day period when shore communications were cut off. In addition to the observers, at least one of the authors, and frequently both, was on duty in the observation room at all times.

Data Coders

Data coders recorded the observational data on IBM data sheets on the site. About 90% of all data had been coded and

[2] Special thanks are due to Dr. Eric Gunderson, U. S. Navy Medical Neuropsychiatric Research Unit, San Diego, California for his assistance in recruiting observers.

punched when Team III emerged from decompression. The coders were seaman apprentices from the incoming unit at the San Diego Naval Training Center. We asked for men with GCT scores of 65 or higher (IQ = 130). Such men were available and they functioned well with minimal on the job training. Their enthusiasm for the project was evidenced by their willingness to serve voluntarily on weekends and on the Labor Day holiday. It should be acknowledged, however, that the work attractions were doubtless augmented by the availability of the beach at La Jolla for a lunch time dip.

Forms

The forms and instructions used are presented in Appendix C. Nearly all forms were designed and the necessary copies multilithed well in advance of the beginning of the project, though we did develop two very simple forms soon after the project started. Data from one of these forms was of very limited value, from the other, totally useless. As can be seen from an examination of the forms, most of the information to be filled in was quite specific and objective in nature with instructions as detailed as possible. The entire experience, including data analysis, has reaffirmed our conviction that first priority should be assigned to the collection of observational data which is quantified and objective, requiring a minimum of judgment. Elucidating comments and a narrative record are of some value but they are of secondary importance. Quantity of data was never any problem and probably will not be in most operations of this type if available opportunities are utilized. The problem is rather in data reduction. Narrative records are unlikely to be digested and analyzed thoroughly, as the task is simply too great and there is no need to reduce comments to numbers if sufficient quantitative data are already available. The investigator who relies solely or primarily on extensive written comments or, even worse, on tape recorded comments designed to capture the "richness" of the developing situation in a large field study will rue his decision when he begins to analyze his data. His study will suffer an acute case of "data poisoning" from which it is unlikely to recover.

Thus, our data forms called for tallies and numbers rather than written accounts. Each aquanaut was given a two digit identifying number which included team as well as man designation. In addition, all forms, and in some cases parts of forms, were given a date-time group according to "SEALAB days" and a 24 hour clock. These may seem like small details and because they are they may not be given adequate consideration, however, life is much simpler if every bit of information is adequately and uniquely identified when it is recorded rather than after the fact. In a large observational study it is vitally necessary to *quantify* and to *keep data recording simple and organized.*

DECIDING ON SPECIFIC OBSERVATIONAL MEASURES

A decision to gather quantitative, objective and specific rather than qualitative, subjective and general data by observation still leaves one many steps away from specifying exactly what tallies are to be made on what forms, when, and how often. For example, how could we be certain beforehand that a particular datum would be available for observation or if a certain datum were available, that it would describe meaningfully behavior under stress? When someone trained and experienced in laboratory research who has only a nodding acquaintance with field research attempts to design a form for collecting observational data, he comes to appreciate fully the myriad and subtle differences between the two approaches. Therefore, in presenting the data collection forms we will attempt to indicate the major considerations affecting the choice of a specific measure, to indicate also what we expected to get from each form, and in general how it came out. That is, how feasible each form proved to be under the prevailing circumstances. Data collection forms will be discussed in the order in which they are listed in Table 3-1.

Order of Arising

As its name implies, this form had a very specific and simple purpose; to make a record of the order in which the aquanauts arose to begin the day. Since reveille was at 7 A.M., it might be expected that all men would appear within a few minutes of each other and that there would be slight individual differences and no meaningful variations; however, the presence of only one toilet and one wash basin were factors which could help to impose meaningful variation on this possible indicator of motivation. Thus, we were looking for individual and group differences within teams and over time which might tell us how well the men were adjusting to their environment.

The major virtue of this measure was its simplicity and ease of collection. As it turned out, things were not all that simple. Cameras failed in the helium atmosphere and new ones were placed at different angles so that even these simple data were not strictly comparable across all teams. In addition, lights near the entrance to the bunk area were frequently not turned on until several men had arisen, out of deference to those still sleeping. Then too, clarity of reception varied considerably over the course of the study. Thus, it proved impossible to judge reliably the moods of the men on arising. Simply identifying who arose when was a task requiring the most careful attention. The main point here is that even this relatively simple measure was not easy to collect, though we do have confidence in the data indicating the mean order of arising. As will be shown in the analysis, this proved to be highly useful information. By "useful", "meaningful" or "good" data we mean here, and in the rest of this chapter, data which are sufficiently robust to allow comparisons to be made. Data may be weak or nonrobust in this sense for a variety of reasons such as insufficient number of observations, large variances, lack of specificity of measurement and the like. It was difficult for us to tell in many cases how well a particular variable had been measured until long after the study had been completed and several reductive operations, such as computing means, variances, deviation scores and blocking had been performed. We were amazed at the robustness of several variables. The moral here is not to give up too quickly on a measure which appears to be failing because of observational difficulties.

Meal Recording

The meal recording form was our most complex and difficult form to complete and we anticipated that our observers would have great trouble recording all the information requested on this form. As it turned out, the viewing conditions, combined with the manner in which meals were served and eaten, made it much more difficult than we had anticipated to determine mood, tension and activity of the group and individuals during meals. However, had conditions been ideal, our observers could probably have handled even this monster of a form quite well. In short, one can expect well motivated observers to handle complex data collection if instructions are sufficiently explicit.

The principal reasons for placing emphasis on recording meal behavior were that we knew it would occur, that at least some aspects could be measured, and hopefully that it would yield a variety of indices of adjustment and social interaction. For example, information on who prepared the meals and who cleaned up could explain sociometric choice. In another field setting, order of being served indicated a pecking order (Smith, 1966). Missing meals and the relish with which meals are eaten are also reasonable indices of adjustment. Failure on the part of some men to share in group affect was another measure we hoped to get from the meal form.

The form yielded considerably less data than it was designed to provide, but in spite of this, it proved to be a very useful instrument. Since groups living in natural settings will always eat, and since this may be one of the few common activities, meal behavior can be expected to yield important information in almost any setting. Whether appetites are robust or not, mealtime behavior as an indicator of adjustment and group processes is.

Location Record

This was the most frequently used of all observational instruments. Recordings were made every half hour for 15 hours. The location report was planned as a still picture of the group. Primary emphasis was given to a simple recording of the location of each man. The virtues of such elementary data should not be overlooked. First of all, it is quite reliable even under relatively poor observational conditions. For several days there was a clear picture from only one camera which covered less than half the capsule. Nevertheless, the observers diligently, ingeniously and reliably located the men either on camera, forward of camera or to the rear of the camera. As with other observational measures, the quantity and quality of data were less than what was hoped. Disappointments during data collection, however, changed to surprised gratification during analysis. These data turned out much better than we had thought they would while they were being gathered. This is another case of a simple but robust measure which stood up well under the degrading influences of day to day difficulties of observation. More complex measures requiring interpretation and even simple narrative comments did not prove as useful.

From the location record we obtained a measure of gregariousness—the amount of time each man spent in the presence of others; a territoriality index—the extent to which a man occupied a given area of the capsule; and measures of time in the work, galley and bunk areas—indicators of work performance and social behavior. Measures of mood were unreliable because of previously mentioned viewing conditions. The measure of activity, whether a man was sitting, standing or moving at the time the record was made, was easy to collect but suffered from the fact that many men could not be seen. In summary, the Location Record yielded good data and illustrates the importance of repetitive, simple, quantified measures of high reliability.

Activity Level

This measure, added after observations had begun, demonstrated to us that it is possible to be too radically simple and quantitative. The circumstances surrounding the decision to gather this measure and the reasons for its deficiencies may have instructive value. This is what happened.

After about 24 hours of observation it became apparent that data would be far less than we had hoped or even expected. Two crucially important measures, communication and diving preparation, had yielded no data and were unlikely to improve. One of the two cameras, the one covering the work area, was sending such a poor signal that men could barely be identified when right next to it. The other camera was transmitting a clearer picture, but the area covered, the galley, was less interesting as a viewing area. Interference on the audio channel, coupled with the difficulties of understanding helium speech and high levels of background noise, rendered that data source virtually useless. We were attempting to train monitors while unable to see and hear much of anything. In short, we could see months of planning effort going down the drain. Very little data were being collected.

In these depressing circumstances one thing was quite clear. It was easy to distinguish who was going back and forth across the camera. As we sat glumly viewing what appeared to be random activity, we began a frequency count of on and off camera excursions of each man. Sure enough, there were individual differences which, after three separate observation occasions, appeared to be regular. Maybe there was something in this behavior. We had little idea what it might be and only vague notions about nervous pacing or differences in work roles occurred to us. But the information was there, so we quickly mimeographed the simple forms required and our observers faithfully recorded on and off camera excursions for each man eight times per day for half an hour each—largely wasted effort as it turned out. Although highly reliable, quantitative with a vengeance and available in vast amounts, these data were related to practically nothing else. We think we have figured out why they were not and we probably could have reached the same conclusions if we had thought about it beforehand. In any case, the probable reasons for their failure to mean much are as trivial and uninteresting as are the data.

There are two morals to this story. First, don't panic and second, improvise cautiously. We were persuaded to employ the activity count because it appeared that most of our planned measures were going badly. As it turned out, even though the data were far below expectations on most measures, they were still good and in most cases better than the activity count data despite the objectivity, reliability and quantity of the latter information. The main reason for the failure of the activity count data was not due to deficiencies in the data as such but rather to the rationale governing their collection. Collected primarily because they were available rather than because of any reasonable certainty that they would indicate anything specific about performance in and adaptation to the environment, these data were a time consuming lesson in the need for careful advance planning.

Night Watch Record

The purpose of this form was to provide data on the solitary behavior of the men in SEALAB. We knew beforehand that watches would rotate among the men, so that each man could be observed in a relatively comparable setting. Unfortunately, men were off camera and light levels in the capsule were reduced much of the time. Nevertheless, we did get information on individual behavior and a record of men who got up during the night as well.

Outside Telephone Calls

This measure was a record of calls originated by the aquanauts to persons outside the capsule not connected with SEALAB, generally friends or relatives. An official record of the calls was kept by the project communication center. There was a wide variation in the use of the telephone by the men. These data were gathered as an index of adjustment and in-group identification, the rationale being that if a man were happy with his lot in SEALAB, relations with his fellow aquanauts and others in the project, he should have less reason to contact persons outside the project. Results indicate that it served extremely well as such an index. This simple measure correlated more highly with more other variables in more meaningful ways than any other single measure we obtained. Since it worked so well, was a bit unusual, and its collection was not planned it bears some discussion.

Outside telephone calls are an excellent example of an *unobtrusive measure* (Webb *et. al.,* 1966). The measure is also an example of taking advantage as a data source of information gathered for other purposes. In planning research on SEALAB, we did not know that a telephone for outside calls would be available. Extensive plans had been made to audit intra-group communication as an indicator of adjustment, group identification and group processes. When it became evident that it would be impossible to record systematically any information on in-capsule communications, we looked for a comparable measure.

Compared to many of our other measures, data on outside telephone calls were ridiculously simple to gather and process. All the information on all three teams took no more than two hours' time to transfer from the official records to punch cards. These data would have been easy to overlook. Measures of this type are probably available in a variety of settings. Based on our experience we advise any field researcher to keep a careful watch for them. Good data may not often by easy to come by, but there is no "law of greatest effort" which says that the data one works hardest to get are always the best.[3]

Diving Log

The diving log was an official project record kept by the aquanauts in the SEALAB capsule. The man on watch recorded divers' names and times of entry and exit on each sortie. Data from this log book provided the principal work criteria—diving time and number of sorties. We felt before the study began that the measures of time in the water and number of times entered would be the best and most meaningful performance criteria available. Data analysis indicated that they were indeed exemplary criteria.

Since good criteria are essential to the descriptive and explanatory success of a field study, it is worth examining why these were good criteria and why we expected that they would be. The reasons for choosing them may be so good as to spoil the intended illustration by example. That is, the reader may say, "Of course, obviously those were the measures to use so why belabor the point." We can only say that these measures did not seem at all obvious to a number of other persons who were involved in SEALAB, and there were other criteria on which we could have concentrated. In short, they did not appear obvious without a careful examination of the total situation. It is probably the case in most field settings that good criteria exist, naturally embedded in the program. *It is far better for a psychologist studying a natural group to use such criteria rather than to intervene in the situation and to try to make something happen which he can measure.*

Why were diving time and number of sorties good criteria? Principally because working in the water was the publicly stated and universally accepted goal of the project. Excursions from

[3] Except perhaps perceptually, *a la* dissonance theory (Festinger, 1957).

SEALAB were a common denominator of performance. While there were some differences in role requirements, that is, some men had more work to do inside than did others, all aquanauts were divers. The dangers and discomforts involved in entering the water are described in detail later. We were studying behavior under stress, and the multiple stresses of the environment reached their peak during sorties. The opportunity for each diver to determine to a marked degree the number and duration of his dives made these measures excellent indicators of motivation and reaction to stress. Finally, the fact that the measurement of the variables was an official part of the record cannot be stressed too heavily in determining the quality of the data. We feel that psychologists are too prone to depend on self-report measures, on asking a man to describe his own reactions on a five or seven point scale. Such measures are necessary in many settings and in some cases are the only data available. If there is no alternative they must be used, but only after a careful search for *unobstrusive, objective* measures of *behavior.*

Daily Activities Checklist

This was a self-report measure completed daily, designed to assess eating, sleeping, recreation and social behavior in gross terms. The measure was intended primarily to provide backup data for our observations in case of inability to observe some of this behavior or of total failure of the audio-visual system. Even though excellent cooperation was obtained in filling out the forms, the data in general were of poor quality and limited utility. In many instances behavior reported on the forms did not agree with our observations. These discrepancies could have been due to a variety of causes including poor design of the forms, lack of consistent set in filling them out, faulty memories, hasty completion, or any of a number of intentional and unintentional, self-serving distortions. In any case, data from this source proved to be of little use.

Mood Adjective Checklist

Each aquanaut filled out a 67 item mood adjective checklist every other day. Developed by Myers (1966), it is a forced choice checklist with three alternative responses for each adjective (See Appendix A). Six mood scales (anger, happiness, fear, depression, psychological well-being and lethargy) can be derived. Despite frequent complaints from the aquanauts regarding the length and repetitious administration of the scale, data from it proved to be excellent. The every-other-day administration was probably a wise compromise in view of the complaints on frequency of administration. For use in field settings, this adjective checklist could possibly be made more palatable without unduly compromising quality or reliability by shortening.

The mood checklist measure was designed to provide a variety of comparative and correlational data regarding moods. There was a comparison of normal topside moods with moods during submersion in SEALAB, with correlations possible between a variety of performance indices and individual differences in moods. Changes in mean moods, and variances for individuals and groups over time were other areas of interest. In short, the mood checklist was expected to yield a variety of valuable data, and it did. We feel that it is an essential measure in studies of this type and for SEALAB it proved by far the best of all the self-report measures, in many respects equal to objective behavioral measures. Because of its robust nature, a good mood checklist should be equally useful in other field studies, particularly those concerned with stress.

Failures of Planned Observations

There may be some illustrative utility in describing briefly two of our complete failures to obtain observational data which we planned and tried to collect. References have previously been made to the deficiencies of the audio and visual signals and adequacy of coverage. The purpose in reporting these problems is to forewarn the field researcher that he should expect such difficulties. However, if data collection plans include a sufficient variety of methods of collection, such problems will not spell complete disaster. On all our observational instruments we planned to collect more subtle and sophisticated data than we were able to gather. However, we also planned to collect relatively simple and robust data which in most cases, we were able to record reliably. While laboratory conditions were not achieved in the control over or quality of data gathered, we feel that the reality of the behavior being measured more than compensated for such deficiencies.

There were, however, two complete failures. One involved the gathering of data on in-capsule, intra-group communications. Extensive plans had been made to record who talked to whom, who initiated each conversation, the length of individual statements, and the subject matter of the conversation. From such data we intended to derive a variety of indications of adjustment, group interaction, leader dependence, group cohesiveness, inter-group differences, and changes over time on all of the above variables. At the minimum, we had hoped to get relatively gross estimates of at least one or two of these variables. We got nothing. The failure had multiple causes, but essentially it was due to unrealistic optimism in planning. Plans to collect data on communications were based on an observation of SEALAB I, but the extrapolation proved unrealistic because SEALAB I had only four crew members compared to the ten in the SEALAB II crews. Also, the SEALAB I capsule was much smaller, and a greater proportion of it was exposed to TV observation. Thus, it was a rather simple matter to determine which of the four men was speaking because they were almost always together in one group. If the speaker could not be seen clearly, enough of his colleagues could be seen so that the speaker could be identified by a process of elimination. In SEALAB II there were frequently two or more subgroups in simultaneous conversation and seldom could the speaker be identified. Three open microphones covered different areas of the capsule and simultaneous monitoring of all three was impossible. We should have realized all this beforehand, but sanguine naiveté controlled plans to collect these data and resulted in wasted time and effort.

The other "big one that got away" illustrates a different problem with field research data collection. This problem is that even with the best of planning based upon a behavioral and practical analysis of the situation, data regarding crucial variables may become unavailable because of contingencies over which the researcher has no control.

Our analysis of the SEALAB operations convinced us that behavior immediately preceding and following sorties into the water would be an important source of data. Preparing for and securing from dives were vital and meaningful tasks which could be observed. Data regarding social interaction (who helped whom to prepare and secure) and individual differences (latencies and order of leaving and returning) could be expected to be revealed best in this situation. The observation forms designed were quite simple and straightforward, but capable of yielding a wealth of data. In short, this was the observational data we wanted most of all. We drew a complete blank. The camera covering the dive preparation area malfunctioned at the exact moment the first team entered SEALAB. It had been functioning very well until that time, but coverage of the area, for a variety of reasons, was never achieved.

We feel that the important point regarding these failures is "Don't put all your eggs in one basket." At the time data collection plans were being made, we knew that we were planning to collect too much. But we also knew that there would be some failures. We did not know that our two total failures would involve what we expected to be the two most crucial sources of data. Despite the fact that these data were lost, others were available. Even though the study was diminished by the absence of these data we still feel adequately compensated for our time and effort. Without an eclectic, multifaceted approach to planning data collection we would have been left with very little information.

POST DIVE MEASURES

Questionnaire

The Post SEALAB Questionnaire was a ten page document covering areas of inquiry such as: adequacy of the habitat as a living and working area; adaptation to helium speech, cold water, visibility and other potential stressors; use of leisure time; and desirable characteristics of team mates. It was designed in collaboration with other operating personnel including persons instrumental in the design of the habitat. Psychometrically it is rather primitive because it was written in less than 24 hours. Mimeographing was completed only an hour before it was administered. The questionnaire was an afterthought in the data collection program and was included principally because we felt data were missing in many areas. As it turned out, most of the information obtained from the questionnaire was either redundant with or contradictory to more objective, and probably better, data available from other sources.

We found that subjective self-report data correlated with other subjective self-report data but not with observations or other records of behavior. The mood checklist data was the outstanding exception to this conclusion. Our results indicate, in general, agreement with the thesis of Webb *et al.,* (1966) that other data are necessary as a check on self-report measures before the researcher can conclude that he has learned anything about behavior in natural settings. Let us make clear that our contention is not that self-report data are completely useless, but merely that intensive efforts should be made to supplement them with more objective measures as a check on their validity.

Debrief Interview

Each aquanaut was interviewed for 30 to 45 minutes at the San Diego Naval Hospital as part of his debriefing. The principal purpose of these interviews was to provide data on work experiences and conditions in the water. Questions were asked regarding interpersonal relations and adaptation to the in-capsule environment. In addition, many spontaneous comments touched on these topics. Standard questions were not used and the interviews were not content analyzed. In general, the interviews have been used to provide illustrative and supplementary material, largely anecdotal in nature.

Leader Ratings

Each of the two team leaders (one man was the leader for both Teams I and II) made ratings of the other nine men on his team(s). These ratings were made on two four-point scales (See Appendix B) designed to assess performance as a diver and willingness to do common tasks and appear to be excellent criteria.

This discussion of data collection has been a lengthy presentation, largely because the study itself was big. But extensive as this research was, the plans were even more ambitious than the execution. We have tried to indicate, however, that this was not a dragnet study. Data collection was based on rational hypotheses and definite goals from which those hypotheses were derived. As we have already indicated, the objectives have only partially been realized, but this will become clearer as the data are presented. It is our hope and intention that some of the lessons we have learned will be of assistance to other researchers planning similar studies. We do not attempt to expound here a comprehensive methodology; rather, we have tried to illustrate by concrete examples in the total framework of one study many of the techniques and guidelines of data collection which are normally discussed in relative abstraction and out of context in methodological treatises.

Below is a summary list of principles, techniques, approaches and helpful hints which have been developed in this chapter. They are meant to apply primarily to large-scale, naturalistic field observations.

1. Plan broadly and deeply. Have backup data sources wherever possible, as it is easier to delete measures than to add them once a study is underway.

2. Plan observations to be as simple, objective, quantitative and systematic as possible. Have recording forms prepared in detail in advance.

3. Measures should embrace a *wide variety* of collection methods. This point is alluded to in several of the other principles in this list, but it is important enough to emphasize by stating it separately. Self-report measures are necessary and valuable but there are a number of reasons for challenging their ubiquity and exclusive use. One of the appealing features of SEALAB as a research opportunity was the variety of measures available. Interviews, questionnaires and standard tests were all used. There were, however, a variety of additional data sources which did not depend upon self-report.

4. Select the observation site carefully. Its location can influence data collection markedly.

5. Focus and structure observations to include behavior which you know will occur naturally, for example eating and sleeping.

6. Identify each datum with a unique signature as it is collected and transfer data to punched cards as it is collected if at all possible.

7. Plan the type of analyses to be done and the quantitative characteristics of the variables. If data are to be processed by computers, be sure that suitable techniques and programs are available.

8. Be prepared to improvise creatively, as illustrated by the measure of outside communications in SEALAB.

9. Be on guard against improvising hastily or with only vague reasons for doing so. This point is illustrated by the time wasted on the activity level data.

10. Be as unobtrusive as possible in measuring behavior. This principle implies at least three points regarding data gathering.

a. Place low priority and reliance on self-report measures.
b. Place high priority and reliance on systematic observations.
c. Take full advantage of records kept for other purposes, particularly official records such as the diving log.

11. Use "real" criteria of performance. That is, determine the goal(s) of the project and attempt to determine the most representative measure(s) of those goal(s). This principal may well be the most important of those presented here. It may also be the most difficult for psychologists to put into practice. In field studies it may be necessary to sacrifice some reliability and other desirable psychometric properties for validity of criterion measures.

12. Use sociometric ratings, but using only positive ratings will probably produce better cooperation.

13. Be prepared for things to go wrong, and don't panic when they do. If the study is basically sound the data will be good despite severe buffetings from a variety of natural causes. Field behavior is far more robust than laboratory behavior.

CHAPTER 4

Stresses of SEALAB

We have discussed briefly some of the characteristics of SEALAB and of the concept of stress in Chapters I and II. While recognizing that the concept of stress is still poorly defined, there can be little doubt that SEALAB II was extremely stressful by commonly accepted situational definitions. The stresses in SEALAB were both physical and psychological, including threats to life, disruptions of physiological homeostasis, and ego threats. They also included hard work, frustration, annoyances and potential misunderstandings due to differences in background and values of the individual aquanauts.

A detailed description of the stressful elements of SEALAB is intended to serve the following purposes: (*a*) To familiarize nondivers with the stresses of saturation diving; (*b*) to attempt an operational definition of the stressful components of the SEALAB situation; (*c*) to provide a background for understanding the men of SEALAB and their behavior; (*d*) and finally, to give due credit to SEALAB II aquanauts and their accomplishments.

In describing the stressful elements we should emphasize that they were unavoidable. The men of SEALAB II were explorers on a frontier. This point was emphasized by Capt. Walter Mazzone, MSC, USN in his report (Mazzone, 1966) on physiological research on SEALAB II, "We are now at the dawning of a new era in deep diving research. Through the centuries, man has been imbued with a strong and compelling urge to explore under the sea, yet be has made few advances in this technology over the past two hundred and seventy-five years. However, a renaissance is now upon us, and more advances in diving techniques have occurred during the last decade than during any other period in the history of diving." Venturing into unknown territory is always hazardous. SEALAB II had been preceded by approximately ten years of laboratory work and experiments involving both animals and humans in tests of the concept of saturation diving. It had also been preceded by SEALAB I, an open sea test near Bermuda (O'Neal, 1965). In SEALAB I, four men lived and worked from a capsule located 193 feet beneath the ocean's surface for a period of eleven days. Unlike SEALAB II conditions, the water was clear and warm, the bottom flat and sandy, and the program of activities much less ambitious. In short, SEALAB II had been preceded by a long and careful program emphasizing safety. Now, however, it was time for a test under operational conditions. Therefore, for SEALAB II, a site had been chosen deliberately in which the water was cold and dark, the terrain uneven, and the bottom clouded by silt. In addition, an extensive scientific and salvage program had been planned. In taking this giant step, the most stringent safety precautions were observed. The dangers and hazards had been carefully assessed; they were well known and allowances had been made for them. The latest equipment and technology available were employed to reduce the dangers to a minimum. Nevertheless, despite all of these efforts, the hazards were considerable.

SOURCES OF STRESS IN SEALAB

Threat to Life

The basic reason for threats to life in SEALAB stemmed from the very nature and purpose of the study—to test the concept of saturation diving. Any sudden ascent to the surface from the

SEALAB depth would have been fatal—speedily, painfully and certainly. In a sense, all humans are constantly in danger. All occupations are hazardous in varying degrees and it is true that most people die in bed. However, some occupations are certainly more hazardous than others. For example, miners, test-pilots and construction workers are clearly more exposed to danger than are teachers, office workers and restaurant employees. On this rough scale, diving is obviously one of the more hazardous occupations and SEALAB was a very hazardous diving venture. As has been indicated, this was true despite the stringent safety precautions which were observed; despite the presence of knowledgeable personnel and excellent facilities to treat any possible casualties. The efficacy of the safety procedures is evidenced by the fact that no one was killed in SEALAB and that the treatment facilities were not needed to minister to victims. These precautions reduced the threat, but they could not remove it. More importantly, they could not dismiss from the consciousness of each diver the fact that he was in danger at all times until he was decompressed. His danger was at a maximum when he left the SEALAB habitat to carry out his work in the water.

Why did the fact of hyperbaric saturation produce such extreme danger? In SEALAB II the body of each diver was completely permeated with gas at 100 pounds of pressure (sealevel pressure is 14.7 pounds per square inch). If external pressure were reduced suddenly to normal, this gas would boil and explode within his body. He could not return to the surface without long and slow decompression. Therefore, when a man left SEALAB his only safe haven was a return to the SEALAB capsule. He had to return to what the divers described as "a mighty small hole in the big Pacific Ocean". What could prevent him from returning to SEALAB?

Breathing Gear

Probably the most critical element in determining a diver's ability to return safely to the SEALAB was his breathing gear.

He was completely dependent upon his source of life-sustaining gas when in the water. Two types of breathing gear were used in SEALAB, the Mark VI SCUBA (self-contained underwater breathing apparatus) and the Arawak or Hookah breathing apparatus. The Mark VI gear enabled the diver to swim free of physical contact with SEALAB and thus to traverse relatively long distances. The Arawak operated with hoses from SEALAB which provided gas. On Arawak, he was breathing the atmosphere from the capsule, which was pumped to him as he swam through the water. When he was wearing Arawak, hoses trailed after him and tethered him to SEALAB. Both types of breathing gear presented their own special problems. We will consider the problems of the Mark VI first.

The Mark VI is known as a semi-closed circuit breathing apparatus. This means that a portion of each breath is recirculated through a cleansing agent to remove the CO_2 (carbon dioxide) before the exhalation is rebreathed. In re-breathing, it is mixed with gas from bottles on the man's back. This cleansing and re-breathing is done in order to conserve gas and necessarily complicates the apparatus. The ability to rebreathe prolongs a man's time in the water. Extending time in the water through the use of a complex piece of equipment is typical of the trade-offs between safety and efficiency necessary in operational situations. It would have been safer to use an open circuit breathing apparatus which is much less complicated than the Mark VI. However, to have employed such an apparatus would have meant that each diver would have had only a very brief time in the water because the available gas supply would have been expended very quickly.

The Mark VI consists of two bottles strapped on the back of the swimmer, a cannister containing baralime (the CO_2 cleansing agent), two breathing bags, one for inhalation, one for exhalation, a mouthpiece, hoses and various valves and regulators. (See photographic insert.) Obviously, it was necessary for each aquanaut to be thoroughly familiar with this complex apparatus. Each Mark VI had to be partly stripped down after each dive, the gas in its bottles recharged, the valves checked, the carbon dioxide purifier replaced, and the gear reassembled before the next dive. This procedure is rather like packing one's parachute before a jump—only far more complex. Several divers commented that they liked to assemble their own apparatus for obvious reasons. These feelings are summarized in the following two quotations from the debriefing interviews.

> "I'd like to see every man that's on the SEALAB have his own Mark VI. Be personally responsible and *nobody* else take care of it. Him take care of it himself."

> "You always had fear with you in knowing that someone else set this up, and I don't like the idea of setting it up. I mean I was always conscious of the fact that if something happened out there with perhaps four units I had set up, it would be a terrible feeling to know that there was a possibility that you are responsible for this. I believe that each man should set up his own apparatus, without a question."

However, for efficiency of operation it was not possible for each diver to assemble his own or to even use the same gear on each dive. Each aquanaut standing the night watch set up several of the Mark VI's for the next day's operation. Assembling gear for each other probably produced feelings of mutual dependence among the divers.

The fact that all men assembled the gear and were thus highly familiar with it was doubtless a mixed blessing in so far as confidence was concerned. Each man knew very well how to handle the apparatus, but each one also knew the potential problems. The effect of this knowledge is illustrated by the following comment.

> "I don't feel confident about any piece of equipment that delicate—it keeps you on your toes—you always have to be aware of it all the time. If you have respect for it and pay attention to it, it's a good piece of gear but if you start treating it like a piece of open circuit gear—once it stops functioning correctly you know it right then and there at the very moment—you get used to that. But a Mark VI you keep on working; at least you think its working and it's not. So I

> have a great respect for the Mark VI and I am scared of it which is the thing to be as far as the Mark VI goes."

Potential and actual problems with the Mark VI were numerous. Almost every diver had one experience and many had several experiences in which the apparatus malfunctioned in a major or minor way. An abnormal functioning meant either that the diver was not getting sufficient oxygen, was inhaling an impure gas, or that his buoyancy was increasing. Whatever the malfunction, the diver had only a few seconds or minutes to take corrective action.

The malfunction resulting in the closest call was caused by a case of over inflation of a rebreathing bag. In this incident the diver was wearing an electrically heated wet suit. This suit was relatively new, having been tested experimentally in pools, but this use in SEALAB was its first open sea test. In this accident, a valve, regulating the flow of gas out of the exhalation bag malfunctioned, causing the bag to inflate. This increase in buoyancy started to carry the diver to the surface. A battery pack used to power the heated suit blocked his access to a valve which he could have adjusted to correct the situation. Because of the poor visibility in the area and the difficulty of communication, it was some time before the man's diving partner recognized the problem.

Let us continue the story in the diver's own words:

> "I made a quick turn to assist my partner and my bypass started free flowing. Well before I knew it—I would estimate I was from 15 to 20 feet off the bottom. My bypass was free flowing and one side of my vest bag popped up. I was swimming to the bottom as hard as I could and I wasn't making any headway for awhile. I decided well the most important thing for me to do is to get to the bottom and I got to that stake we were driving in and held on. My partner said are you in trouble and I said yes. I quit trying to fool with the bypass and went ahead and let the bag flop up in my face. So I swam to the bottom and he assisted me to get started and I swam along this line to the visibility range and cable. I didn't leave that cable because I knew that cable would lead right back to the habitat. Quite frankly—I don't think I have ever been as frightened

in the water. I was quite apprehensive about the next dive. I was quite relieved when everything went well, and that dive was over."

This incident emphasizes some of the trade-offs which characterized SEALAB—between absolute safety and operational efficiency. It illustrates also the dangers and the realistic apprehensions and fears which were the major stresses of SEALAB.

Let us analyze those factors which combined to make this incident and every dive from SEALAB a stressful experience. First, the man was saturated with gas at seven atmospheres pressure. Had he not been so saturated, he could simply have gone to the surface when the trouble first occurred. His over inflated rebreathing bag acting as a float would have made his surfacing an effortless ascent. The second factor was the coldness of the water. If the water had been warm, as it was in SEALAB I he would not have been wearing a heated suit. If he had no heated suit there would have been no battery pack to interfere with his taking corrective action relatively easily. Too, if SEALAB II had not been a research and development operation, the heated suit would have had the problems, such as the location of the battery pack, ironed out. If it had not been necessary for him to conserve his gas supply, the offending rebreathing bag would have been unnecessary. Finally, if visibility had been better, as it was in SEALAB I, his diving partner might have been able to come to his assistance sooner. Assistance from the diving partner would have been more readily available if adequate communications had been possible. Improved diver-to-diver communications are one of the major research goals of undersea work and therefore probably will be available on future projects.

By analyzing this accident we have attempted to show that the stress produced by danger was at a very high level in SEALAB because of the project's experimental nature. In future operations many of the equipment and communication problems revealed in SEALAB II will have been solved or partly alleviated. SEALAB II was a milestone in diving history. Because it was such a milestone it was of necessity dangerous.

The incident described above was perhaps the closest call in SEALAB but there were numerous other malfunctions involving the Mark VI. Another is described by a diver:

> "I jumped out, I threw my on and off lever to give me gas—stepped outside, started swimming. I took a breath of air and got nothing but my bag collapsed, so I started heading back and I got real whoozy—rockets started going off and I didn't think I was going to make it, and I got hung up in the damn doorway—I didn't think I was going to get back in. I was on the verge, I think, of going out. I have fainted a couple of times in my life. You get that tingling. I was just about ready right then. I got inside. Didn't talk straight for a few minutes, just stood there and breathed real hard. Told them my rig wasn't working . . ."

The failure of the air purifier led to another close call:

> "I came in one night after a night dive, the Mark VI was flooded, the cannister was completely flooded. When I got up in the entryway I stood maybe 5 minutes or so to hyperventilate. I might of got a CO_2 buildup or something—I don't know. I was way, way behind in my breathing. For awhile things were kind of spinning."

Uncertainty about the amount of gas remaining was a source of anxiety while in the water. The potential danger of this is illustrated in the following quote.

> "Because of the angle of SEALAB our flow meter ball was sticking on the tube—and we were getting a wide variance in leader flow—this always should be able to be calculated mathematically and we'd be off 1,000 pounds (a factor of ⅓) in our calculations, which scared us quite a bit. I'm not sure we've really solved that problem yet."

Perhaps the attitude of the aquanauts towards the Mark VI and its problem is best summed up in the comments of two of the most experienced divers.

> "It's a wonderful piece of equipment. It needs some modifications but basically it is sound."

> "Using the Mark VI under these conditions is altogether different than (diving) it from the surface, if it malfunctions on you (under normal conditions) you know that you can make your way to the surface. I thought about it several times—I'd look up and say, if anything happens this is the wrong thing to do and I know everyone else did too."

The other breathing gear was the Arawak or Hookah. This device had 100 foot hoses connected to a pump in SEALAB, thus the diver breathed gas from SEALAB while he swam. The virtue of the Arawak was that it permitted theoretically unlimited time in the water. That is, the gas supply would not run out as it did on the Mark VI. However, it had two major drawbacks, one being that it limited a diver to a range of 100 feet, the other that the hoses became fouled, tangled, kinked and subject to cuts by sharp objects in the area. A diver comments on problems with Arawak.

> "The Arawak hoses became tangled severely, constantly . . . they float and any time you have as many lines hanging around SEALAB as we have, such as trolley lines for buoys and this, that and the other thing, all coming from the surface, this Arawak tangles, and the man who is swimming is moving around and not paying any attention to what lines he is going around or how he goes around them . . . This was no fault of the diver . . . You start swimming around and you are going around lines. Also, they took a lot of turns because a diver, when he is moving around, he will make a turn this way and the hose goes with him, that is one turn. Then he will move around a little more; if he turns a lot pretty soon he is tied in a knot."

There were numerous incidents involving the Arawak, for example:

> "Well, you know I had an emergency on the Arawak . . . You just have to use it to know how it tangles. You see with the Arawak you have no safety whatsoever. When a hose kinks off, you stop breathing. Your bag level is gone. It's just like clapping a hand over a child's mouth."

> "I got tangled up quite a few times going out of the entrance way. I got my regulator hose completely pinched off two or three times

for 20 or 30 seconds 'til I could get it clear and, of course, all the time you're wondering, you know, am I going to get it clear or not."

"One time I was out on the Arawak. I took in a lung full of air and I just didn't have any. I grabbed onto the hose and I looked toward the surface and I tried again to breathe and there just wasn't a drop of air coming out there. Well, I could see the hose was kinked but there was no way in the world I could unkink it so all I did was I rolled over, pointed my head down and straightened my legs out and I really headed for the entry way. All I remembered thinking while I was going back, I hope that hose don't hang up because if that hose hung up on nothing I'd of never, never made it back."

Most divers preferred the Mark VI breathing gear. Their reaction is best summed up by the following comment:

"I hate the damn Arawak. It was a clumsy piece of equipment for me to use. When I wore the thing the bags bulged up around me—it was hard for me to maintain my position. You couldn't control the amount of gas in your bags and they were normally much more inflated and up around your neck."

It should be emphasized that each diver was trained thoroughly in the use of this breathing apparatus. He knew exactly what to do when trouble arose. In addition, he was always in contact with SEALAB through safety lines radiating from it. Also, whenever he left SEALAB, every diver was accompanied by a buddy who could assist him in case of trouble. One of the specific ways in which assistance could be provide was by means of a "buddy breathing" apparatus. This procedure enabled a diver who was in trouble to breathe the gas of his diving partner. Despite the extensive safety precautions and the thorough knowledge and training of the divers, however, this was a first of type operation, and as is seen above the dangers were real and well known to each diver.

OTHER STRESSES

Entering the water from SEALAB was stressful in a number of other ways. Even if the impossible had been achieved and there had been no problems with breathing apparatus, there were other factors which would have made work in the water stressful. Among these were the cold, poor visibility, difficulty in establishing orientation, hard work, problems of communication, and dangerous marine life.

Cold

The water temperature in the vicinity of SEALAB ranged from 46° to 55° F.—debilitatingly cold. Mention was made above of the use of a heated suit. This equipment was experimental and was used for a few dives only. Most dives were made with ⅜ inch or ¼ inch wetsuits, which provided some thermal protection, but not much. Furthermore, the insulating quality of the material was degraded severely by the 100 pounds pressure which compressed them. When the suits were first taken into SEALAB, they were squeezed paper thin and it took approximately one week for them to re-expand to their normal thickness. Cold had been anticipated as a problem but most divers reported it not to be as limiting as they had expected. To say this, however, is merely to say that the cold did not make work impossible, merely very uncomfortable. There can be little doubt that extreme cold is stressful in and of itself and it was cold diving from SEALAB. Reactions to cold are illustrated by comments of several divers.

> "Pretty soon you realize that the water is just doggone cold and I think you accept the fact that part of the day is going to be spent being miserable and that period is going to be the latter part of your dive. Once you accept that fact you don't feel so sorry for yourself. You learn to accept it to a certain extent. I worried about the cold water less and less and worried about getting the work done more and more as the days progressed, but I tell you I got awfully, awfully cold some days."

> "I won't say it got unbearable—it wouldn't be to the point that if an emergency arose that you couldn't stay out there, but you had the feeling of wanting to get back in there and getting under that

hot shower. Once you got up in the entry-way, sat down for a few minutes while the pots were being loaded, you'd start shaking uncontrollably; you weren't that cold, you weren't that uncomfortable but you just couldn't stop shaking."

"The cold probably wouldn't kill you for a long, long time if you were doing useful work. On a busy day when we were really hustling along I would spend easily an hour and 20 minutes or an hour and a half doing pretty good work before I would start shaking so bad that I really wasn't getting much done."

"By warm, I don't mean comfortably warm. I was staying workably warm."

"I didn't get cold as long as I was working, but whenever you stop, of course, you do."

"It isn't like swimming down in Panama City, Florida or Bermuda."

Visibility and Orientation

Another source of stress in the water was the possibility of getting lost because of poor visibility. Some days and under certain conditions visibility was near zero, both because of the poor ambient light (the sun's rays do not filter down very well to 200 feet in water which has a good deal of marine life and other translucent and opaque light diffusers) and because of the silt stirred up from the bottom. Getting lost meant not being able to find one's way back to SEALAB before the gas ran out. Thus, the problems of orientation and maintaining physical contact with SEALAB were ever present. Knowledge of position was of equal importance to the proper functioning of breathing gear. The divers discussed their difficulties in this area in the debriefing interview.

"The 300 foot dive I made I had no visibility at all. It was just total darkness. Even the light wasn't helping much."

"Some days you could get fair visibility with the lights on. I guess you could get off 35 or 40 feet and turn around and see the lab. Other days you could get off the same distance and just see a very dim glow of the light. Other days you couldn't see anything."

"I think I could get back from some directions without a tether, but anybody that didn't take a tether would be a fool."

"When we went out getting core samples we would stir up the bottom and you couldn't see anything. All we did was just stop where we had a line attached. But if you made a few circles it would be very easy to lose yourself down there."

"If you are swimming in the Mark VI it should be a law to have a tether back to the lab. Never rely on sonar for something like this."

"A person has an active mind, you're always thinking about situations that can happen. You're always a little more apprehensive because of the fact that you cannot afford to get lost."

"If the water was very cloudy I always kept my hands on the lines. When you start working on something—not sitting on the bottom—you always attach a line to the line and move around with it attached to you personally."

"When we'd work on a new site we'd always make sure we had a safety line from the site going right back to the habitat. I don't think there was ever a place where we had to swim more than 15 feet, or say 10 feet without a line that we couldn't see the habitat. It was just too risky."

"I always had in the back of my mind the fact that I had to get back to the SEALAB, and I always took precautions to insure that I did. I only really was apprehensive on this one occsasion when, as I said, on a very early dive I found that I had lost physical contact with SEALAB and lost sight of it, and I realized that this was a possibly dangerous situation. I noticed from my own experience diving in shallow water that it's very easy to get turned around when you're in a silty situation, and this was a silty situation."

"I did get disoriented when I was not on the line, and this was about 15 feet away from the SEALAB. I looked back over my shoulder to see the SEALAB and didn't see it. I was a little apprehensive, then I looked around and I saw it. I was looking in the wrong direction."

Marine Life

"Scorpion fish" proved to be a rather unexpected hazard. These marine creatures had poisonous spines with which they could and did administer painful stings to aquanauts. The direct effects of the stings were not fatal, but they could produce seizures, which under SEALAB conditions would have been fatal. While the chances of such seizures were remote, their possible occurrence and the uncomfortable direct effect of stings made the divers very wary of these fish. Foreign objects in the sea attract forms of marine life, scorpion fish included, thus, these creatures were numerous and a number of divers were struck by them. One diver describes his encounter.

> "The bottom is completely covered with them (scorpion fish). I got hit with one the first week we were there. I stayed in the water—you bleed quite a bit. It cut clear through the rubber glove. The hand felt real numb for about 30 minutes, but I kept using it—made myself use it more than normally and by the time I come out of the water it was all gone. Another diver not too long ago, he had one hit him 3 times—got him in the face, the chest and the stomach. This is before he came to SEALAB. He said it made him violently sick."

Even if a man was not hit, knowledge of their potential effects influenced him as is illustrated in this comment:

> "I don't like those fish . . . I was scared of those fish. I don't like the idea of going out there and getting zapped and not knowing if the effects of that fish are going to prevent you from getting back inside the lab because you can get stung like that, go into a type of fit . . . so I was always in fear of touching the bottom."

A quantitative assessment of the problem was provided by still another diver.

> "Near the end I counted 27 scorpion (fish), in one meter square . . . and this is a carpet of spines."

Work Difficulties and Frustrations

Underwater work is always difficult; in SEALAB the difficulties reached a peak. A number of factors combined to produce feelings of frustration regarding work. SEALAB divers were a group of hard driving, dedicated men who wanted to accomplish more than they were able to do under the circumstances.

What were some of the factors limiting the amount of work which could be accomplished? First and foremost was the matter of safety. The dangers of SEALAB have been cited above. In addition to the dangers, there were traffic jams in the SEALAB entrance. It was necessary always to leave the way clear so that a diver in trouble could get inside quickly. This meant that, for the most part, only two divers were in the water at any one time. Another limiting factor was the time needed to prepare for a dive. In total time it took nearly an hour to prepare for and possibly another hour to secure from a dive. This meant that it required three hours of time to be in the water only one hour as is illustrated in the following assessment.

> "Well, I spent a good half an hour rigging my Mark VI—then it takes about 15 minutes to get your gear on. Then when you make your dive and you come back in and then you have to tear your Mark VI down—wash it off real good with fresh water, and taking your suit off takes about 5 minutes maybe, so you shot another 30 to 45 minutes, after the dive. So to make an hour's dive you can figure you invested about three hours."

The frustratingly long time it took to perform simple tasks in the water is vividly described by the following comments of several of the divers.

> "It takes, it takes a long time to do things in the water and I don't know why. You don't move as fast, first of all. You get tired sooner—you get cold sooner. You can't see as well. You've got gloves that interfere with your manual dexterity. Things float away—lines get in your way—you get your gear fouled-up with equipment and you worry about stepping on the fish . . . and all these things put together make every task take a long time. I mean you want to drive something down in the ground, you're not heavy enough to do it . . . and so forth, it's more difficult, it's hard work, it takes a long time to do simple tasks in the water."

> "I'm sure you've heard this before from everybody you've talked to. It's unbelievable how difficult a minor task is. For example some of the equipment we were sent to work with—to unwrap it took 20 minutes—to find it might take an hour—just to find it. And you say it's right by the shark cage. Well hell, that might be 20 square feet of silt, you know, with maybe 200 or 300 scorpion fish to kick out of the way."

> "It takes a good hour to replace a bulb. It takes time to go out and get the light, bring it inside, dry it off, take it apart and splice it, and it takes time to take it back out and set it up."

In addition, a particularly annoying problem in accomplishing work was the difficulty in communicating between divers in the water.

> "When you are out there you can't really communicate with anyone—you can grunt and point your finger. If they understand—fine, but if they don't you have to come back in and talk it over with them. It is just little things like that and over a period of time they build up a delay—actually it isn't a delay—where you are comparing it to the surface where I can say 'well hand me the wrench, this thing doesn't look like it is going to fit—what do you think about it?' That particular communication may take 15 minutes."

The multipurpose nature of the work in SEALAB was another factor limiting the amount of time which could be devoted to any one project. Such time limitations were effected in several ways. First of all the different projects competed for the limited time available in the water. That is, because of the traffic jams in the work area which made it difficult to get more than two men in the water at anyone time, there were severe restrictions on the time that any one man could be in the water. The multipurpose nature of the project also meant that a variety of materials had to be transferred from SEALAB to surface and back. This transfer required time in the water and thus cut down on the time available for other work. Consequently, most divers were disappointed with the amount of time they had available for work which they considered their own, as is illustrated in the following comments.

> "I was very disappointed, because, I think everybody was in a sense. They had so much they wanted to do and knew they could do, but then when you get down there, there was so much just, what do you call it, housekeeping, or survival work that had to be done, that kept you from doing your work."
>
> "The jobs that have to be done that aren't related to your work really cut down your work time—your personal work time."

All of the factors listed above added up to a condition which produced feelings of frustration and lack of accomplishment.

> "I wasn't satisfied, because I devoted so much of my time to activities that I wasn't directly related to. I felt they were not part of my function. Very definitely, probably 30–35% of the time down there was devoted to what I wanted to do."
>
> "I look back and I don't see where I accomplished anything but, boy, my days were awful full."

The crux of the problem of working in the water is probably best summed up by one of the divers, who said:

> "I was extremely disappointed but I realize now I expected too damn much."

Thus, working in the water in SEALAB was stressful. The stresses included dangers from malfunctions of breathing gear, becoming lost, or being stung by scorpion fish. Added to these were the debilitating effects of the cold water, the problems of visibility, and the hard and frustrating work, all of which were compounded by difficulties in communication. This was not the whole story however, for there were tremendous rewards. On balance, most of the divers felt that SEALAB II was the greatest experience of their lives. That is, they did cope with these stressful stimuli and adjusted to them at a very high level. Why they were able to do this we will consider later. The point here is that the conditions detailed above add up to a highly negative complex of stimuli. Moreover, there were many conditions inside the capsule, where most of the aquanauts' time was spent, which further complicated life and work.

STRESSES INSIDE SEALAB

Life inside SEALAB presented problems in addition to those faced in the water. While the distractions and debilitations inside SEALAB were much less dramatic than those in the water, they would rank as severe in the extreme when compared with conditions in industrial or laboratory settings which have been shown to degrade performance significantly. We are speaking here of stimuli such as noise, temperature, humidity, and overcrowding (Mackworth, 1950; Chiles, 1958; Broussard, 1953; Broadbent, 1957; Helper, 1957). Added to these were a variety of stimuli unique to SEALAB such as the exotic atmosphere which the men breathed. Finally, SEALAB was the aquanaut's home as well as his place of work. Consequently, this was not a situation which a man could leave after his work day. Under the category "*Stresses Inside SEALAB*" we will consider first those associated with the unique atmosphere of the capsule.

SEALAB's Atmosphere

The respirable atmosphere of SEALAB was abnormal both with respect to its pressure and its composition. We have already noted that the pressure in SEALAB was approximately 100 pounds per square inch. Because of this great pressure, the composition of the SEALAB atmosphere had to be altered significantly. The normal atmosphere of the earth is approximately 20% oxygen and 80% nitrogen with fractional percentages of carbon dioxide and traces of other gases, but this sea level atmosphere transferred to 205 feet beneath the ocean's surface at ambient pressure would have resulted in a mixture seven times as dense in oxygen and nitrogen making the effective levels of these gases 140% and 560%, respectively. Such concentrations of nitrogen and oxygen would be lethal. Therefore, the concentrations of these two gases were lowered by substituting helium, used both because it is inert and because it is light. The fact that it is inert means that it passes through the body with no deleterious effects. Its lightness means that the density of the overall mixture is reduced, making it easier to breathe. The atmosphere in SEALAB was approximately 3.5% oxygen, 18% nitrogen, less than 0.4% carbon dioxide with the balance, about 78%, being helium. Multiplying the atomic weights of the gases in this mixture by the pressure and comparing it with normal atmosphere shows a density of the atmosphere which was about 1.6 times normal. The atmosphere used in SEALAB had been tested previously in laboratory experiments and in SEALAB I. It was known to be capable of supporting life with no detectable deleterious effects if the gases were maintained within a few percentage points of the values listed above. Maintaining the mixture within these limits was a constant and exacting task requiring the attention of monitoring personnel, both on the bottom and topside. The atmosphere was successfully controlled throughout the entire period of the study, however the mixture was abnormal; and this abnormality produced a variety of stressful, annoying, amusing and disrupting if not toxic effects. What were some of these effects?

Perhaps most noticeable was the effect on speech. Helium, being a very light gas, affects the vibration of the vocal chords and the resonance of speech tones. This resulted in a "Donald Duck" like quality to all speech. Most men felt that they adapted to the altered nature of vocal sounds produced by themselves and their teammates within three to four days so that they could understand speech relatively well. However, this meant that they could understand well when they were close to the person and when vocabulary and sentence structure were simplified. The difficulty of understanding helium speech was further complicated by the high ambient noise levels from the equipment; therefore, communication was effortful as is illustrated in the following comments of the aquanauts.

> "It became easier to understand people in about 2 or 3 days, and after about 7 or 8 days it was very easy to tell who was talking

> without turning around and looking in almost all cases. However, I noticed that there was still a great deal of difficulty at the end to get across fine points or to use an uncommon word. This, I think, delayed us a hell of a lot in deciding what we were going to do on the diving, making sure what you were going to do on a specialized process. I felt there was still a communication problem at the end—added to this there was a lot of noise in the lab. The Arawak was being used more often later, I think."
>
> "I'd have to ask them to repeat to the point of embarrassment—you'd think, well, I'll just nod my head "yes"—I still didn't understand what he said."
>
> "One of the most interesting problems to me was this lack of ability to localize the sound. We all adapted to that reasonably well, but not totally—I think there was still a slight tendency not to localize too well, but it wasn't nearly so apparent after two weeks."

The effects of helium speech did have some positive aspects as well. It was a source of amusement for all men, thus relieving some of the tensions generated by living in close contact.

> "It was a funny problem at first. It was hard to talk because it was hard not to laugh at each other. I've noticed people hiding their mouth, you know, when I was telling them what to do because they couldn't keep from laughing at me, I sounded so silly, and I did the same thing. We accommodated to this in a couple of days."
>
> "I had one little amusing incident; we were standing at the sink one day. He pointed to this can that was open which contained gelatin dessert and he said (at least this is what I thought he said) 'yellow and hot water is a good drink'. I looked at it and it was raspberry and I said 'no it's red'—he said 'no yellow' and I said 'no it's red' and we batted this thing back and forth several minutes there. I thought hell, I better get this guy out of here—he's gone."
>
> "I found myself talking to myself lots of times—just wanting to hear this strange voice. That is why I did a lot of singing down there—I was rather amused at myself."

The lightness of helium means that it has high thermal conductivity. This characteristic results in rapid body heat loss which made it necessary to maintain relatively high temperatures, about 85° F.

Because of the open hatch to the sea in the diving area, and heating of this area by radiant electric heaters, the amount of moisture entering SEALAB was great, resulting in a relative humidity of 60% to 90% (Cannon 1966). While these ranges of temperature and humidity produced *subjective comfort* for the most part, they also wreaked havoc with the human thermostat. Disruptions in heat balance within the body were particularly noticeable while men were asleep, probably because of low activity at that time. They would wake up shivering while sweating even though they were covered with several blankets. The reason for this reaction is not completely understood; however, it is clear that disruptions in heat balance did interfere with sleeping and with other activities as well.

A variety of relatively minor complaints could be attributed to the atmosphere, including skin rashes and ear infections resulting from the high temperature and humidity. Headaches, noted mainly upon waking in the morning, were a frequent complaint, and could have been caused by a buildup of carbon dioxide and possibly carbon monoxide in the bunk areas. Curtains were provided for privacy but when a man drew them in order to shut out other sights and sounds, the air circulation in his bunk was impeded, thus allowing an accumulation of carbon dioxide. Mention was made above of the greater than normal density of the SEALAB atmosphere, which meant that each breath required excess effort. Finally, because of its composition, the SEALAB atmosphere would not support an open flame, which made smoking impossible. Many of the aquanauts had been smokers prior to their submersion.

OTHER POTENTIALLY STRESSFUL CONDITIONS

Diet Restrictions

There were several restrictions on the permissible diet in SEALAB. Because of the nature of the atmosphere, the aquanauts were unable to fry, broil or roast any meats, as such processes would have released toxic molecules which would have contaminated the atmosphere permanently. Therefore much of the meat consumed was of the canned variety. In addition, there was little time devoted to meal preparation because the men were extremely busy; and there were no specially trained cooks. Cooking was shared relatively equally among all the men. Some culinary triumphs were achieved in the face of these difficult conditions by some chefs, but most of the meals were quite dull and ordinary. In addition to problems in preparing the food, there were also problems in consuming it. The dining room was supposed to be located in the bunk area with the men sitting on bottom bunks and eating from a table in the middle of the aisle; however, because of the angle at which SEALAB sat on the bottom, the dishes slid off the table, so that eating was done either standing up or sitting in a chair holding the bowl of food in one's hand. The result of these conditions was that food was far from being a major source of gratification in SEALAB as it has proved to be in other isolated groups such as those in the Antarctic and on fleet ballistic missile submarines (Gunderson & Nelson, 1966; Navy Times, Oct. 1966). However, the less than gourmet diet and less than posh dining facilities were not a problem, as indicated by few complaints in the post experiment interviews. More variety would have been appreciated, but the most typical reaction is summed up in the following comment:

> "Actually, meals were a bother. Up here you enjoy it, but down there it is a nuisance. You get hungry so you have to eat real quickly and you get up and you get back to work. I would say we would spend 10 minutes on breakfast and maybe 15 apiece on lunch and dinner. We didn't care about it. It just wasn't important."

Thus, a restriction which would very likely have been quite annoying under more normal circumstances was seen as being of little consequence in SEALAB II.

Noise

Studies of work efficiency in industrial psychology have shown the disrupting effects of high noise levels on productivity and morale

(Broadbent, 1957). While decibel ratings of the noise inside SEALAB are not available, it is safe to say that the capsule environment was uncomfortably noisy, the chief offender being the Arawak pump. When this apparatus was running, as it was several hours each day, communication was all but impossible. In addition, there was a loudspeaker carrying communications from the surface which was used periodically, as well as a variety of other machinery that produced noise. These sounds, added to the chipmunk-like babble of ten men confined in a 12′ x 57′ capsule combined to produce a distractingly high level of noise. The effects of noise were perceived, and as in the case of the restricted diet, they would doubtless have been a major source of annoyance had not they been masked by other more stressful stimuli.

Crowded Conditions

As with noise, overcrowding has been shown to have a variety of disruptive effects, ranging from reduced efficiency to complete breakdown of normal biological processes (Helmreich, 1960; Calhoun, 1963). SEALAB was crowded. Had the capsule been bare of any equipment there would have been fewer than 70 square feet of space per man in this combined home and workshop under the sea. (The U.S. Navy recommends 90 square feet of floor space for each enlisted man's berthing area alone.) But the capsule was not bare, much of the floor space being taken up by bunks, stove, refrigerator, sinks, counters, gas and electrical monitoring equipment, showers, water heater, and so on. In addition, a large amount of necessary gear had to be stored within the capsule, such as wetsuits, and bulky gas bottles and Mark VI units, tools, equipment, scientific samples and food. Consequently, there was a shortage of space in which to move around, not to mention space for work and recreation. The major problem was the entry area. The crowded conditions in the entry were listed by the divers on the debriefing questionnaire as the number one problem in the entire operation. Their sentiments are summed up in the following two comments:

> "That habitat is big enough to live in but it is not big enough to work in."
>
> "There was too damn many men in this. I think ten is five too many. You get ten men in a confined space and you got problems, just getting in each other's way, more than anything else."

Because of the crowded conditions, there was no private space, no chance to be alone, and almost no storage space for personal gear. These problems were also mentioned by the men.

Tilted Capsule

SEALAB rested on the ocean floor with a six degree tilt in two directions. To have leveled the capsule would have taken weeks of valuable time; therefore, it was decided to live with the unlevel condition. The "Tiltin' Hilton" was the sardonically humorous name the aquanauts gave to their home under the sea. This tilt produced many problems. It has been mentioned above that it was impossible to eat from a table or counter because of this condition. It was also necessary to tie pots onto the stove; writing reports was difficult and drawers would slide open or shut—whichever status was least desired, it seemed. The difficulty in walking around while wearing 120 pounds of diving gear under these conditions had to be experienced to be appreciated. The fact that setting up Mark VI breathing gear under these conditions might have affected the adjustment of the flow meter meant that, indirectly, this tilt could have contributed to fatal accidents. All in all, the unlevel situation of SEALAB was a hindrance that the aquanauts could well have done without.

Fatigue

Long hours of hard work, combined with difficulties in sleeping produced extreme fatigue in many of the aquanauts. Difficulties in sleeping were caused by the exotic atmosphere, the need for standing around the clock watches in order to monitor the gas and electrical equipment, and probably also in part by high arousal from the multitude of stressful stimuli. Nearly all of the divers stated that they became very tired by the end of their fifteen day stay. The following comments are typical of the general reactions.

> "I found sleeping a problem. I was always perspiring in my sleep and yet usually cold at the same time. So, although I woke up frequently in the night, I didn't get up. I'd wake up and toss around. I think I only got about 5 hours of real sleep a night. I spent much more time in bed at night."

> "I would like to go down again, but not right away. It takes a lot out of you, like sleep. I got only ten hours sleep the whole time I was down there. That was my only problem, just sleep. I ate good . . . everyone had trouble sleeping. I was relaxed, it wasn't that you were bothered that way. You would lay there and you would toss and turn and you felt like you were sweating, you were hot and you were cold."

> "I would guess I slept only 4½ hours a night. I became increasingly tired and then one day I got hit with that sting, and I slept all day long, and actually that was a blessing because I needed the sleep."

Other Annoyances, Deprivations, and Potential Disruptions

In addition to all of the above, there were a variety of other conditions in SEALAB which could have interfered with normal and efficient functioning. It should be pointed out that while these conditions are considered relatively minor here, each of them could have been severely limiting had its salience not been obscured by the more pressing stimuli discussed above. Among these other factors were the status of the aquanauts as experimental subjects, the heterogeneity of the group, the lack of familiar topside stimuli, and the possibility of unknown deleterious physiological effects.

The aquanauts' status as experimental subjects was annoying in a variety of ways. Blood samples were reluctantly given daily by some of the men and on a less frequent schedule by others. In addition, there were routine physiological tests to undergo. A major source of complaint was the requirement of filling out forms and repetitious questionnaires which interfered with the divers' "own work" or recreation.

There was the possibility of unknown physiological changes of a permanent and irreversible nature. Previous physiological tests in SEALAB I had shown no untoward effects; however, it was still unknown what effects might result from living and working for this length of time under the ocean. Just as the effects of weightlessness and radiation could only be estimated before man actually ventured into outer space, so could the effects of living and working under pressure only be estimated and extrapolated from previous research. This point has been made by Captain Walter Mazzone (Mazzone, 1966) in discussing the findings of physiological research in SEALAB II, "It is apparent that man, when subjected to severe environmental stresses in SEALAB operations, did not manifest untoward responses indicative of biological rejection of a new mode of life, life under the surface of the sea . . . above all, one must exercise extreme reluctance in accepting superficial interpretations of results. Although for SEALAB II all results were essentially within normal limits, it must be remembered that these normal limits have been stipulated for conditions on the surface, with normal atmosphere, the design criteria established for the development of man."

While Capt. Mazzone is speaking here of the results of SEALAB II and their application for the future, the same comments could have been made previous to SEALAB II regarding the findings from earlier studies and their application to this situation.

OTHER DANGERS

We will close this discussion of stresses by describing two dangers not mentioned earlier because they were not associated with work in the water. These dangers were rather like the sword of Damocles hanging over the heads of the aquanauts, as they were completely outside the control of the divers. One was the danger from a sudden flooding of the capsule caused by a broken port hole. This threat is described by one of the men:

> "One of the things that created a mental hazard for all of us when they were raising the TV tripod or something that was coming close to the habitat. That just the legs hanging from that port can knock it out . . . If something would come through one of the ports, a massive flooding would occur there. I doubt if anybody could get to the electrical system in time to turn them off."

The other danger lay in the transfer to the surface at the termination of the experiment. Briefly this is what occurred in transfer. The personnel transfer capsule (PTC) sat on the bottom about 40 feet away from SEALAB. At the termination of the study the men swam to and entered the PTC. In order that it could be handled more easily, the PTC was barely large enough to accommodate the ten men. Conditions inside it were very cramped. Once the men were all in, and had put on their football helmets and tightened their seat belts (used in order to reduce the possibility of head injuries should the capsule suddenly lurch), the hatch was sealed. It was then hauled to the surface on a cable dangling from the end of a crane on the support vessel. When the PTC emerged, it was swung across the deck of the support vessel, and the legs were then detached so that it could be lowered onto the deck decompression chamber (DDC). When the legs had been detached, it was swung across the support vessel again to the DDC. During these operations, when the PTC was in the air swinging free, it could have collided with the support vessel or its structures, the cable could have failed, or the tackle might have slipped dropping the PTC onto the deck or back into the sea. Because of these dangers, a calm sea was required for the operation. Another crucial part of the operation was mating the PTC to the DDC. Once this seal was made, the hatches in the two chambers were opened and the men climbed down from the PTC into the DDC to start their 35 hours of decompression. The transfer to the surface was regarded by many of the men as the most dangerous part of the operation. In many ways it is similar to the reentry of astronauts into the earth's atmosphere, except that it required a much longer time. The reactions of most aquanauts were typified by the following comments:

"That ride in the PTC where they got—each team—10 people in there and trying to (mate) that thing to the DDC. If you lost the seal you might just kill all the men. That's the tricky part of the whole maneuver in my estimation."

"The PTC was a dreaded piece of equipment to me, that's the only part of the operation that I was actually afraid of. I realized how much you depended on shackles and men slipping shackles on. This is what I fear—human error up there."

The fact that this operation occurred at the termination of the experiment meant that this threat hung over the men throughout their stay on the bottom.

REACTIONS TO SEALAB

What were the reactions to the situations described above? How did the men perform with reference to work and social interaction? What were their emotional reactions? In general, the aquanauts of SEALAB coped very well with their highly stressful environment. Both individuals and groups worked effectively; social interaction was harmonious; and emotionally, the men weathered the stresses very well. There are several types of evidence which bear out these general conclusions, derived chiefly from comments given in the debrief interviews, from comments of team leaders and topside supervisors, from the impressions gained by psychologists in TV and audio monitioring and from quantitative measures of reactions to the environment. The present discussion is relatively general in nature, as more specific data, particularly those data bearing on individual reactions, will be presented in Chapter 6.

Comments of the Aquanauts

From the post-experimental questionnaires and interviews there are a number of indicators of excellent adaptation and adjustment. That the aquanauts perceived the stresses in SEALAB is evident.

Along with these perceptions of stress however, they also felt that they could and did cope adequately with the situation. A general answer to the question of their ability to cope is provided by responses to the post-experimental questionnaire. The men were asked: "Would you undertake another prolonged submergence in a SEALAB type capsule?" Responses to this question were requested on a five choice scale ranging from "definitely not" to "definitely yes", with "maybe" in the middle. Twenty-six of the twenty-eight aquanauts answered "definitely yes" and only two said "maybe". None said "probably not" or "definitely not". In answer to another question, most men said that they would have liked to have stayed much longer. This general reaction is amplified in the following statements made in the interviews.

> "I had a real good time—I enjoyed every bit of it. If I had to stay another 15 days I could have without any problems whatsoever. I was ready—I could have stayed. I think any of the other guys could have stayed."
>
> "I think it was a wonderful experience and . . . I'm certainly appreciative of having been given the opportunity to do it."
>
> "I was very, very excited, like I told those reporters. I was extremely excited when I left. It is hard to stay in this state for two weeks, but I did."
>
> "I don't think I've ever been as motivated as I was in SEALAB."
>
> "I sure wish we could have stayed down another two weeks."
>
> "That was the hardest I have ever worked in my life. And it is the busiest I have ever been. I would go back right now. I didn't want to come up. I wish I could go back. I would like to go back for 45 days."
>
> "I enjoyed every minute of it, even though I was sleepy, I was so fascinated by the whole thing and so, so motivated too, to do it right and safely and well, that I got by with less sleep and worked harder and enjoyed it at the same time."

To be sure, there were some negative reactions in the area of social relations. They were, however, relatively minor and definitely not the dominant theme. These negative reactions were of two types. Some men felt that others on their team did not understand them and what they were trying to do or that they did not understand others or their roles. Some men felt that this lack of understanding hindered them in carrying out their work or resulted in nonparticipation in what might have been thought to be common work. These two reactions generally went together and the following comments are typical.

> "They thought we were goofing off and they did not understand (it seemed to me anyway). They didn't understand that we were down there to do another job."
>
> "There is nothing wrong with any of them in the water, they are all good divers, every one of them . . . we had a lot of good times together. It is just that they are not used to our type of work is all it is. You could stand there and look them right in the eye and ask them to give you a hand, and they would look right through you. Not that they were not hearing you, it was just that their mind was 50 miles away someplace."
>
> "They weren't carrying their share of the load and I did, at the time, resent this. But this is just my personal opinion."
>
> "When you put two men in the water, you must take them back out and get them squared away before others can get ready to go. They didn't quite understand this."
>
> "We had no friction of any kind at any time really, but we did have times when we didn't understand what each other wanted to do, and we butted heads a couple of times, and really we were trying to do the same thing and didn't know it."

Such attitudes are perhaps inevitable in a multipurpose project such as this which brought together men of widely varying backgrounds and interests. It is remarkable that these attitudes assumed such a minor role in the overall reactions. Furthermore, even those who felt most strongly that they were misunderstood or who did not understand the role of others said that they enjoyed and appreciated the experience, that personally they liked the other divers, and that they found SEALAB II highly rewarding.

This general perception of favorable adjustment was supported by the feeling that things were improving as time passed. Most men felt that they adapted quite well to the cold, but whether this adaptation was physiological or due to the expanding wetsuits is unclear as is revealed in the following comments:

> "I would say we adapted because the first day I went down to get into the SEALAB when I had that U.S. divers suit and we didn't do too much . . . I was quite chilled before I got into the SEALAB. When we left (at the end of two weeks) we all skinned out of the lab into the PTC and we didn't use any suit and didn't feel too chilly with no suit on."
>
> "I most certainly did adapt. After the first few dives we were real happy to come in. As the time progressed some of the guys were just putting on a shortie vest and skinning out to get pots and stuff like that. I definitely noticed that we were getting acclimated to it."
>
> "I think when we first got there—the first couple of days it was cold. It always is. But after awhile you can actually get accustomed to it—an adaptation takes place towards the cold—I think it is about as much psychological as it is physical."
>
> "This is a strange thing. It's not a progressing thing. It fluctuated. I learned to accept the cold water. I don't think my body drew up a layer of resistance to it. I learned to accept it more than anything else."
>
> "I don't know whether I adapted to the cold. I think not. I think the suit improved its performance rather than my adapting to the cold, but I may have adapted, I don't know.

There were few divers who felt that they did not adapt, and these men said that the cold never did bother them.

Another circumstance which made for improved performance was the fact that men became better oriented as time went on, as illustrated in the following two comments:

> "Another diver has an expression that he calls marinemanship which is a takeoff on the old expression woodsmanship. You know you can take a hunter and put him in a strange forest and after a little while

> he will adapt to it. He will navigate and find his way around. Well, I'm sure we all develop some of this."
>
> "The last day we went out to take a visibility measurement it was just like walking across the street."

In addition to becoming more familiar with the area, confidence increased and apprehension decreased as time passed.

> "Getting away from the lab the first week was a test for everybody . . . Getting away—a long distance away from it. I found myself progressively doing this with more ease as I stayed down there."

So, in general, operations went more smoothly as time went on. Many of the men felt that they were just hitting their stride at the time they had to come up and would have liked to have stayed longer.

> "I was just getting started good. I mean, I really believe that if we had had another two weeks down there we could have done twice as much work in the second two weeks than we did in the first two weeks."

The above comments present a picture of men who were working very hard and, although they were becoming increasingly fatigued, felt that through better organization and coordination of efforts, increasing confidence and adaptation to the cold, and orientation to their environment they were able to work much better as time passed.

Reports of a very high level of group harmony and cooperation were unanimous. We discuss group harmony in detail later on and attempt to analyze the reasons for good relations. At this point we merely report it as a universal perception. The following are typical reactions.

> "You were elbowing and eyeballing each other. If we hadn't had a real compatible group there might have been a lot of hard feelings. Everybody was very cooperative. They all worked and helped each other as much as possible. I think it was a real good group."

> "Definitely the group did get along. There wasn't a cross word said between anybody down there in the 15 days I was there and that's pretty remarkable."

Of course, some men did recognize that group relations were so good as to be almost "abnormal" or "unnatural".

> "Well, it was pseudo-cordiality. We weren't all that friendly, let's face it. There were a couple of guys down there that sort of disliked each other. We were concerned that they were actually going to have a knockdown, dragout fight. But both of these guys are professionals and when we got down there, they were sickeningly sweet to each other. Everybody was putting themselves second and putting things important to the project first."
>
> "I feel morale was good. Yes . . . because we just made it that way. I know a lot of people that would have been more independent about it and perhaps voiced a lot of complaints while it was going on, but I didn't exactly feel I should do it."

These latter comments, however, support the general impression of excellent group relations. Group harmony was not achieved without effort, but the necessary effort was expended. The men *did* censor and restrain themselves in expressing irritations and hostilities in the interests of overall good relations.

Evaluation by Leaders and Top Side Supervisors

The divers' perceptions of excellent performance and social adjustment were shared by underwater team leaders and by top side supervisors who observed repeatedly that machinery and equipment failed and malfunctioned but that the men of SEALAB never faltered. Equipment failures and malfunctions ranged from humorous incidents such as the mess resulting from the accidental *implosion* of a bottle of cocktail sauce to an extremely dangerous electrical short which cut off the power and nearly caused termination of the project. Included in these incidents were malfunctions of breathing gear which have been discussed in detail, diving lights which failed to last, TV cameras which leaked helium and failed, underwater sound gear which went dead, incompatible metals which soon rusted, rendering machines useless, positively buoyant tools, and a seemingly endless list of other problems. The equipment was repaired, replaced, substituted, used anyway, or done without, depending on the nature of the problem. Therefore the official evaluation of a high level of functioning seems well justified.

In short, the overall mission was accomplished and the study was regarded as a success by all concerned. It is significant in this respect that the full planned underwater duration was achieved. A termination of the project was never contemplated because of demands on the men, and no man requested a shortening or termination of his own stay. While many tasks were not completed and some were not begun at all, the overall accomplishment was outstanding. The planned salvage tasks in particular went very smoothly, requiring less time than had been anticipated. The scientific divers also accomplished a great deal. Time in the water was limited, but it was not limited by the capability or motivation of the men. The official reaction is perhaps best summed up by the comments of one of the team leaders who said:

"I feel we did as much as it was humanly possible to do."

Thus, the aquanauts themselves, their leaders and topside supervisors all agreed that performance and adjustment were excellent. One could ask if these "public" reactions expressed the "true" feelings of the aquanauts, and if they did, how enduring these feelings were. Furthermore, while these evaluations may be a complete and accurate account of the situation, most students of human behavior working in the last half of the twentieth century recognize that similar reactions could be expected regardless of the actual circumstances. That is, a variety of conscious or unconscious mechanisms of perception or report, acting singly or in combination could bias the evaluation of a project such as this. It is therefore desirable to supplement these reactions with other detached observations and with objective data. Fortunately such observations and data are available.

Observations by Psychologists

The psychological observation station was manned 24 hours per day by monitors. In addition, both of the authors spent many hours each day watching the TV from the capsule and listening to the audio signals. While the principal reason for this monitoring was to record data objectively, a running log of comments was kept and general impressions were formed. Objective data will be reported in detail in Chapter 6 and gross objective data will be presented immediately following this subsection. Here we are concentrating on the global impressions which we formed from our observations. As observers, we had the advantage of being less involved than the aquanauts or their supervisors, but we also suffered from the limitations of being far less informed and knowledgeable. We could see only a limited area of the capsule, as could all topside personnel, and could understand only limited portions of conversations. Also, there were channels of communications open to supervisors but unavailable to us. For much of the time we had no specific knowledge of what was happening, or of the detailed meaning of what we saw and heard. However, we could observe the emotional atmosphere and the general work pace, and we had the advantage of being able to sit and observe without having our attention constantly diverted. These observations then, should be considered in view of their advantages and limitations. They are offered not as a substitute for other observations or objective data but rather as one more view of a very complex situation.

Our observations supported the accounts of favorable adjustment and performance given by the men and their supervisors. We observed no evidence of interpersonal hostility or overt aggression in any of the groups. We did observe the good-natured kidding and banter reported by the aquanauts in the interviews, but at no time did we see these interchanges flare into hostility. On the contrary we noted much friendly and cooperative behavior. The emotional climate of all three teams was euphoric and aroused rather than depressed and lethargic. Most of the discussions between men were businesslike and neutral in affect, but there was also a good deal of smiling and laughter. Since a great deal of the conversation from SEALAB could not be understood because of the high level of background noise and the distorting effects of helium, we relied principally on facial expressions and the sounds of laughter which could be seen and heard.

With reference to work, we had the impression of groups which were working hard and were constantly busy. There was little chance to relax in SEALAB, because there was a variety of tasks which constantly demanded the attention of the divers. If they were not in the water, the men had plenty of other work to do. Some men would, for example, be assisting others entering the water or helping them out at the termination of a dive, while another man would be suited up and ready to go into the water as a standby diver. Numerous hours were spent in preparing the Mark VI breathing gear, in bringing in the heavy pressure pots in which material was transferred to and from the surface, in writing reports, in taking pictures, and in gathering medical data. In addition, there was a great deal of housekeeping to be done, which in SEALAB, meant not only cooking, washing the dishes, vacuuming, and straightening up but also replacing and repairing many items of equipment, changing the chemicals in the dehumidifier and the air purifiers and monitoring the life support equipment. The above are the kinds of activities we observed. Although we could not always tell exactly what a man was doing, we could observe when he was at work. In short, our observations squared with the self-reports of a harmonious and busy group.

Objective Data

Data of a more systematic and objective nature lend further support to our observations and to the self-reports. Several types of measures reflect work performance, and social and emotional reactions indicating favorable adjustment.

The best objective indicator of the perceived increase over time in the quantity and quality of work is the record of diving time. For each of the three teams diving time increased from the first week to the second week. These increases were, for the three teams, 25%, 25% and 21%. The average increase for the three teams from week 1 to week 2 was 24% ($t = 24.7$, 2 d.f., $p < .02$ for difference scores for the three teams). Thus, time in the water for each team increased markedly. The same is true for the number of sorties, that is the number of times a man went into the water. During the second week, more dives were made and the average length of each dive was longer than during the first week. These data provide strong support for the impressions reported above. The divers' comments that they became better oriented and adapted to the cold are borne out by the increase in the length of the dives. The increases in diving time and in number of sorties also meant a concomitant increase in many other work activities. It meant that more Mark VIs had to be prepared to support the men in the water, a major time consuming task. It also meant that more men had to be suited up and assisted in getting into and out of the water. This work was also extensive, as it meant more reports to be written, more samples to be labeled and processed, and more standby divers for a greater length of time. Thus, the increase in diving time and in sorties is hard evidence for increased individual and team adaptation, organization, and performance. It is clear that, rather than being overwhelmed by the multiple stresses in the situation and reacting with deteriorating performance, the men and crews of SEALAB coped with and demonstrated an increasing mastery of their stressful environment.

Measures of social interaction are consistent with the evidence of favorable work performance in indicating good adjustment. The clearest evidence of good social relations, in addition to and in support of the post-interview comments, is a significant increase in team cohesiveness from pre to post measures. Data measuring cohesiveness are provided by the sociometric questionnaires. Recall that the pre and post-sociometric measures asked each man to choose five from among the 27 other SEALAB divers with whom he would most like to be in SEALAB. Cohesiveness is defined here as the number of men who were chosen from within a man's own ten man team. The more men chosen from within a man's team, the more cohesive the team. According to the pre-dive ratings, own team members were not over chosen. 35% of all choices for the three teams were from within a man's own team. By chance we could expect that 33% of his choices would come from within the team, since other team members numbered nine out of a total group of twenty-seven others. Sociometric choices showed a marked increase on the post measure, 54% of the choices being own team members, that is, the men with whom he had been on the bottom. An even greater increase is shown if weighted choices are used. By weighted choices, we mean applying a weight of 5 for the first choice, 4 for the second, 3 for the third, 2 for the fourth and 1 for the fifth. Using weighted choices the number of points assigned does not change for the pre-measure, it is 35%; but for the post-measure it rises to 62%. It should be pointed out here that assignments to teams were not made by sociometric choice. The different specialties required on each team meant that many natural friendship groups had to be ignored in composing teams. The change in pre to post measures meant that in some instances, own team members were chosen in preference to men whom a diver may have known for a number of years, and this fact may account for the difference between the weighted scores and the unweighted scores. That is, the old buddy was not dropped completely from a man's list of five choices, but he was lower in the order than he had been previously. Thus, this quantitative measure of group cohesiveness agrees with the subjective impressions of group harmony reported by the divers.

One other bit of objective data provides an additional measure of social interaction, the record of outside telephone calls. An increase in the number of outside contacts could have meant a decrease in group cohesiveness. The data, to be examined later by individuals, will show that there are strong reasons to believe that better individual performance is associated with fewer outside phone calls. For the groups, there was no increase in number of outside phone calls over time.

Data for emotional reactions also indicate no deterioration in adjustment in this respect. Emotional reactions were measured by an adjective checklist which was administered seven times (every other day) for each team. Comparing three 5-day blocks of mood data over time no significant changes in emotional state were observed. It should be pointed out that increased knowledge and confidence was accompanied by an increase in time in the water—where the greatest danger lay. Also, there was an accumulation of incidents which kept the very real dangers of SEALAB salient. Finally, as time wore on, the trip to the surface, regarded by many divers as the most dangerous aspect of the entire project, was approaching. All of these factors would tend to elevate level of fear—all other things being equal. Therefore, it is considered that lack of change in these measures indicates favorable emotional adjustment.

Two other measures provide indirect indications of no deterioration in emotional adjustment. A count kept of the number of missed meals showed no increase over time in the number of meals missed. Observations were also made of the time men got up in the morning. While reveille was sounded at a scheduled time, it would have been easy to depart from this routine. For example, if the men had said that because of the fatiguing environment more sleep was needed, they would have been encouraged by topside supervisors to sleep later in the morning. Thus, they could have delayed facing the overwhelming stresses of a new day if they had so desired, but they did not. The data indicate that there was no change in the time at which men arose.

One final indicator of favorable reactions to SEALAB II remains to be cited. This is the volunteer rate of SEALAB II divers for SEALAB III. SEALAB III is scheduled to be placed at around 430 feet in 1968. Equipment and diving conditions will be better than they were in SEALAB II, but the general level of stress will not be appreciably lower. All divers from SEALAB II who are available for duty have volunteered for SEALAB III. There has been attrition from the SEALAB II team caused by retirement from the Navy, changed duty assignments, changes in planned projects, and the like. But there has been no attrition due to lack of interest or motivation.

CHAPTER 5

Costs and Rewards in Exotic Environments

In the previous chapter we described the dangerous and demanding environment of SEALAB. We have called this situation stressful because it contained a large number of severely negative aspects, including threats to safety, painful and unpleasant stimuli, interferences with goal directed activities and disruptions of physiological homeostasis.

All other things being equal, an adult human having full knowledge of this situation should have avoided it; however, a number of adult humans who had such knowledge did not. All divers in SEALAB were volunteers; moreover, after their participation they called their stay a great experience and said that they would go again if given the opportunity. Clearly then, all other things were not equal. In this chapter we will propose a conceptual framework in which the attraction to SEALAB can be understood. But first, we give a brief demographic description of the aquanauts as a group to use in analyzing their responses to SEALAB within the proposed conceptual framework.

THE AQUANAUTS

In examining selected demographic characteristics of the SEALAB II aquanauts one is struck with the heterogeneity of the group. They varied widely in a number of characteristics. For example, ten of the men were civilians and eighteen were in the Navy. Of the Navy divers two were commissioned officers. Data on civilian-military status are presented in Table 5-1 and, as can be seen in Table 5-1, the total group and the individual teams were very similar in composition according to civilian–military status. That is, each team contained approximately the same proportion of civilians and military divers as did the overall group. This composition was dictated by the diverse nature of the project. It should be apparent from this difference in status that there were concomitant differences in interests, values and reasons for participating in the project. Differences are discussed in greater detail later; at this point we merely note that they were present.

The one characteristic that all aquanauts had in common was their interest in diving and experience as divers. Even in this respect, however, there were wide variations as is indicated in Table 5-2. Data in Table 5-2 show that this was a very experienced group of divers. The differences between the teams in mean years of diving experience are not significant. The apparently high number of years experience on Team III is due to the presence of one very experienced man on that team.

TABLE 5-1
Civilian–Navy Status SEALAB II Aquanauts *

Status	Team I	Team II	Team III	Total
Navy Enlisted	5	5	6	16
Navy Officer	2	1	1	2
Civilian	3	4	3	10
Total	10	10	10	28

*In all tables in Chapter 5, totals are based on $N = 28$, since two men were on two teams each.

TABLE 5-2
Years of Diving Experience of SEALAB II Aquanauts

Years of Experience	Team I	Team II	Team III	Total
0-4	4	2	1	5
5-9	0	4	2	6
10-14	3	2	3	8
15-19	3	2	3	8
20-29	0	0	1	1
Total N	10	10	10	28
Mean	9.4	9.2	12.5	10.96
Range	17	14	28	28

Numbers of years of experience, impressive as they are, cannot adequately convey the importance of this experience to the success of the project. Included in the more than 300 years of accumulated diving experience of the SEALAB aquanauts were many unique and outstanding achievements. One of these illustrates well the nature of such experiences. One SEALAB II diver was a man who had made a free ascent from a submarine escape trunk when the submarine was at a depth of slightly greater than 300 feet. It may be helpful to explain briefly the background of this adventure so that its significance can be better appreciated.

For many years, one of the principal problems in rescuing men from submarines has been the inability of men to surface from damaged or disabled vessels when they are relatively close, that is, within a few hundred feet of the ocean's surface. Various methods and types of equipment have been used to facilitate the safe ascent of men trapped at such depths. Perhaps the simplest method of making an emergency escape from a disabled submarine is the one first demonstrated by Captain George Bond, MC, USN and ENC Cyril Tuckfield, USN. The two men entered the escape compartment of a submarine which was 300 feet beneath the ocean's surface. The compartment was then sealed and flooded until the air pressure inside equaled the ambient sea pressure (approximately 150 pounds per square inch). They then took a deep breath, opened the hatch and floated to the surface, exhaling slowly as they ascended. In this pioneering demonstration they wore no breathing gear of any type, depending on the air supply in their lungs for the oxygen needed during the ascent. Since their lungs contained air under high pressure for less than two minutes decompression was not required. Had they retained the air in their lungs by failing to exhale on the ascent, they would however have experienced an explosive, and very probably fatal, embolism. From this brief description, it is obvious that the successful accomplishment of this feat required brave and experienced men; men with confidence in their knowledge of diving and in their own abilities. One of the men who made this ascent was a diver on the first team of SEALAB II, the other was the principal investigator on the project and medical supervisor who kept watch topside during the entire project. The ties developed from this shared experience cannot be overestimated in their contribution to mutual confidence between topside supervisors and support divers and the aquanauts in SEALAB. These ties were duplicated many times over in similar experiences shared by other aquanauts and support personnel.

Many if not most of the SEALAB divers had experienced highly stressful environments previous to their SEALAB participation. Their biographical sketches include numerous references to combat experience. A list of their decorations and citations would fill two or three pages of this report if cited. Most of the military divers had experienced isolation and confinement in the submarine service. The crew leader of teams one and two had been the second American astronaut to orbit the earth. In short, the aquanauts had collectively experienced a wide variety of exotic and dangerous environments prior to their sojourn in SEALAB. There can be little doubt that these experiences helped them to anticipate and cope with the multiple stresses of SEALAB.

In addition to the differences in military and civilian status and the wide variations in diving experience, there were similar

TABLE 5-3
Age Distribution of SEALAB II Aquanauts

Age	Team I	Team II	Team III	Total All Teams
20-24	1	0	0	1
25-29	1	1	3	4
30-34	1	2	2	5
35-39	4	5	4	13
40-44	3	2	0	4
45-49	0	0	1	1
Total N	10	10	10	28
Mean	35.2	35.9	34.0	35.1
Range	20	12	25	26

variations in age and education. The data for these two variables are presented in Tables 5-3 and 5-4 for the total group, and are broken down by team. In general, the civilians had more years of schooling than the military participants with the exception of the officers. However, among the Navy enlisted men, there were men who had had some college education, with many of the Navy divers being much better educated in many areas than their formal schooling would indicate. Mention has already been made of their con-

TABLE 5-4
Education of SEALAB II Aquanauts

Education	Team I	Team II	Team III	Total
Less than H.S. Grad	1	0	2	3
H.S. Grad	4	4	4	12
Some College	1	1	1	3
College Grad	3	2	1	5
Advanced Degree	1	3	2	5
Total	10	10	10	28

TABLE 5-5
Marital Status SEALAB II Aquanauts

Status	Team I	Team II	Team III	Total
Single & Divorced	2	0	2	4
Married—No Children	1	0	1	2
Married—Children	7	10	7	22
Total	10	10	10	28

siderable knowledge of the breathing gear which supported them in the water. Their study and understanding of this equipment meant that they had acquired extensive knowledge of mechanics and physics. Basic physiology, particularly applied to mixed gases under pressure, was another area in which many of the Navy divers had extensive knowledge, and their association with the sea had sparked interest in marine biology and oceanography. Underwater acoustics, heat transfer and underwater propulsion were additional areas in which many of the Navy divers were amateur experts.

Two other demographic variables are of interest. These are marital status and size of hometown which are presented in Tables 5-5 and 5-6. It is apparent that the men of SEALAB were not unattached; they did not approach this study free of any family responsibilities. On the contrary, nearly all of them were family men.

TABLE 5-6
Size of Hometown of SEALAB II Aquanauts

Size of Community	Team I	Team II	Team III	Total
Farm or Village under 5000	2	2	4	8
Small City 5000-50,000	3	5	3	10
City 50,000-500,000	4	1	2	6
Large City—500,000+	1	1	1	3
Total	10	9	10	27

Also, as a group they came from relatively small towns. The possible relevance of this variable to their success in adapting to SEALAB will be discussed later.

SEALAB COMPARED WITH OTHER ENVIRONMENTS

In an attempt to understand the favorable reactions to the highly negative environment of SEALAB, it may be helpful to compare it with other environments. Rather than considering other environments at random, this analysis will focus on field, simulation, and laboratory studies involving isolation and confinement, which are here very broadly defined to include settings in which the individual or group is cut off from the rest of society for a relatively long period of time. An excellent recent review of studies of isolation and confinement has been written by Fraser (1966).

In simulation studies and laboratory experiments involving isolation and confinement, the negative or stressful elements are many fewer in number and much less severe than they were in SEALAB (Fraser, 1966). That is, danger, heat, humidity, high noise levels, overcrowding, fatigue, heavy work loads and frustration of goal directed activities are, if present at all, much less intense than they were in SEALAB. In field settings such as exploration parties (Lester, 1964; Nordhoff & Hall 1934), military combat units (Stouffer, *et al.,* 1949), paratroop training (Basowitz, *et al.,* 1955), mountain climbing (Lester, 1964), and the like, many of the stressful elements of SEALAB are also present. On the response side, reactions range from attraction to rejection, frequently accompanied by other indications of good or poor performance and adjustment. For example, laboratory studies of isolation and confinement are frequently marked by high abortion rates (Haythorn & Altman, 1966), by interpersonal difficulties where groups are involved, and by decrements in work performance (Adams and Chiles, 1961; Haythorn & Altman, 1966). If the mission is not aborted before its scheduled completion, there is no indication in the reports that the stay was enjoyable or that the situation was desirable for the participants. In brief, subjects have usually found simulation and laboratory studies of isolation and confinement highly undesirable. In field studies the opposite is generally true. While there are accounts of negative reactions to stressful field situations, it is more often the case that volunteers who undergo the high stresses of real life situations tend to react more favorably than do men experiencing the lesser objective stresses of laboratory and simulation studies. Men and crews frequently maintain high levels of performance, establish close and warm interpersonal relations, and remember the experience as an outstandingly positive event in their lives. Furthermore, there appears to be very little, if any, correlation between severity of stress and favorability of reactions within field studies. Although it is impossible to calculate a correlation with precision on the basis of presently available data and conceptual analysis, a rough examination of field studies suggests that the correlation might even be negative.

In other words, projecting from laboratory and simulation studies involving isolation and confinement, one would have to predict that it would be impossible for humans to endure the stresses of field settings if one assumed a linear correlation between objectively specifiable stresses and negative reactions to the situation. The above analysis does not have to be limited to the studies involving isolation and confinement, although such studies have been used for comparison in an attempt to simplify the discussion. A similar analysis could apply to a wide variety of situations.

To this point, we have presented only a partial picture in posing the lack of correlation between stressful or negative elements of a situation and negative reactions to the situation. The question is why men are attracted to dangerous and demanding situations and why they make successful adjustments and perform well in highly stressful situations; correspondingly, why they reject, make poor adjustments and perform poorly in less stressful situations.

COSTS, REWARDS AND OUTCOMES

It is quite apparent that any analysis capable of explaining the lack of correlation between negative elements in a situation and attraction toward it must also take into account the positive elements of that situation. Such an approach has been developed by Thibaut and Kelley in their book, *The Social Psychology of Groups.* In their analysis, Thibaut and Kelley discuss in broad terms the attraction of persons to groups, focussing principally on social interaction leading to attraction and rejection; they also briefly consider tasks and environmental factors. An application and extension of their major concepts to the present discussion is the purpose of this section.

Thibaut and Kelley have conceptualized social interaction in terms of cost, rewards and outcomes. They define these terms as follows (Thibaut and Kelley, 1959, p. 12 and 13).

> "By rewards, we refer to the pleasures, satisfactions, and gratifications the person enjoys. The provision of a means whereby a drive is reduced or a need fulfilled constitutes a reward. We assume that the amount of reward provided by any such experience can be measured and that the reward values of different modalities of gratification are reducible to a single psychological scale.
>
> By costs, we refer to any factors that operate to inhibit or deter the performance of a sequence of behavior. The greater the deterence to performing a given act—the greater the inhibition the individual has to overcome—the greater cost of the act. Thus cost is high when great physical or mental effort is required, when embarrassment or anxiety accompany the action, or when there are conflicting forces or competing response tendencies of any sort. Costs derived from these different factors are also assumed to be measurable on a common psychological scale, and costs of different sorts, to be additive in their effect.
>
> The consequences or outcomes for an individual participant of any interaction or series of interactions can be stated then, in terms of the rewards received and the costs incurred, these values depending upon the behavioral items which the two persons produce in the course of their interaction. For some purposes it is desirable to treat rewards and costs separately; for other purposes it is assumed that

> they can be combined into a single scale of "goodness" of outcome, with states of high reward and low cost being given high-scale values and states of low reward and high cost, low scale values. Admittedly, such a scaling operation would be a very ambitious enterprise and would present a number of technical difficulties. However, the present interest is in the theoretical consequences of such an operation (real or imaginary) rather than in its technical properties or even its feasibility."

With this cost–reward analysis, the desirability of a given social relation for an individual can be determined. Two standards or criteria of acceptability of outcomes are proposed by Thibaut and Kelley. These standards are called the *comparison level* (CL) and the *comparison level of alternatives* (CLalt). The CL is an absolute standard by which the attractiveness of a relationship is judged in terms of what the participant feels he "deserves." The CLalt is a relative standard used to judge whether or not the person wishes to remain in a relationship. The alternatives are other possible relationships in which a person could participate at any given time. In other words, the CL determines whether or not a person is doing as well as he should be in his present situation. The CLalt indicates whether or not he is doing as well as he could considering all possible relationships.

The concepts of costs, rewards and outcomes can be expanded to include all aspects of a situation which tend to make it attractive or unattractive. For purposes of the present analysis we propose the following definition:

Costs—The sum total of all stimuli which a person perceives as negative components of the total stimulus environment.

Rewards—The sum total of all stimuli which a person perceives as positive components of the total stimulus environment.

Negative is defined here as any perceived stimulus which, all other things being equal, a normal human adult would avoid. Such stimuli may be physical or psychological. For SEALAB, the negative stimuli have been presented in the previous chapter. Similarly, positive elements are defined as any perceived stimuli which, all other things being equal, a normal human adult would desire. Such stimuli are principally psychological in nature, examples being recognition, a sense of accomplishment, acceptance by significant others, and satisfaction of any of a variety of personal motives.

While dependent principally on Thibaut and Kelley's model, the presently employed cost–reward analysis has been influenced by a number of other sources as well. Though only a few of the more relevant influences will be cited here, a number of accounts of natural groups working in isolation and confinement have been considered. The work having the most influence on the present analysis is the continuing research on Antarctic wintering over parties by Eric Gunderson and Paul Nelson of the U.S. Navy Neuropsychiatric Unit in San Diego (1966). Another influence has been the research of Lester on the 1963 Mt. Everest expedition. The work of Sells (1965), who has recently developed a descriptive classification of variables affecting isolated groups, has also proved very useful in directing attention to the total social system in which individual reactions occur.

We have called this attempt to analyze responses to SEALAB in cost–reward terms an analysis within a conceptual framework rather than a theoretical analysis. This analysis is admittedly somewhat loose and speculative, because it must be. We do not believe that social psychology is as yet capable of providing a comprehensive and detailed analysis of group behavior in natural settings. In later chapters we will examine more closely some specific aspects of behavior such as work performance, emotional reactions, leader and peer choice in terms of narrower and better defined concepts. In this chapter the intent is to present a global view, giving it as much structure as appears possible at this time.

REWARDS

What were the rewards of SEALAB? What did the men get out of it? In terms of the definition provided above, what were the positive stimuli in the situation? Rewards in SEALAB were highly subjective, as no special monetary rewards or privileges were granted to the aquanauts. Since the rewards were mostly subjective, their determination depends upon an analysis of the total system and of the men involved. We have attempted to determine the intrinsic rewards in terms of the backgrounds of the aquanauts. This account will depend heavily upon the comments of the men to substantiate the analysis. In brief, we take the position that behavior is a function of both the person and the environment. We have described the negative aspects of the environment and have given a brief description of the men. We will now describe the positive aspects in an attempt to account for the favorable reactions. There were many rewards in SEALAB; some were concrete and easy to identify, while others were dependent upon dynamic interactions between men and the environment, the sources and courses of which can only be inferred. The order in which the reward characteristics are presented below does not imply a ranking according to importance. Also, the rewards listed below do not apply equally to all the men; while some of these factors were important to all, others had idiosyncratic effects. In this attempt to identify reward characteristics we have doubtless missed some, because of the complexity of the situation, but all of the positive elements which are identified below have specific referents either in the behavior or in the comments of the men.

Participation in SEALAB

There are a variety of indications that the mere fact of participation in SEALAB was highly rewarding, mention having been made previously of the place of SEALAB in diving history. Saturation diving is capable of opening up millions of square miles of the continental shelf to study and exploitation of a type previously unknown. The exploration of the sea may very well prove to be of greater importance economically, scientifically and militarily than the exploration of outer space. While the fulfillment of the potential of the concept of saturation diving is an empirical question which will be decided in future decades, the promise and potential did exist for SEALAB II. The attitudinal effects of this great potential were a significant factor in making participation in this project rewarding in and of itself. There was a sense of excitement, of being in on the ground floor of something really big. A man can endure a great deal if he feels that he personally is contributing significantly and uniquely to the expansion of human knowledge and to economic and military progress. In short, Project SEALAB II had great potential significance, all the aquanauts knew that it did, and they were proud to be part of the project.

There were a number of tangible reminders of the significance of the project. President Johnson's call to Commander Carpenter at the termination of his stay in SEALAB was the most significant, but there were others as well. For example, the Gemini V space capsule was orbiting the earth at the time SEALAB was on the floor of the ocean and NASA and the Navy arranged a telephone contact between Aquanaut Carpenter and Astronaut Cooper. Also, at the time SEALAB II was under the Pacific, the French engineer–explorer Jacques Cousteau had placed a similar capsule, Conshelf III, on the floor of the Mediterranean. A call was arranged between SEALAB II and Conshelf III. The fact that the French aquanauts attempted to converse in English and the Americans in French, and that neither could understand the other because of the severe speech distortion caused by the exotic atmospheres did not detract from the reward value of this communication.

Other evidence of SEALAB's importance was afforded by press, radio and TV coverage. SEALAB was national news. Letters from the aquanauts' friends and relatives around the country provided evidence that the project was receiving national attention. More important, the local press gave excellent coverage to the story. SEALAB was front page news in the San Diego press, and the newspapers were sent down to the capsule so that the aquanauts could read about themselves as they were making news. Also, they had a TV receiver in the capsule and could observe their teammates and supervisors topside as they were interviewed on local news programs.

It is probable, however, that this recognition served more as a reminder of the significance of the project than as an actual reward in and of itself, since the divers were already well aware of the importance of the project. An indication of their perception of its status is provided in the following comments from the debriefing interviews.

> "You still get a, a big sense of accomplishment anyway; you feel that you're part of something that is big and growing and that just not everybody you feel could live down there, anyway for 15 days even if you didn't do a damn thing."
>
> "There are an awful lot of rewards. The biggest reward was being able to participate in the project."
>
> "I'm really motivated with the project because I know that we are still in the development stage. What we do now is later going to pay off."

Pride in Accomplishment

In addition to the rewards associated with the fact of participation in the project were the satisfactions derived from pride in accomplishment of difficult and demanding work. The aquanauts were all career divers which gave them a knowledge of the problems which they would encounter in SEALAB. In short they knew what they had to do and they were confident in their ability to do it as is illustrated in the comment of one of the team leaders:

> "The men are all career divers . . . and they knew that they were going to be able to do a predetermined quota. Now this is something that some of the people were enthused about—And they were very aware that the accomplishment was necessary for it to be a success . . ."

Because SEALAB was a first of type operation, the men were doing work which others had never done before and which few other men were capable of doing. The sense of accomplishment derived from the demanding nature of the tasks, in the pioneering character of their work, and in overcoming hardships. The following comments are typical in illustrating these types of reactions.

> "That 300 foot dive was my highlight—personal highlight—it was a test of guts, there's no doubt about it. It was total darkness—it couldn't have gotten any darker. It was a nice thing to know that I did have the intestinal fortitude to go out there and do it."

> "Then suddenly I realized that we made it. It was a real great sense of well being, by golly, something like the Northwest Passage on a very tiny scale. We made it and even though it was only 250 feet from the habitat it was a real accomplishment. It was very pretty. It wasn't pretty as far as the scenic value, but it was beautiful in that it was what we were fighting to get to. The canyon rim."

> "Q. Any one experience . . . thing that sticks in your mind the most?
>
> A. Oh, I think probably the excursion dive was.
>
> Q. Why?
>
> A. Well, we'd tried a long time to do it, and it was deeper than anybody had gone, and we saw some different territory. I don't know, maybe it's just because it was different than anything else."

> "Q. I take it that you would like to go again?
>
> A. Yes. If I thought there were a challenge for achievement, but repeat the same thing, I don't think so. It would have to be something that's more of an adventurous challenge or hasn't been done. or needs to be done to be expanded on."

> "It's quite a feeling when you come up. You say 'well nobody's been that deep before for that long'. And to know that deep down inside that if your rig was set up right you could of went four, five hundred feet down; this is something 'cause nobody knows what's down there you know, and it's something to look forward to."

Peer Group Support

The peer group was very important as a source of reward in SEALAB. It is difficult to overestimate the importance of group acceptance or rejection in determining adjustment to isolated and dangerous environments. The significance of group support is well summarized in the sentiment expressed by a member of an Antarctic wintering over party who said: "If the rest of the guys get fed up and stop talking to you . . . that is worse than when they go off and leave you in a crevasse" (Rohrer, 1960). In a variety of direct and indirect ways a man's fellow participants defined and provided the rewarding aspects of the SEALAB experience. For example, only another aquanaut could appreciate fully the accomplishments of the individuals and the groups in this environment. The fact of excellent group relations, which has been discussed previously, was a significant positive aspect of participation in SEALAB.

Many of the men commented favorably on the ability of the heterogeneous crews of SEALAB II to work well together. They were amazed at the spirit of cooperation which prevailed despite the diverse backgrounds, interests and goals of the participants. Several of the men contrasted the favorable group relations in SEALAB with other less harmonious groups of which they had been a part.

> ". . . I don't think you could of got anybody that jelled any better than we did.
>
> Q. Was it more harmonious than a demolition team then?
>
> A. Yeah. Which surprised me. You got all different backgrounds. We got guys with a grade-school education, and you got guys with Masters degrees down there, and all come from different family backgrounds too, really surprising."
>
> "I think we got along great. To my knowledge there was not a serious, not even a semi-serious spat during the whole time down there. I was amazed we really got along well. I have seen it a lot worse on oceanographic cruises."
>
> "I spent over 20 years aboard submarines—you would get a lot more people if you wake them up to go on watch or something, they are grouchy. This whole crew here—you didn't have to hardly even call them. You would just say 'hey, it is time to go on watch—' and they would greet you with a 'good morning' and 'how are you'—Everybody was just real friendly—well, they were well motivated. Got along real fine I think."

"Q. Do you think there was any animosity between the two groups?
A. There was, but it was not really too obvious. It didn't break through.

Q. It was pretty well equal give and take?

A. Both of us gave quite a bit; I'm pretty proud of both sides."

"We were getting in each other's way, some of us didn't see why some of these projects had to be done. You just pitched in and helped them, and it's outstanding when you figure it that way. Now on the Polaris missile boats there's an awful lot of unkind words said in a 60-day patrol because you're down into a routine . . ."

Consideration for others, high esprit de corps, and mutual respect were cited by various divers as their estimate of group interaction.

"The one thing I got a kick out of was, a guy would go out to make cocoa or something and he would make enough for 6 or 7 guys without even thinking. It was just automatic, you count how many people there were and you make that much. We got along good, we really did."

"People were nicer to me than they were on the surface. And I was nicer to them than I am on the surface. This SEALAB bunch, we have got a hell of a high esprit de corps. We all respect each other. And this is something. Even though you hate a guy's guts, you respect him."

"If anything new came up it was a new respect in most cases for, for everyone. A lot of things were revealed about every man that were good that I hadn't seen before . . ."

The fact that the men were aware of the potential dangers in group disruption, that they consciously took steps to forestall potential problems, and that their efforts succeeded were seen as significant accomplishments of which the men were very proud.

"I expected to see some tempers flare—I think I saw some—it is hard to tell. I may have saw some flares for about two seconds before the guy caught himself and everything was all fine and dandy again. Worked real good together."

"I personally was amazed at how well we did get along under such cramped conditions. It seemed to me everybody just went out of their way to be nice. You were bumping into people and knocking their stuff over and they were bumping into you and knocking your stuff over. It seems to me that everybody was just overly polite about it because they realized this condition existed and if dissension ever once did get started it would spread like wildfire."

"Q. You censored your emotions?"

"A. I censored my emotions. I don't know about the rest of the fellows. I sure did."

"I think we all deserve a real commendation for staying harmonious because we had plenty of opportunities and reasons, I guess, on all sides for becoming unharmonious. It may have been our own understanding of this being a situation in which things could deteriorate pretty rapidly if we let them."

Hostile external forces have been noted as factors in producing group cohesiveness, though most attention in the literature has been focused on other competing groups as sources of such hostile forces. In SEALAB, the dangerous and difficult physical environment was the common enemy. One of the aquanauts considered the effect of danger in producing group cohesion.

"Maybe we were all welded together a little bit by the fact that it was a dangerous situation and maybe that makes men better friends."

In the final analysis, the characteristics which the aquanauts had in common may have become more important than any differences.

"Everyone of those guys down there are basically the same type of person I am. We might not think exactly alike but we must think alike in many of our ways or we wouldn't be underwater."

We have described a group in which norms of hard work, cooperation and mutual assistance prevailed. A number of examples will illustrate ways in which the particular characteristics or abilities of a man made him a valuable member of the group. These illustrations are based on inferences from a variety of sources, such as conversations which were only partially heard over the open microphones; post-experience anecdotes which were, unfortunately, not tape-recorded; patterns of sociometric choice which substantiate some of these specific examples, and observations of the aquanauts in a variety of settings. In other words, the following vignettes are documented with less precision than we would like them to be, but we feel that their presentation is useful to an understanding of the reward value of peer group relations. They are intended to convey some of the specific ways in which reinforcement was provided by various team members to each other.

Ability to perform work of a type essential to the success of the entire group is an important way in which an individual can demonstrate his value to the group. By the nature of their work divers are jacks-of-all-trades, and the divers on SEALAB, since they were veterans, possessed a variety of skills in working with diving equipment. An incident involving the Arawak breathing equipment illustrates aptly one of the ways in which such skills were used. The Arawak was performing sluggishly in the early days of the underwater stay. Two of the veteran divers dismantled and repaired the unit in the SEALAB habitat. Their work made the equipment safer to use and prevented delays which would have cut down on diving time. A number of other divers commented on the skill and ingenuity of the men who performed this work. Because of their skill these men received the admiration of the group and the other divers received the benefits of safer equipment without loss of time.

Photographers in SEALAB crews worked relatively alone, but their jobs were such that mutual rewards were provided between the photographers and other group members. Photographers provided ego enhancement for all aquanauts by recording significant events and the subjects of their photographs were ready admirers of the photographers' work.

Each team had one or more men who could be seen buoying up spirits with their stories and humorous comments on the day's happenings. Sociometric choice and comments of the men revealed that these natural wits were valued members of the crew.

The wide age differences in the crews noted previously resulted in a number of dyads in which interactions were mutually reinforcing in quite subtle but predictable ways. Some of the dyadic relationships in the SEALAB crews assumed some of the characteristics of father–son or pupil–teacher interactions. In such dyads, the younger man gained more knowledge and confidence from the assistance given by the older man in preparing for and during his dives, while the veteran derived his rewards from the respect shown him by the younger man and from helping the younger man to succeed.

Differences in interests also provided the basis for rewards, similar to rewards derived from differences in age. Several of the Navy men became quite skilled amateur marine biologists under the tutelage of the civilian scientists. These quasi pupil–teacher relationships seemed mutually rewarding from the comments of several of the men.

The leaders of the SEALAB crews were highly qualified, dedicated and hardworking men who were admired and respected by their team members. The fact that the crews had good leaders helped to give men confidence in the ability of the group to function well, while the leaders were rewarded by having subordinates who fulfilled assignments willingly and above and beyond the call of duty.

The doctor and the corpsman were kept busy responding to minor complaints, and the knowledge that they were there in case of emergency doubtless reassured the men. Their being needed was in turn rewarding to the medical specialists.

Men with culinary skills made special efforts to prepare good meals when time permitted. Their efforts were greatly appreciated by other men as is indicated in many of the comments which were overheard.

There were others who anticipated the needs of their fellow divers, particularly those needs connected with tending to the numerous details of preparing for and securing from dives. The mutual rewards here were the respect and gratitude gained on the one hand,

and the essential assistance in performing one's own duties on the other.

Finally, there were a number of rewards associated with diving together; all of the men dived at least once with all of the others. These dives were not always successful. We have already indicated how often work efforts were frustrated. There were a number of pairs of divers in which men dived together for the first time, in some cases performing work of a type which they had not done before, but finding it enjoyable and rewarding. In other cases, they found that they worked together very well with men with whom they had not dived previously. A number of off the record comments indicate that for several of the men their experiences together in the water aided in establishing warm friendships.

The above vignettes represent the type of rewarding interactions between men and groups in SEALAB. Individually, each incident of the type described here made only a small contribution towards offsetting the many negative aspects of the environment, but collectively, these and many similar activities wove a strong fabric of mutually supportive interactions which enabled SEALAB teams to cope constructively with their hostile environment.

Life on the Bottom

There were numerous rewards associated with living on the floor of the ocean, the primary one being the opportunity to observe marine life. Any foreign object placed in the sea attracts sea creatures, and SEALAB was no exception. Scorpion fish were a nuisance and a hazard but many of the other marine creatures were a source of enjoyment. Since SEALAB had eleven port holes from which the surrounding water could be viewed, there was never a dull moment in the "marine game preserve" of which they were a part, and the aquanauts had grandstand seats to view sea life as it had never been seen before.

A sea lion, Sam or Samantha (the question was never finally settled) became an especial favorite of the aquanauts. The sea lion would swoop down from the surface scattering fish in all directions as he approached. On several occasions he even appeared in the open hatch of the SEALAB capsule. Tuffy, a trained porpoise, participated in the study by demonstrating his ability to carry tools from the surface to divers on the bottom.

At times, life outside was quietly fascinating as men contemplated mysteries of a new and different world.

> "That was very interesting. These little particles suspended in the water—they would be passing by the port from left to right and five minutes later they would be coming down. An hour later they would be going up. It's a very strange phenomena."

At other times the action was much livelier.

> "With those ports open, man, it's great. In fact I was so interested in those ports I couldn't get to bed . . . You'd see a rock fish come up and grab a squid and tussle at this thing, and the squid would grab hold of the glass, and the scorpion fish would try to pull it off, and there'd be a fight right there. Stuff like that just kept you on pins and needles."

But at all times it was interesting.

> "We would sit and would watch those animals out there by the hour. We also thought we were part of this, this was our little world and all. We were in our own back yard."

Many of the divers became quite at home with life on the bottom of the ocean. The extent of their acclimatization is illustrated by the following comment.

> "I didn't realize this but when you wake up in the morning, without knowing that you do it, you go look out the window, you don't make a special point to do it but as you walk from the bedroom to the bathroom you kinda glance out of the window to see whether it's raining or sun shining and that sort of thing, you know. You look at the outside world in a very cursory manner but it doesn't take

very much. You get some quick idea as to what's out there. And I found out that I was visualizing the concept outside in the sense that I just mentioned it, as being green and watery—the view that you got as you came out of the shark cage was what I thought instead of the air and sunshine. This actually happens. I got to where I guess I was beginning to transfer in that sense. I would wake up and look out of a porthole immediately and I'd just unconsciously get some concept of dirty, light, dark, you know, and then when I'd go outside I would sort of know what to expect."

In some cases the transfer from the topside orientation was so complete that they were sorry to have to return to the surface.

"I didn't miss what I thought I was going to miss. I thought I was going to miss the sun, the clouds, and I didn't miss the sun once, nor the clouds, nor the sky. Because it was another world. It was topside. We had our world down there. Our daylight started around 8 and ended around 3:30. We got adjusted very, very rapidly to that. And our nights were much more beautiful than yours. We had much more to see, and we became very, very self-centered. I liked it down there, just as well as up here. When those guys came down there for the third team, I thought they were intruding. And I hated to see them come in because I realized that was the end."

Freedom to Work

An important reward of living on the bottom of the ocean was the advantage of diving from SEALAB over other diving which the men had experienced previously. One difference, favoring diving from SEALAB, derived from the breathing mixture which was used. In diving from the surface, breathing normal air, a man is in danger of suffering nitrogen narcosis, a mental and physical state similar to that produced by consumption of alcohol. The SEALAB atmosphere was a distinct advantage in this respect.

"I was elated, and it was a good feeling to be able to do it. You were so clearheaded in the mixture. I have done quite a bit of very deep diving and I know the limitations at this depth of air."

However, the most important advantage of diving from SEALAB was the time in the water which a man had available to him. An increase in effective "bottom time" was, of course, the basic purpose of the program. The frustrations of working in the water have been described previously, and while SEALAB diving time was limited, it was still far greater than it would have been had the men been diving from the surface. This was seen as a distinct advantage.

> "There is the tremendous advantage of being able to start a job and then finish it . . . Whereas, say a guy could drop down from the surface and maybe have 20 minutes on the bottom he could be just two or three minutes away from completing the job and his time would be up and he'd have to quit and they'd bring him up and put somebody else down."
>
> "Q. How does this experience compare with previous diving that you have done on salvage dives?
>
> A. There's just no comparison. You just can't compare it. You go out of that lab, you have no concern about decompression whatsoever."
>
> "On a surface dive you would never be able to complete a job. Down there, you know you can finish it. A man really likes to do it."

Having the needed equipment close at hand was another related advantage of SEALAB.

> "The big stumbling thing on your research diving is you get out there and you say 'I didn't bring a hammer' or you got a million dollar horse and you didn't bring the saddle. This way you can run back in the house—it takes 3 minutes. Have a cup of coffee, gather up some wires and pliers and go back. It's really great. Or you are working on something—it's like doing something at home, if you don't quite finish you know in a few hours you can come back."

Center of Attention

In addition to receiving recognition from society at large in the form of publicity, rewards were also derived from the atten-

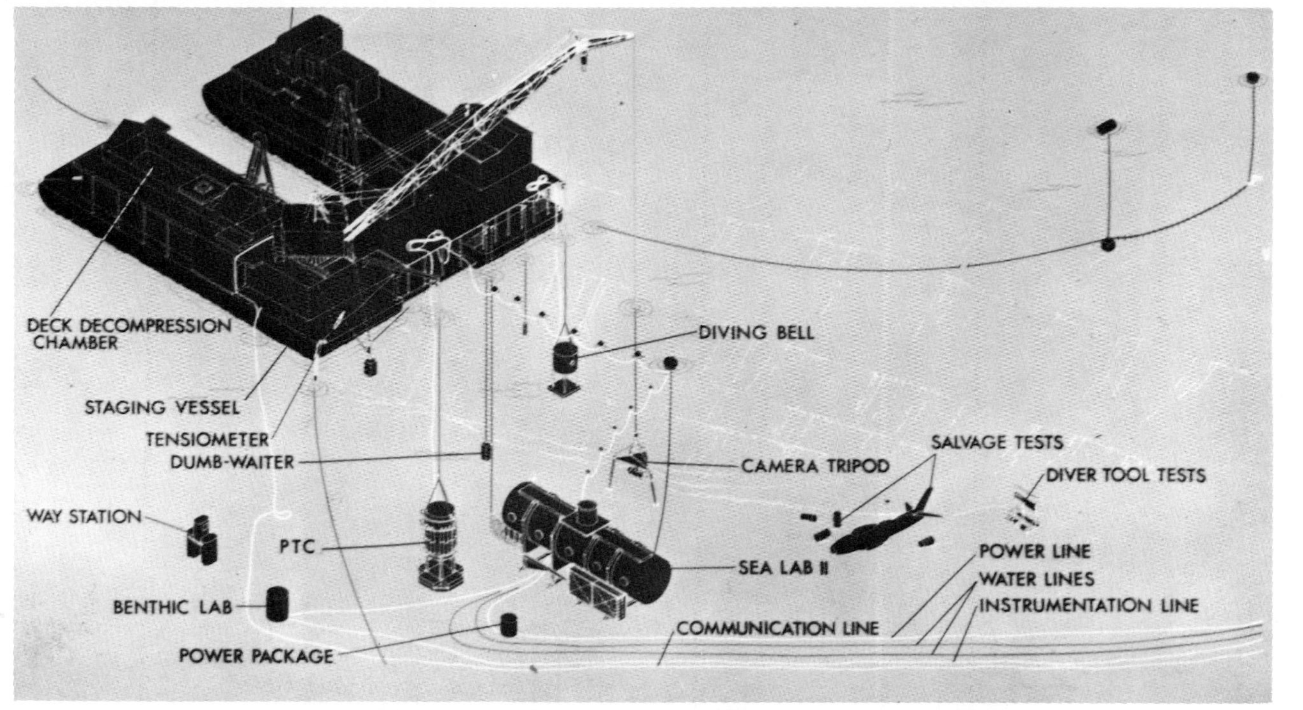

Schematic diagram of SEALAB capsule, showing surface and underwater support equipment. *(Official U.S. Navy photograph.)*

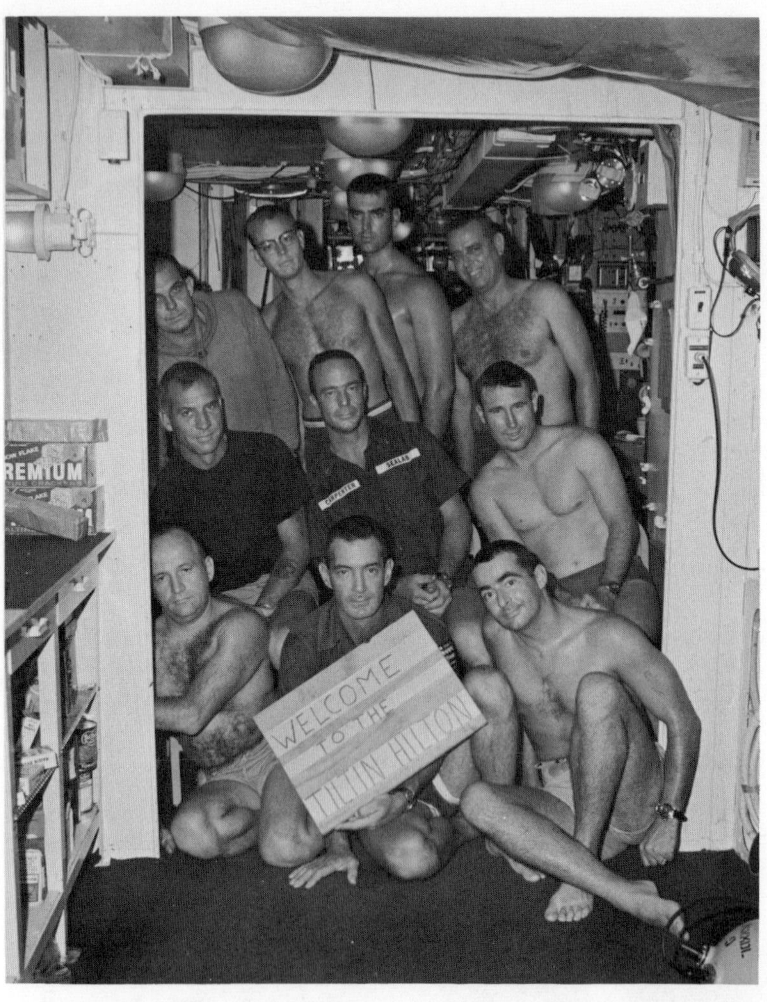

Team I Aquanauts at the entrance to laboratory area inside SEALAB capsule during submergence. Angle of men gives sardonic emphasis to tilt of capsule. *(Official U.S. Navy photograph.)*

Personnel Transfer Capsule being lowered to deck of support vessel after returning aquanauts to surface. *(Official U.S. Navy photograph.)*

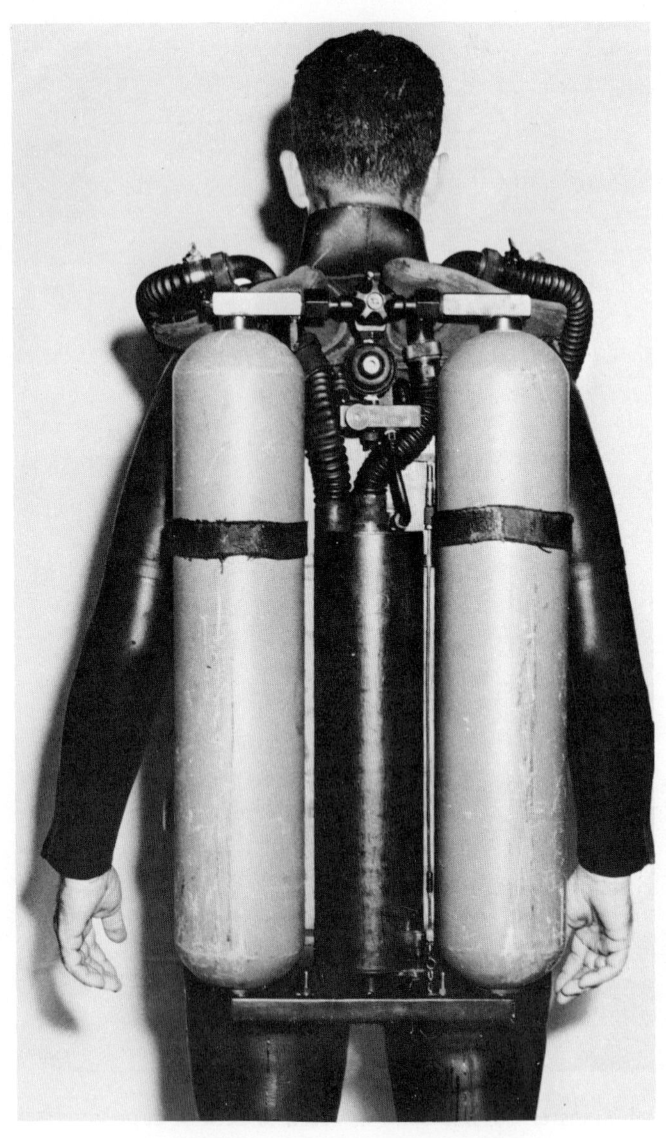

Back view of diver showing Mark VI SCUBA equipment. (See page 54.)
(Official U.S. Navy photograph.)

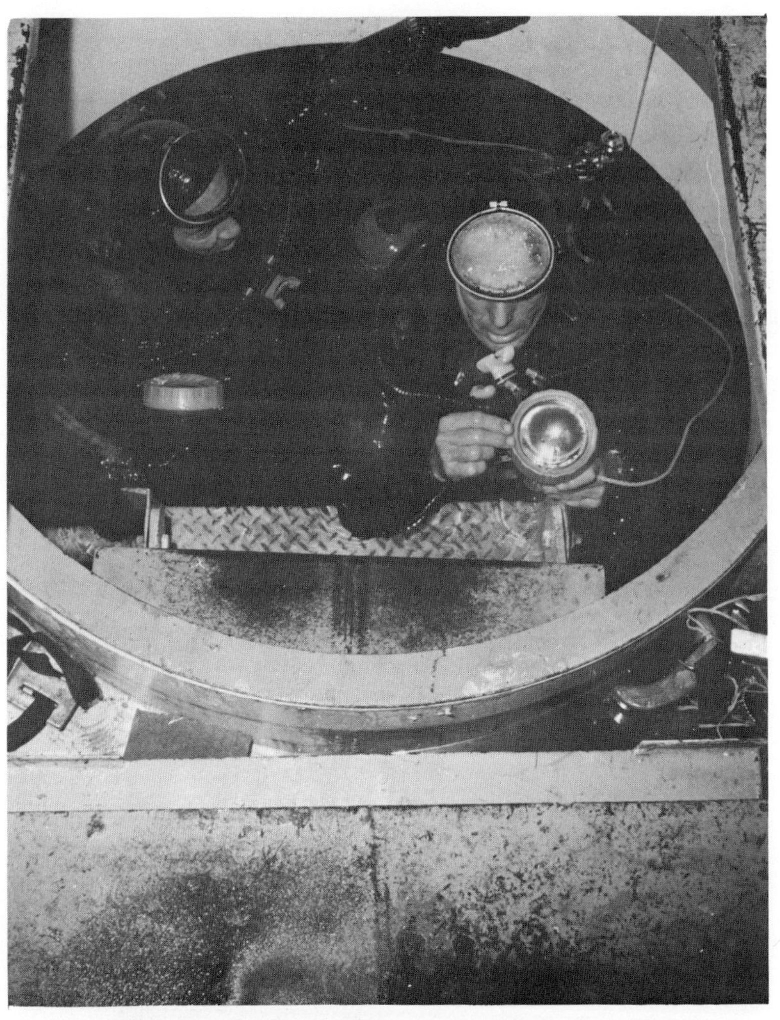

Aquanauts returning to SEALAB through entry hatch.
(Official U.S. Navy photograph.)

Relaxing in SEALAB. *(Official U.S. Navy photograph.)*

Differences in choice of attire illustrate varied reactions to the exotic atmospheric environment in SEALAB (See page 71). *(Official U.S. Navy photograph.)*

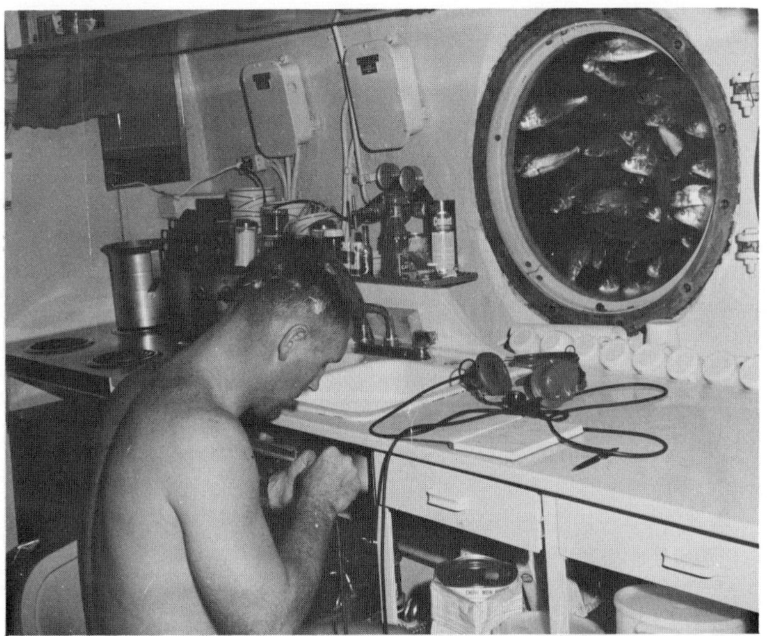

Aquanaut working in laboratory area of SEALAB capsule under the watchful eye of natives. The crushed noodle can shows the effects of pressure at 200 feet. *(Official U.S. Navy photograph.)*

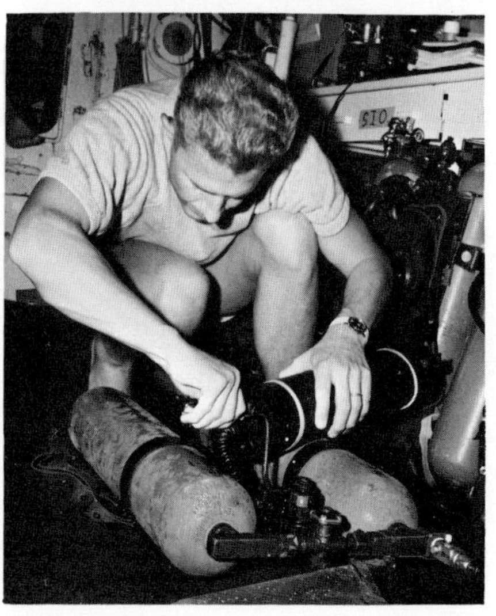

Preparing Mark VI equipment under crowded conditions in the laboratory area. *(Official U.S. Navy photograph.)*

Diver working in capsule under the watchful eye of video camera.
(Official U.S. Navy photograph.)

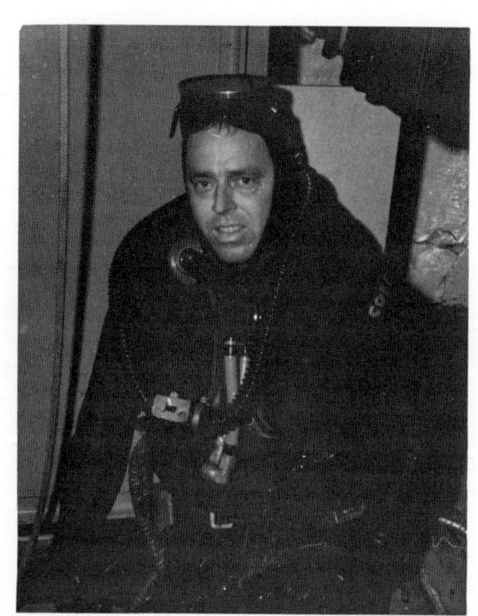

Thoroughly chilled aquanaut returning to capsule after dive. *(Official U.S. Navy photograph.)*

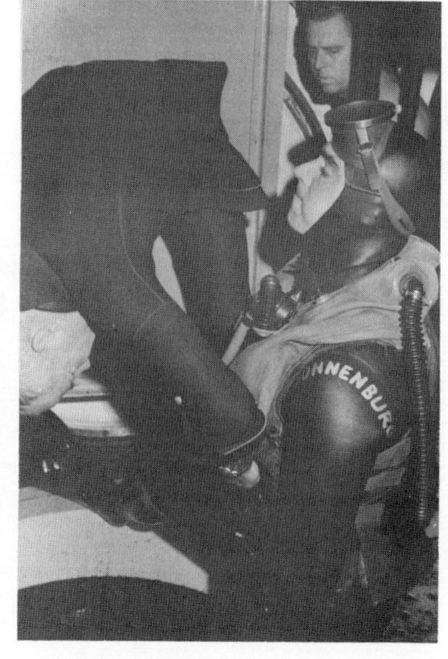

Adjusting breathing equipment prior to dive in the cramped diving area. *(Official U.S. Navy photograph.)*

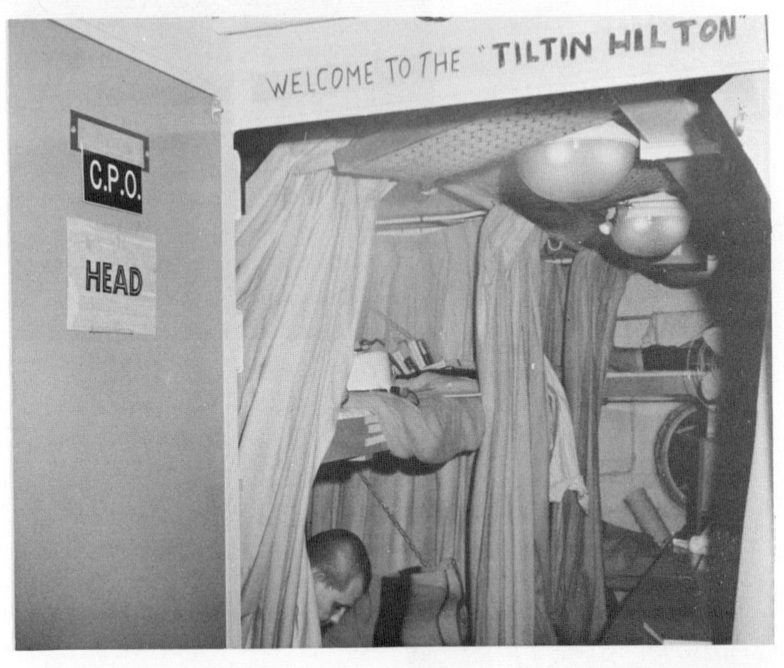

View of crowded berth area. *(Official U.S. Navy photograph.)*

Flash photo of aquanaut swimming in murky water near SEALAB.
(Official U.S. Navy photograph.)

Aquanaut using foam salvage tool to raise submerged airplane.
(Official U.S. Navy photograph.)

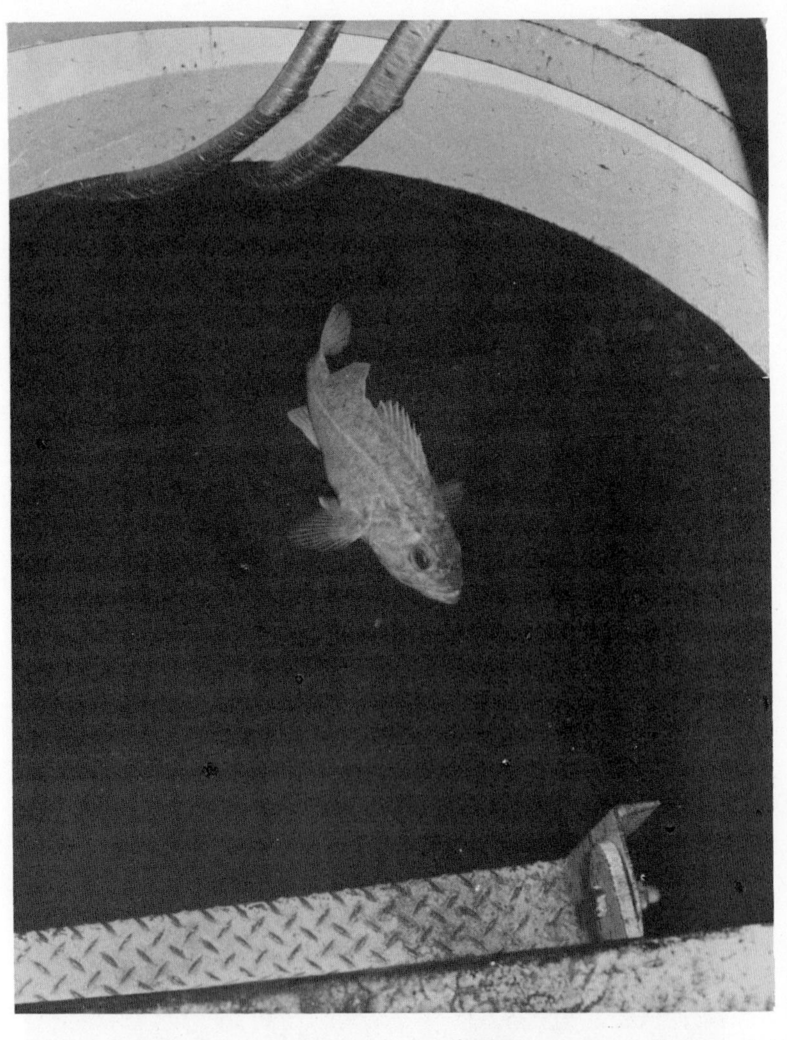

Finned friend visits entrance to SEALAB. *(Official U.S. Navy photograph.)*

tion and consideration manifested by supervisors and personnel on the support vessel. All the time he was on the bottom, the aquanaut was the most important man in the project. There was daily and continuing evidence of the fact that "somebody up there cares about me," which doubtless made the stresses of SEALAB easier to tolerate. One perceptive aquanaut describes this aspect of SEALAB.

> "I thought that topside cooperated more with SEALAB than SEALAB did with topside. Because we were all prima donnas down there and I think we all put on a little bit and played the part, that we were going to be wined and dined and humored. And I think we all took advantage of it to a certain extent. It is kind of nice to be catered to."

It is interesting to note the contrast of this perception of the attention given during the stay on the bottom with the perceived consideration for providing creature comforts during the decompression phase of the study. It should be emphasized that the decompression operation required and received constant attention to atmosphere control and to the reactions of the men to the decompression process. In fact, the men were watched more closely during decompression than while they were on the bottom. Despite this constant and careful monitoring during decompression, there was a difference in the type of attention given, which resulted in a perception of being ignored compared to their experiences while on the bottom.

> "We came up from that thing and our morale was high. And we all felt that we had really done something great. When we got in the DDC, we were ignored; we couldn't get this and we couldn't get that. This was anticlimatic as the devil to come up there in that DDC and everybody forgot about us."

Career Benefits

Of potentially great importance to the aquanauts was the effect of participation in SEALAB on their future careers. Reference has been made above to the place of SEALAB in the history of diving, but whether or not the careers of SEALAB participants will be favorably influenced by their participation in this pioneering effort, the expectation that they would be was doubtless of considerable value to each aquanaut. Perhaps the expectation of such benefits is expressed in part by one of the aqauanauts who, on being congratulated after coming to the surface, responded "Hell, I'm no hero. I didn't do anything that a thousand other Navy divers wouldn't have given their right arm to do."

These, then, were the rewards in SEALAB which we were able to identify. This list is obviously incomplete, since it would be impossible to determine and identify categorically all of the factors which produced favorable adjustment to SEALAB. It is recognized that the list itself and the distinctions between the various reward characteristics are arbitrary. While recognizing the incompleteness of this list, we hope to have identified at least the major rewards; however, even if we could have identified all rewards, we would still not have a complete account of the counter-stress factors. There were numerous characteristics of the men and of the situation that enabled the aquanauts to withstand the stresses (or costs) of SEALAB. Many such characteristics were very likely unique to this environment or relatively idiosyncratic in nature, and thus their effects would be difficult to identify or of little general relevance if they could be identified. However, an attempt to account for favorable adjustment to the situation would be incomplete without a brief mention of a few of the more general and important of these factors.

NONREWARD FACTORS CONTRIBUTING TO FAVORABLE ADJUSTMENT IN SEALAB

Experience of the Men

In the section on the biographical description of the aquanauts, reference was made to the high level of diving experience in the group. This high level of experience is probably characteristic of pioneering groups. For example, the age of the 1963 American Mt. Everest climbing team is quite similar to that of the SEALAB aquanauts both in mean and variance (Lester, 1964). Early Antarctic wintering over parties, for example those of the International Geophysical Year 1957–58, tended to have men in their thirties as participants. Scientists who were members of the IGY groups were established scholars, most of whom had Ph.D. degrees. Ten years later the scientists tend to be graduate students in their twenties with Masters degrees, men who are working for their PhD.'s. More will be said later about the contrast between the maturity and experience of men in pioneering groups and of participants in later phases of expanding and developing programs.

The high average experience of the SEALAB participants probably operated in a number of ways to counteract the stresses they experienced. Although they have been mentioned previously, these effects are important enough to summarize again for emphasis. The benefits derived from knowledge of equipment and techniques, confidence in ability, the good judgment which derives from maturity, and other similar characteristics which are associated with experience, all played a role in the adjustment to SEALAB. In the next chapter, data will be reported indicating that age and experience are not correlated significantly with performance and adjustment in SEALAB. This lack of correlation most probably means that the average level of experience was sufficiently high to mask its effects; that is, there may be a threshold of level of experience necessary to produce all the favorable effects which experience can contribute, and experience greater than that threshold will not contribute measurably to adaptation and adjustment. Other explanations of the lack of correlation are possible, such as the countereffects of reduced stamina and resiliency which would accompany advancing age. Whatever the reasons for the lack of correlation between performance and adjustment and experience in SEALAB, however, the conclusion cannot be drawn that experience is unimportant. Rather, it is probably of such crucial importance in selecting men for pioneering studies that its use as a selection criterion tends to mask its effects for individuals. Considering the effects globally and for groups as a whole, there is good reason to believe that experience contributed importantly to the success of SEALAB groups.

Volunteer Status

The volunteer status of the aquanauts certainly influenced their acceptance of the stresses they experienced. In recent years, dissonance theory (Festinger, 1957) and experiments derived from it (Brehm & Cohen, 1962), have provided an explanation of post-decisional cognitive restructuring following the commitment to a course of action which is relevant here. The decision to volunteer for SEALAB, affecting as it did the vital interests of the men involved, can be expected to have resulted in an increase in the salience of positive elements and a decrease in the salience of negative aspects of the situation.

Definite Time Frame

The aquanauts stayed in SEALAB for fourteen or fifteen days. One man was on the bottom for thirty consecutive days, while another was down for two fifteen day tours. Perception of time is a subjective and relative matter, and considering the conditions prevailing in SEALAB, fifteen days cannot be said to be a brief time. There is no evidence that the men counted the days and many of them said that they could easily have stayed much longer; however, the fact that the length of time was known, and that it was two weeks rather than two months or two years, plus the fact that the aquanauts were very busy during the entire time, probably contributed to the feeling that they could endure the experience successfully. Research on isolated and confined groups in which the effects of time have been considered lends general support to this conclusion (Fraser, 1966; Weybrew, 1957, 1963; Gunderson, 1963).

Confidence in Topside

Reference has been made above to rewards derived from the attention and recognition given by topside personnel. A less tangible but, nevertheless important aspect of topside relations, was the confidence the men had in the monitoring personnel. SEALAB II was a relatively small program, and many of the men involved had been associated with it for several years. Thus, for most of the divers, topside personnel were old friends and trusted associates. Divers had the feeling of being watched over by men they knew and trusted. In addition to the key topside personnel, who were on duty 16 to 18 hours a day throughout the entire study, members of the two teams who were not on the bottom were also on the support vessel much of the time. Feelings of security engendered by such friendship ties were doubtless an important counterstress influence.

COST–REWARD DISCUSSION

SEALAB has been described as a high cost, high reward environment. In Chapters 4 and 5 we have documented the principal costs and rewards of the situation, but since the description is lengthy and detailed, a summary of the major costs and rewards is given in Table 5-7.

This cost–reward analysis was stimulated by an apparent paradox, namely, the attraction to and excellent performance and adjustment in the highly stressful SEALAB II environment, in contrast to negative reactions toward much less stressful environments, particularly those of laboratory and simulation studies of isolation and confinement. In this discussion we will consider several implications of the cost–reward analysis, first presenting a diagramatic representation of a conceptual model which may help to clarify the discussion. Next, an implication of this cost–reward model for the relation between laboratory and field research on isolation and confinement is presented. An hypothesis that rewards are subjective and costs are objective in isolated and confined groups is discussed,

TABLE 5-7
Cost and Rewards in SEALAB

- I. Costs
  - A. Danger of death from sudden decompression
    1. Potential failure of breathing gear
    2. Getting lost
       - a. Disorientation
       - b. Silt and visibility
       - c. Darkness and visibility
    3. Scorpion fish
    4. Smashed porthole
    5. Transfer accidents
  - B. Work difficulties and frustrations
    1. In the water
       - a. Cold
       - b. Poor visibility
       - c. Communication problems
       - d. Limited time
       - e. Buoyancy
       - f. Cumbersome equipment
       - g. Multipurpose projects
       - h. Exertion required
    2. In the capsule
       - a. Crowded conditions
       - b. Noise
       - c. Time to prepare for dives
       - d. Scheduling
       - e. Tilted capsule
       - f. Required maintenance and life support functions
  - C. Exotic atmosphere
    1. Speech problems
    2. Maintaining thermal balance
    3. Humidity
    4. Sleeping
    5. Headaches
    6. No smoking
  - D. Other Costs
    1. Diet restrictions
    2. Fatigue

TABLE 5-7 *(continued)*

3. Experimental subject activities
4. Heterogeneous backgrounds and interests
5. Possibility of unknown effects

II. Rewards
  A. Participation benefits in SEALAB
    1. Potential of exploration of the continental shelf
    2. Recognition
      a. President Johnson's call
      b. Publicity
      c. Contacts with Gemini and Conshelf III
    3. Pride in accomplishment
      a. Unique achievements
      b. Overcoming difficulties
      c. Utilizing skills
  B. Peer group support
    1. Excellent interpersonal relations
    2. Mutual assistance and recognition
    3. Realizing advantages of heterogeneity
    4. Comaraderie
    5. Leadership
  C. Living on the bottom
    1. Observation of marine life
    2. Contrast with surface diving
      a. Time to finish jobs
      b. Absence of nitrogen narcosis
    3. Center of attention
  D. Potential career benefits

---

and from this is derived an hypothesized lability of rewards and stability of costs in such environments. Implications for reactions to various environments involving isolation and confinement are also considered. We discuss in particular, the implications of these hypotheses for social systems as they progress from a pioneering developmental phase through a more mature and stable phase. The crucial role of the leader in determining the cost–reward ratios in such systems and an analysis of the leadership role in terms of social power conclude the discussion.

Laboratory and Simulation Studies

In considering the cost–reward characteristics of laboratory and simulation studies of groups in isolation and confinement, such environments, in contrast to SEALAB, are relatively low in both costs and rewards. In most such studies there is little, if any, objective danger, although there are exceptions (Fraser, 1966). Crowding is generally characteristic of laboratory and simulation studies, but such problems as high or low temperature, humidity, noise and work difficulties are generally much less severe than they were in SEALAB. On the opposite side of the equation, the rewards in simulation and laboratory studies are also quite low. Generally, the only rewards are those derived from testing equipment in simulation studies or from contributing to scientific knowledge in the case of laboratory studies (Haythorn & Altman, 1966). Almost completely absent is the sense of exhilaration over having accomplished unique, outstanding and unusual feats which seems to be a characteristic response to hazardous and demanding natural environments.

While SEALAB could be compared to any of a variety of work situations on a cost–reward matrix, the main emphasis up to this point has been on laboratory and simulation studies in order to give focus to the discussion. We return to this emphasis after presenting and discussing briefly a matrix in which the two concepts are considered. For purposes of illustration other groups are included in the cost–reward matrix as shown in Figure 5-1.

Cost–Reward Matrix

In Figure 5-1 we have attempted to locate various groups on a cost–reward matrix. It should be emphasized that the placement of these groups represents a crude "arm chair" approximation of their

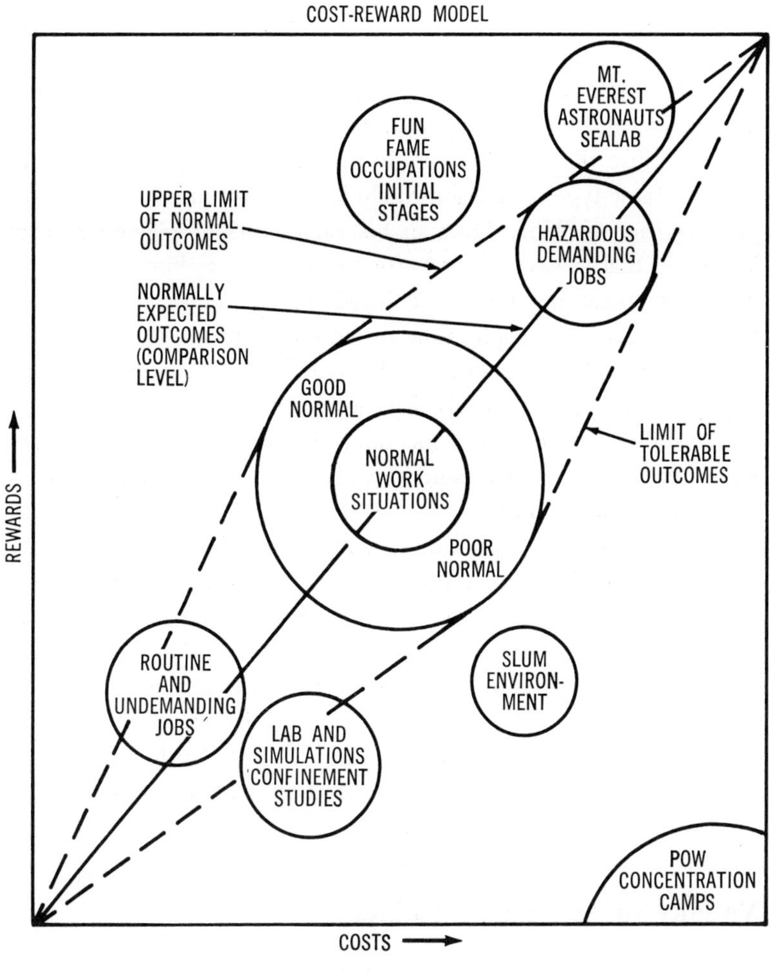

Figure 5-1

location, as data simply are not available to give an exact placement for any of the groups involved. In general, the farther to the left and above the diagonal line, the more desirable the situation for a person or group. Correspondingly, the farther to the right and below the diagonal line, the less desirable are outcomes and therefore, the situation. The area below the dotted line in the lower right half of the matrix is intended to define situations in which a person would not remain voluntarily, such as slum and ghetto environments and concentration and prisoner of war camps. Similarly, outcomes above and to the left of the upper dotted line are those which seldom occur because they yield normally unattainably high outcomes. The fun and fame type occupations included here are meant to cover such cases as that of Willy Mays in his early years of playing baseball. Willy felt that it was ridiculous for someone to pay him, and pay him well, for something that he enjoyed doing and would have done free. The fact that people came to see him play and then applauded him added to the favorability of his outcomes. In recent years, however, even though his salary has gone up, the Giant center fielder may no longer be enjoying the fantastically high outcomes he once knew because of his increasing age, changes in life style and changes in expectations in general.

The principal purpose of this matrix is to present a schematic representation of the cost–reward concepts. Note in particular the placement of the circles representing SEALAB and laboratory and simulation studies of isolation and confinement. The placement of these groups on the dotted lines means that SEALAB is highly attractive, while the laboratory and simulation studies are situations of low attraction. These estimates of attraction are based principally on the previously noted differences in satisfaction with the two situations as reported by the participants.

Validity of Laboratory Studies

This analysis in cost–reward terms has interesting implications for the important question of the validity of laboratory studies in examining the variables involved in isolation and confinement. Obviously, it is not feasible to produce in the laboratory the levels of stress (in present terms, the high costs) found in field studies. This characteristic of laboratory studies has been noted frequently and has long been recognized. But, prior to the present analysis, it seems to have been less well recognized that the rewarding characterestics found in natural environments are not present in the laboratory. A recent symposium on stress research did begin to focus on this aspect of laboratory and field differences, principally in emphasizing the rewarding aspects of dangerous and demanding natural life environments (Appley & Trumbull, 1966). In comparing the two situations within this framework, we find that, when studying groups in isolation and confinement in laboratories, we are subtracting from both sides of the cost–reward equation, thus achieving a rough level of equality between the two situations. To clarify this point further, if it were true that the only differences between laboratory and field studies were those in costs between the situations, then laboratory studies would have severely limited utility in the study of variables related to isolation and confinement. However, if it is recognized that many of the rewards found in natural environments are not present in experimental settings, it would seem to redress somewhat the imbalance between the two settings. It may be that the ratio of costs and rewards is more important than the absolute level in its effect on a variety of responses over a relatively wide range of cost–reward conditions. If indeed it can be demonstrated, conceptually and by a comparison of similar data, that group and individual adaptation to and performance in isolation and confinement are dependent upon the ratio rather than upon the absolute level of costs and rewards, this finding would provide a basis for generalizing from laboratory findings to field settings. In advancing this argument, we do not imply that laboratory and field results are thereby equated; rather, that this analysis provides a framework in which the differences and similarities between the two settings can be better appreciated. Further, this analysis suggests that attempts should be made to determine as nearly as possible what aspects of behavior are dependent upon cost–reward ratios and, in general, just what is left when a subtraction is made from the positive and negative aspects of real world situations. In other words, we feel that it is necessary to make a careful conceptual analysis beginning with the global concepts employed here and proceeding to finer analyses as indicated by comparisons of laboratory and field findings. It would seem, for example, that social interaction variables are more affected by cost–reward ratios than they are by absolute levels.

Subjective Rewards

The rewards which we have identified in SEALAB are for the most part subjective in nature, since they are composed of attitudes and perceptions, psychological entities, rather than the physical stimuli, which, for the most part, characterize the costs. We contend that this subjective characteristic of rewards is true generally of situations high in physical costs. Two examples will serve to illustrate this point. These illustrations have been chosen mainly because they are quite different both from each other and from the SEALAB environment. They are intended to indicate the generality of the phenomena under discussion.

The first example concerns the reactions, twenty-five years later, of World War II veterans to their combat experiences. This account appeared in the Washington Post on the 25th anniversary of Pearl Harbor (Pett & Loh, 1966). Four men who had seen extensive combat duty, all of whom were holders of awards (including one medal of honor) signifying their valor under fire, were interviewed by Associated Press correspondents. The negative aspects of participation in war time combat are obvious, and they were at a very high level for these men. Despite the dangers and deprivations they experienced, all of these men remembered World War II as the high point of their lives. The reasons for these reactions, as summarized by the authors of the article, illustrate the subjective nature of the rewards these men experienced. "None of our four middle-aged lions misses the violence of war, but all of them miss the sense of doing something of value for their country, the feeling of being part of an importance, of being wanted, of being surrounded by brave men in common peril." This reaction was substantiated and amplified by one of the men as follows: "The Marine Corps was the high point of my life. Everything since has seemed a little paler. Nothing will match it." Another man reacted similarly in discussing his life since the war. "Since the war, nothing I have done has seemed important. I have lost my ambition. I don't feel I am accomplishing anything that benefits many people." Still another summed up his reactions in the following manner. "I've had my disappointments, I know I haven't reached my goals. I won't accomplish anything big in my life—climb a mountain or cure a disease. But I am content. I was one of 14,000,000 men in World War II who held their ground when it needed to be held. It may not seem important to most people now, but it was to me, and is."

Thibaut and Kelley, in considering costs and rewards, discussed the phenomenon of a halo effect which applies to the remembrance of past events. Very probably the halo effect is operative in the reactions quoted above; however, it is also quite probable that the rewards derived from doing something of significance in the company of supportive and cohesive peers did in fact compensate for the high objective costs of war time combat.

The second illustration concerns more recent events and affords comparative information on the reactions of two groups of volunteers serving in the Peace Corps. It seems that the Peace Corps has tapped a sort of secular missionary spirit in young Americans, and in some older ones as well, in the early 1960s. In its earliest years, the Peace Corps has had a phenomenal rate of success as indicated by the high proportion of volunteers completing their two year tours of duty in difficult and demanding jobs far removed from the affluence of 20th century life in the United States. A mere one-half of 1% of the first 1,000 Peace Corps members assigned to overseas duty requested to be returned before their two year tour was completed (Hobbs, 1963). In recent years, the rate of returnees has been somewhat higher, and it is interesting to compare differential rates of noncompletion according to differences in circumstances.

Information on differential rates was reported in a discussion by Peace Corps selection personnel at the 1966 convention of the American Psychological Association. One of the speakers noted that there were highly contrasting rates of return from the countries of Costa Rica and Colombia. Costa Rica had a relatively high socioeconomic level and many of the Peace Corps personnel were working in urban settings quite similar to those in which they might have worked had they remained in the United States. Colombia is a country with a low socioeconomic level and the volunteers worked in primitive rural areas. Furthermore, nearly all of the volunteers had been physically assaulted or robbed during their stay in Colombia; while they were unmolested in Costa Rica. The rate of return for Costa Rica was one-third, while in Colombia 100% of the volunteers completed their two-year tour of duty! Many other comments in this discussion revealed that Peace Corps volunteers characteristically are disappointed when they land in easy, plush positions as opposed to those which are more demanding and difficult. It appears that one of the principal attractions and satisfactions of the Peace Corps is the demonstration of one's ability to succeed in the face of great obstacles. While the rewards associated with these attitudes and perceptions are intangible and subjective, their effect is seen in a very tangible differential return rate for varying situations.

Objective Costs

In contrast to the subjective quality of rewards, the costs which have been identified in SEALAB are largely objective in nature. That is, the variations of temperature, overcrowding, high noise levels and daily reminders of danger were physically real elements of the aquanauts' environment. It is possible to specify quantitatively how cold the water was, the number of square feet available to each man in the capsule, and the decibels of noise. Even the danger can be quantified in terms of the reliability of the equipment and the probability of surviving a malfunction. This contrast between the objective nature of costs and subjective nature of rewards appears to be characteristic of a variety of natural environments which are remote and isolated from normal society.

What are some of the implications for performance and adaptation in such situations?

We should point out that the intention here is to limit consideration to environments involving separation from normal society. Generally such environments are quite demanding in energy output and hazardous as well, though other types of high cost environment may have quite different reward–cost characteristics on the objective–subjective and stability–lability dimensions.

For example, the "executive suite" and the "valley of the dolls" (the land of Hollywood starlets) may be considered high cost environments. The negative aspects of these environments however, are generally subjective in nature, involving the pressures of responsibility and maintaining an image. Rewards include subjective elements (prestige and recognition) but they also include objective status indicators such as jewelry, expensive automobiles and residences, and physically positive stimuli such as good food and drink and air conditioning. Rewards and costs are not solely of one type or another in either environment, the executive suite or SEALAB, but the emphasis seems clear. The following discussion assumes only that the principle costs, in number and intensity, are objective while the rewards are subjective in the class of environments considered.

Stability of Costs and Lability of Rewards

From the hypothesized physically real and objective nature of costs and psychological and subjective nature of rewards in isolated and confined groups in hazardous environments, we can further derive the hypothesis that costs will be relatively stable and rewards will be highly unstable in such groups. We expect that the stability of costs and the lability of rewards will be revealed when a social system is considered longitudinally as it develops and matures, or when groups subjected to relatively the same physical conditions are seen to differ radically in performance and adjustment. It is predicted that, as time passes and additional groups are subjected to relatively similar environments, the cost–reward ratio will be altered so that costs will exceed rewards.

For purposes of illustration let us consider the possible development of the SEALAB environment in the Man-in-the-Sea program. As the program develops and progresses from the pioneering research stage to a more settled and mature operational phase, there will doubtless be numerous improvements which will serve to reduce the costs in the situation. For example, as more experience is gained and new generations of equipment are developed, the operation will become safer. The development of heated suits will certainly make the diver more comfortable in the water; operations will become easier and more convenient in general as newer methods of transferring materials to and from the surface and/or storing and using them on the bottom of the ocean are developed. Better tools will also make work easier. In short, as the program develops, improvements can be expected to reduce the costs in a variety of ways. By the very nature of the project, however, this decline in costs will reach an asymptote very quickly. Because saturation diving is involved and men will be exposed to high pressures, the situation will still be extremely dangerous. Also, due to the expenses of lowering large objects into the sea, filling them with the proper gases, and maintaining pressure, the capsules will be relatively small and crowded. Such factors as noise, work difficulty and exotic respirable atmospheres will still be present and decompression requirements will necessitate isolation from normal society. The same circumstances are true of a wide variety of isolated and confined groups. That is, groups widely separated in either time or space from normal society will always be in highly unusual and therefore high cost environments.

As the system matures, rewards in the situation may decline much more rapidly than the costs. The sense of personal achievement associated with early ventures and the recognition from peers and from society at large will diminish rapidly. The 100th or 1,000th man to accomplish a given feat cannot be accorded the same recognition as the first man to accomplish it no matter how difficult and dangerous that feat. Along with the decline in rewards associated with sense of personal achievement and recognition by society at large, the rewards from a warm and supportive peer group may change from plus to zero or even to a minus value depending upon the nature of group interaction. Thus, attitudes and perceptions and interpersonal relationships which are very favorable in pioneering phases of groups in challenging environments may be altered rapidly so that they no longer compensate for the costs which remain at a relatively high level.

This shift in the cost–reward ratio will be accompanied by a shift in outcomes of the situation. Thus we predict a shift from a highly cohesive group to one in which cohesion is low. This follows from defining group cohesiveness as the resultant of all forces acting to attract and repel group members. Highly attractive groups, environments or situations are characterized by numerous attributes which combine to produce rewards for the members. For example, such groups have high rates of application for positions, resulting in good selection ratios and high rates of retention, so that experienced personnel are available. Members of such groups are distinguished by high levels of self-motivation and good group relations, morale is high and there are "good" group norms centered around task effectiveness. In highly attractive groups there would be little evidence of desire to leave the group, therefore symptoms of desire to leave such as sick call rates and "goldbricking" would be low. Few disciplinary actions would be required. For groups with low attraction the opposite would apply.

This analysis has important implications for understanding the adaptation and performance of groups in developing social systems in high cost environments. It applies especially to weapons systems (for example Polaris submarines or SAC bombers) as they progress from early research and development stages to mature and stable systems. It may be that, in the early phases of such systems, men and crews are studied to determine how they react to the new environment. The question in general terms is: "Can man stand the stresses to which he is subjected in this uniquely difficult and challenging environment?" The answer is likely to be that men can stand the stresses quite well, for example, Kinsey (1959). Morale and performance are rightly judged to be outstanding. Such results may lead to the conclusion that no personnel problems should be anticipated in future phases of the operation. Such a conclusion is quite logical and is supported by the assumption that as a system is shaken down and the bugs are ironed out, conditions will improve generally. Furthermore, the initial phases of the program provide a cadre of experienced men who are available to lead and train those who will follow after. Focussing only on these factors, the assumption is quite reasonable that if the rigorous conditions of the early phases can be endured successfully, the improved conditions of later phases should present no problems.

So the system becomes operational with possibly cautious but nonetheless sanguine expectations regarding the personnel. As time passes personnel problems may appear and grow. Such problems may be blamed on the inferior personnel who are available compared with men employed in the earlier phases of the operation; and the quality of personnel available is doubtless an aggravation to the declining reward situation. First of all, many more men are required to man the system as it grows from a few units to many, and the men available are younger and less experienced. The increasing numbers of men required and the apparent decline in motivation, morale and performance of crews may result in intensive programs centered around improving the environment, recruiting, training and screening of personnel, upgrading ratings, offering premium pay along with other similar activities. Such efforts are essential and doubtless have significant beneficial effects which, however, may be obscured by the declining rewards in the system.

The cost–reward analysis of SEALAB suggests that primary attention should be given to within-group rewards for crews in maturing systems. While easy to propose, the implementation of this course of action requires a careful study and analysis of each specific situation. (An example of such a study will be presented later.) Increase in, maintenance of, or even deceleration in the rate of decline of rewards as a system matures, may be very difficult to achieve. The principal point is that since the reward characteristics of the situation may decline very rapidly, they are of potentially crucial importance to performance and adjustment.

Bolstering rewards in later stages of development of a system cannot be simply a matter of reinstating those rewards which characterized the pioneering phases of the system, rather, alternate sources of reward must be found. One obvious method of increasing or maintaining a stable level of rewards is through increasing monetary payment. This method has received wide recognition in the form of extra pay for hazardous duty. In commercial enterprises, whatever remuneration is required may be possible, but for a variety of reasons the situation in military operations is not comparable. It is unlikely that increases in pay will be utilized to the same extent in military operations as they are in nonmilitary hazardous duty occupations.

With regard to pay, there is an interesting contrast between military and civilian applications of saturation diving. In pioneering commercial applications of the SEALAB concept of saturation diving, pay rates have been quite high compared to the remuneration received by SEALAB divers. Further, it is interesting to note that SEALAB II divers, upon entering training, lacked the assurance that they would receive even the modest premium pay due them as divers. Because saturation diving is a new concept, Navy regulations for diving pay did not cover the SEALAB operation, and an exception was necessary to permit diving pay for SEALAB II divers. Fortunately, the exception was granted and diving pay was received by each diver for his entire time in the project. However, SEALAB II divers appeared willing to participate in the project even without assurance of extra pay which they would have received routinely had they been working anywhere else in the Navy as divers. Hazardous duty pay is certainly important as a reward and the present analysis suggests that it will be more important as the system matures and, paradoxically, as hazards decrease. However, the relationship between monetary reward and performance is not a simple one. See, for example, a recent excellent review by Opshall and Dunnette (1966).

Leadership Role

It is obvious that the leadership role is important in the changing cost–reward structures of developing social systems of the type under consideration here. We now attempt to analyze ways in which the leadership role may interact with the changing cost–reward structure of the social system. This discussion depends upon an excellent conceptual analysis by French and Raven (1960) entitled "The Bases of Social Power." French and Raven distinguish conceptually five bases of the power of a leader to influence behavior of group members: (*a*) reward power, based on the member's perception that the leader has ability to mediate rewards for him; (*b*) coercive power, based on the member's perception that the leader has the ability to mediate punishment for him; (*c*) legitimate power, based on the group member's perception that the leader has a legitimate right to prescribe behavior for him; (*d*) referent power, based on the group member's identification with the leader; and (*e*) expert power, based on the group member's perception that the leader has some special knowledge or expertise. For each of the five types of power, the more of an attribute the leader has, the greater his power. Given equal strengths of power for each of the five types, the greater the number of bases of power available to the leader, the greater his power. In normal circumstances, several types of power are available to a leader. Also, there are interactions among the various power bases such that the utilization of one type can increase or decrease the strength of another type.

Let us consider some possible differences in the bases of power and strength of power for pioneering groups in contrast with groups in more mature stages of system development. It is likely that the power of the leadership role will decline as a system develops. For example, it will be relatively easy at first for the pioneering leader to utilize reward power by congratulating his men for their achievement under very trying circumstances, while in later stages it will not be possible to reward men with praise for unique and unusual accomplishments if, in fact, their accomplishments are not of that nature. Such a use of reward power will interact to increase the referent power of the leader. That is, men whose efforts are genuinely and enthusiastically appreciated can identify closely with the agent of such rewards. Also, in pioneering groups, the leader may have outstanding expert status. Such expert status was true of SEALAB leaders. While the expertise of the two leaders depended on differing types of knowledge, their abilities were apparent to the crew members. In other groups, the expert knowledge of explorers such as Byrd, Peary, Ross and Shackelton illustrates the characteristics of the type we have in mind here. Also, leaders of pioneering groups are likely to have a high level of legitimate power. In the case of the military, they may be relatively high in rank, and in military and non-military groups alike, they may be somewhat older than the leaders of later groups. Rank, and normally age as well, are the main sources of legitimate power. If reward, referent, expert and legitimate power are all high, the potential for coercive power will be high also, although it may never be necessary for the leader to employ coercive power in influencing the behavior of group members.

In later stages of development of systems in high cost environments it is quite likely that the four bases of social power on which early leaders rely will decline in potential effectiveness. While they may be more expert than the leaders of earlier groups in absolute terms, since they have the benefit of knowledge gained in pioneering phases of the system, leaders of later groups may be relatively less expert in that others share the knowledge which they have. Also, as indicated previously, it is likely that they will experience a decline in reward and legitimate power as well. Such a decline in other sources of power will necessitate a greater reliance on coercive power, the result being that more disciplinary actions will be necessary in more mature groups in comparison to pioneering groups. The need for greater reliance on coercive power accompanying a decline in the strength of other power bases will, of course, result in a sharp drop in referent power. Thus, in the early stages of a social system operating in a high cost environment, interaction with the leader may provide significant rewards and few costs for group members, however as the system develops, the present analysis indicates that there will be a significant decline in the reward potential of interaction with the leader. If it is necessary for the leader to rely on coercive power to a great extent, the sanctions and punishments involved may represent significant increases in costs to group members.

Up to this point we have painted a rather bleak picture of the prospect of success for groups in high cost environments when the system is relatively mature. The analysis indicates that it will be quite difficult for groups to function smoothly in such environments, and the leader is presented with a particularly challenging complex of problems. But we also know that groups do function and are productive in such environments (e.g., the Antarctic). The question is how such groups can function successfully. Even to begin to answer such a complex question, comparative data are needed. That is, data on groups with relatively similar personnel, facing relatively similar environments and differing in their reactions to their environment, are required. Fortunately, a highly relevant study containing such data is available.

An Illustrative Study

The crucial role of the leader in influencing the cost–reward structure of the system and through it group performance and adaptation is illustrated in a recent study of Aircraft Control and Warning stations in the Arctic (Sells, 1965). The principal reason for undertaking the study was to attempt to explain marked differences in morale and performance at various sites. Eighteen different sites were studied intensively, with participant observers studying the groups for two or three months, interviewing personnel and gathering data from objective records. In terms of the cost–reward model these stations represented a relatively high cost situation, since the men were working at remote sites under adverse environmental conditions and the work was dull and monotonous. In terms of objective costs, all groups were roughly comparable. Personnel were comparable also, since the men came from a common pool. Finally, since the system had been in operation for a number of years, it can be considered mature.

The major reason for the differences in performance in the good and poor groups is summarized as follows: "By far the overwhelming factor, which stood out above all others, is the behavior of the commander in setting the pace and determining the standards and the social atmospheres of the site. Specifically, there is clear-cut evidence indicating a number of characteristics of commanders at sites rated high by headquarters which were either not found or observed only to a moderate degree at the sites rated poorly."

It is clear from the citation of the characteristics of successful commanders that they maximize the rewards available in the environment. This maximization of rewards is accomplished in two ways, directly, by the personal efforts of the leader, and indirectly, by contributions to group harmony and productivity which resulted from policies implemented by leaders. Perhaps the most important reward available in isolated and confined groups stems from the satisfactions of performing a job—the extent to which each man can take pride in his own accomplishments. Successful leaders of AC&W sites enhanced job satisfaction in a number of ways. First of all, they set a good example by "an extremely positive attitude toward their own job, and by application of their own time primarily to their own executive duties, leaving actual supervision of the work to supervisors as far as possible. Successful commanders are not one man shows." These attititudes toward and performance of their own jobs are accompanied by "overt pride in their organizations and in their men." These characteristics are grounded in an "emphasis on the mission above everything else." Possibly the crucial element in this area of leader behavior was "use of recognition and reward. Successful commanders seemed to have a knack of complimenting men for good work when appropriate and of making frequent use of recognition and reward in their personal contacts."

Further rewards were provided by training, by emphasis on a thorough training program, including on-the-job training, general education courses, and related training. Such a training program not only increased rewards by insuring a man's success on his present job, but had potential long term benefit as well. After his stay in the Arctic, a man could look forward to enjoying the benefits of his increased work skills and general education either in the Air Force or in civilian life. It is interesting to note that, despite the maintenance of a permissive and accepting attitude regarding personal problems of the men, leaders could not be described as soft or easygoing since they were strong on "discipline and strict in adherence to regulations concerning conduct and dress." Furthermore, rather than trying to make work easier, (reduce costs due to hard work) successful leaders utilized "maintenance of a heavy work load, long work schedules and much overtime, and in some cases made an advantage of undermanning." This theme of keeping men occupied and promoting group cohesion by intense group activity was furthered by "full utilization of existing recreational facilities as an additional means of maintaining morale and combating boredom."

Complementing this accentuation of the positive were attempts to eliminate the negative by "reduction of restrictions on mobility and alleviation of feelings of isolation and confinement. These included efforts to keep a steady flow of incoming mail, removal of curfews, maintenance of 24 hour recreational activities for shift workers and provision of food and coffee around the clock."

These policies resulted in "five results observable among subordinates at better sites, which were: (*a*) supervisory behavior supporting the policies of the commander; (*b*) comparatively few gripes directed at the site; (*c*) few signs of severe hostility among the personnel; (*d*) group cohesiveness evidenced by solidarity and closeness among group members, informal behavior supporting the group and its mission and the very noticeable absence of cliques; and (*e*) finally, clear cut evidence of positive attitudes toward other members of the group."

Thus, for the most part, the efforts of successful AC&W commanders were directed towards and had the effect of increasing rewards available within the environment. It should be obvious, but is important enough to stress, that these efforts resulted in much more than static and additive reward components. They resulted in dynamic and multiplicative beneficial interaction processes within the groups. Leaders of poor groups were not able to set processes in motion, even though they worked with similar personnel in similar environments. Thus we have a situation in which costs were stable across groups, the rewards were quite labile and the outcomes were influenced accordingly.

To review this chapter briefly, we have presented a cost–reward model for use in understanding behavior and the adaptation of groups under extreme psychological and physical stress. Admittedly, the model outlined here is extremely crude, and in one sense may be thought of as no more than a truistic explanation of the data. That is, if one asks why do people enter hazardous or other high cost environments, the answer has to be that, barring forced entry caused by conscription, capture or calamity, they will enter voluntarily because of perceived potential benefits. However, it is hoped that the analysis and discussion have advanced somewhat beyond truisms. In pursuit of that hope we have attempted to specify the nature of costs and rewards in one environment by discussing the implications of the cost–reward analysis for laboratory studies of isolation and confinement. We have proposed the hypothesis that costs tend to be relatively stable and rewards quite labile in environments characterized by negative physical stimuli. In developing social systems high in such costs, it is proposed that rewards will decline more rapidly than will costs. This relatively rapid decline of rewards in comparison with costs can be expected to have negative effects on performance and adjustment in such situations and on volunteer and retention rates as well. The leadership role in relation to the cost–reward structure was analyzed and evidence in support of the analysis was cited.

CHAPTER 6

Performance, Adjustment and Inter-Personal Relations [1]

OVERVIEW OF THE RESULTS

As reported in Chapters 4 and 5, the most striking conclusion drawn from both objective data and subjective impressions is that adjustment was very good throughout the period of life underwater, despite extreme crowding and high levels of perceived danger and psychological stress. There were significant increases in the cohesiveness of the teams, with little or no evidence of overt friction. On being interviewed after the dive, several of the aquanauts expressed surprise at the group cooperation and spirit, "I, personally was amazed at how well we did do under such cramped conditions. It seemed to me everybody just went out of their way to be nice." Differences among the three teams in adjustment and interpersonal relations were remarkably small, each team seeming

[1] The data reported herein were collected as part of a research project sponsored by the U.S. Navy and are in the public domain. The interpretations of the data are solely those of the authors and should not be construed as official and as reflecting the views of the Navy Department.

to maintain an optimal level of adjustment throughout its sojourn underwater.

Despite the high level of adjustment, there were marked individual differences in adjustment, performance and in relations with other divers. Such differences will be examined in an attempt to draw conclusions about antecedents and correlates of adjustment under stress.

CHANGES IN GROUP COHESIVENESS

Collins and Guetzkow (1964, p. 142) proposed that "under conditions of common fate, individuals will develop interpersonal attraction." We felt that this should be reflected in increased group cohesiveness. It was also assumed that the stressful nature of SEALAB should increase this effect, as increases in attachment to the primary group are widely reported in field studies of stress (Grinker & Spiegel, 1945; Janis, 1951; Schmideberg, 1942; Stouffer *et al.,* 1949). The hypothesis that sharing the "common fate" of the SEALAB environment would result in increased group cohesiveness was strongly supported by the sociometric data. As discussed in Chapter 4, the index of change in cohesiveness was the difference in choices of teammates between pre and post-submersion administrations of the teammate sociometric questionnaire. The results show a highly significant increase in the choice of teammates after the fifteen day immersion ($t = 4.10$, $p < .005$).[2] Sociometric means are presented in Table 6-1.

The "common fate" aspects of being separated from the world by the impenetrable barrier of 200 feet of water were emphasized by several men who reported feelings of isolation from the outside world. One amusing instance of this was a period of referring to surface personnel as "earth people." On one occasion, a diver, in his squeaky Donald Duck voice, said "I have a message for the earth people. Fuck you!"

[2] All p values reported throughout are two-tailed.

TABLE 6-1
Means for Sociometric Choice of Team Mates[a]

	Overall Means (N = 28)		
	Pre-dive	Post-dive	Mean Difference
	4.892	8.321	+3.428
	$t = 4.095$	$p < .005$	
	Team Means (Team N = 10)		
Team	Pre-dive	Post-dive	Mean Difference
I	4.70	10.20	+5.50
II	2.90	5.10	+2.20
III	6.60	9.90	+3.30

[a]Sociometric choices were weighted 5 for 1st choice, 4 for 2nd, 3 for 3rd, 2 for 4th, and 1 for 5th. Results for any diver could thus have a range of 0-15.

A comparison of team cohesiveness scores indicated that Team I showed the greatest increase in cohesiveness and Team II the smallest. (Team I mean increase—5.5, Team II—2.2. However, the difference between teams did not reach the .05 level, $t = 1.58$, $p < .10$).

Observation by closed circuit television supported a view that Team I was somewhat more cohesive than Team II and that Team III was intermediate. Divers on Team I spent more time interacting as one large group—sitting around the laboratory area eating or engaging in conversation. There was little evidence of pairing in this group. In Team II, on the other hand, while there was no overt bickering, there appeared to be less total group activity and more interaction between pairs of divers. Observed group differences were, on the whole, slight.

Team I might be expected to have a stronger sense of group identity, having been the first group to face the experience. However, being in the first group was not reflected in higher levels of reported fear.

An attempt was made to see if level of reported fear was

related to attraction to the group, as widely reported in the clinical literature (Grinker & Speigel, 1945; Schmideberg, 1942; Stouffer *et al,* 1949). Mood checklist fear scores were dichotomized at the median on reported fear and mean choices of teammates compared. The results were in the expected direction (Low fear mean, 7.57; high fear mean, 9.07) but did not reach the .10 level. It is perhaps reasonable to expect little differential effect of level of fear on attraction to the group at the extremely high levels of stress found in this experience.

CRITERIA FOR ADJUSTMENT

Nine years of intensive research by Eric Gunderson and his associates (Gunderson & Nelson, 1966) have resulted in the isolation of three sets of factors determining the adjustment of individuals to the stress of wintering-over in Antarctica. Gunderson and Nelson found that their criteria fell into three major areas—task orientation, emotional stability and social compatibility. We felt that these three ge ıeral factors would also be dominant in SEALAB. Consequently, we sought specific criteria which could be classified under these headings. Individual diving time and the rating of each diver by his team leader were the measures of task orientation. We felt that diving time in particular was an excellent measure of motivation as each diver was expected to log a maximum amount of time in the water and the actual time achieved was largely determined by individual motivation. The leader rating was simply the numerical sum of ratings of motivation and achievement for each diver by his own team leader.

Under emotional stability, the diver's self-report of fear on the mood adjective checklist and the number of meals missed during the fifteen day period were used as indices. Under social compatibility were listed gregariousness (the measure of the amount of time spent in social interaction with peers in the SEALAB capsule), time spent in the laboratory work area, post choice of each man as a peer on the sociometric questionnaire, number of phone calls to the surface (the measure of activity directed away from the group) and time spent assisting in preparation of and cleanup after meals.

The criterion measures were highly intercorrelated. This is not surprising, since in a task-oriented and isolated group such as this, men would need to score high on all criteria to achieve optimal adjustment to the environment. For example, it is unlikely that an individual who did not perform well would be highly rated by his leader and highly valued by his peers as a comrade. The intercorrelations of criteria are listed in Table 6-2.

A principle axis factor analysis (Harman, 1960) was performed on the criteria. Following extraction of the initial factors, a Varimax rotation was performed and three orthogonal factors accounting for 72.9% of the variance were obtained. On the basis of the predicted high intercorrelations of the criteria, it was felt that the first unrotated factor would be the best composite indicator of overall adjustment and that each diver's factor score would provide the most discriminating measure of adjustment. This factor accounted for 32% of the variance. Correlations with it will be discussed to provide an overview of individual differences in adjustment. Relationships with specific criteria will be discussed in later sections.

The loadings of each variable on the first unrotated factor in descending order are given in Table 6-3. From these loadings, a clear picture of the high scoring diver emerges. The aquanaut with a high score was highly regarded by his leader as a worker and was highly chosen by his peers as a desirable teammate. This diver was also a good performer (on the basis of achieved diving) and reported a low level of overt fear. He also spent little time communicating with people outside SEALAB and a good deal of time in interaction with his teammates, while spending little time lounging in the laboratory area. The high scoring aquanaut also missed few meals.

TABLE 6-2
Intercorrelations of Criteria

	1	2	3	4	5	6	7	8	9
1. Diving Time	1.00*								
2. Leader Rating	.40*	1.00							
3. Fear	–.50**	–.47*	1.00						
4. Meals Missed	–.24	–.22	.35	1.00					
5. Gregariousness	.50**	.10	–.24	–.06	1.00				
6. Time in Work Area	–.37*	–.47*	.28	.00	.36	1.00			
7. Sociometric Peer Choice	.27	.59**	–.22	–.40*	.14	–.28	1.00		
8. Outside Calls	–.50**	–.44*	.40*	–.37*	–.18	–.29	–.41*	1.00	
9. Meal Preparation	–.10	.04	–.16	–.44*	–.38*	–.11	.19	–.16	1.00

*$p < .05$
**$p < .01$

TABLE 6-3
Factor Loadings on First Unrotated Factor

Leader Rating	+.75
Outside Phone Calls	–.74
Diving Time	+.72
Fear (Mood Checklist)	–.68
Sociometric Peer Choice (Post-dive)	+.65
Time in Work Area	–.60
Gregariousness	.49
Meals Missed	–.49
Meal Preparation	+.01

It should be emphasized that differences in performance and adjustment discussed here are relative differences. Individual differences were found, but they do not imply a lack of success on the part of any of the aquanauts. The SEALAB team was a highly select and well-qualified group; and all men performed and adapted well in an extremely hazardous and challenging environment. The appearance of individual differences means only that some men deviated from a norm of outstanding group performance by a measurable amount.

VARIABLES RELATED TO OVERALL ADJUSTMENT

Personality measures given prior to the dive were disappointing in their almost complete failure to predict adjustment in SEALAB. The FIRO-B, The Allport–Vernon–Lindzey Scale of Values and The Strong Vocational Interest Blank failed to show any significant correlations with the adjustment criterion. Of the other personality measures, only the scale of achievement motivation (Appendix A) correlated significantly ($r = -.44$, $p<.05$). The correlation in this case was counterintuitive as the best adjusted and performing divers were the ones with the least expressed achievement motivation. The scale of delinquency correlated $+.33$ with the criterion ($p < .10$). Out of the large number of computed correlations, it is highly likely that these two significant correlations emerged by chance.

The possibility existed, of course, that the failure to obtain significant overall correlations was due to differing patterns of scores on the personality measures obtained by subgroups of divers—for example, civilian and military divers might show different patterns of successful adjustment. Comparing obtained scores on the adjustment factor for civilian and military divers, the means were not significantly different. There were, however, several personality scales on which differing patterns of correlations were obtained for civilian and military divers, most of these differences centering around values, as measured by the Allport–Vernon–Lindzey Scale of Values. In particular, a high economic orientation was associated with adjustment for civilians while the opposite trend was found for military personnel (civilian r: $+.57$, military: $-.27$, difference $p < .01$). The social scale showed the opposite pattern. For civilian divers a low score on the social scale was associated with adjustment while there was a small positive relationship for military divers (civilian r: $-.55$, military r: $+.18$, difference $p < .01$). The only other significant difference was found on the scale of maturity where the correlation between maturity and adjustment was $-.39$ for civilians and $+.49$ for military aquanauts. The differences between these scales and their relationship with adjustment for the two major subgroups may be a reflection of differing motivations and orientations towards the SEALAB experience. In general, however, the strongest conclusion is that paper and pencil personality measures fail miserably in predicting adjustment to this stressful situation.

This failure of standardized personality tests is quite consistent with earlier studies which have demonstrated the lack of predictive validity for such measures. In particular, Holtzman and Bitterman (1952) failed to find any significant relationships between personality factors and success in the stressful situation of flight training. This finding has recently been replicated by Peterson, Lane and Kennedy (1965). Speculating on the failure of psychologists' most cherished tools, we might advance the hypothesis that the situation in an experience such as SEALAB is so strong that environmental variables assume overriding importance, obscuring most of the differences measured by conventional tests. Some support for this view is found in the fact that observational measures and demographic variables, which are more stable, show consistent and significant relations with adjustment to this type of stress.

Another factor which may have reduced the effectiveness of the paper and pencil personality measures is "demand characteristics" of the SEALAB program. After having been selected from a large number of highly qualified divers, the aquanaut may have felt intense pressure to "look good". This could have been reflected in making the most socially desirable answers on all measures having face validity. Some support for this is found in the fact that the FIRO-B, which can be considered most susceptible to the influence of social desirability failed to show even trends in correlation with objective measures. Motivating forces characteristic of other volunteer populations can be expected to produce results similar to those obtained here with regard to personality measures.

Three major demographic variables were considered as probable predictors of successful adjustment in SEALAB—age, birth order and size of home town. Age was positively correlated with adjustment (+.31) but failed to reach the .10 level of significance. Birth order was correlated +.56 ($p < .01$) with the criterion, indicating that laterborns showed a higher level of adjustment to the environment that did firstborns. Size of hometown was correlated −.43 ($p < .05$) with adjustment. Thus, laterborn divers from small towns adjusted best to the multiple stresses present. A more detailed consideration of birth order differences will be found later.

Two additional mood scales, well-being and happiness correlated significantly with adjustment. (Fear was included in the criterion factor on an *a priori* basis.) The interrelations of mood scales and their relation to specific criterion variables will be considered later. Happiness was correlated $-.74$ ($p < .01$) with adjustment indicating that those divers who reported themselves most happy were least successful in adjusting to the SEALAB environment. The implications of this finding will be discussed later. Well-being was correlated $+.74$ with adjustment indicating that the divers perceiving themselves as most vigorous and alert showed the best adjustment.

Post choice on the sociometric questionnaire as a preferred leader was correlated $+.35$ with the adjustment factor. This finding reaches only the .10 level of significance.

No differences between the three teams or between civilian and military divers on any of these variables were significant. Overall correlations among predictors and the composite criterion for all divers and civilian and military subgroups are found in Table 6-4.

TABLE 6-4
Correlations With the Composite Criterion

Variable	Overall (N = 28)	Civilian (N = 10)	Military (N = 18)
Age	.31	.12	.43
Birth Order	.56**	.61	.53*
Size of Hometown	–.43*	–.38	–.47*
Maturity	.18	–.39	.49*
Order of Arising (Post)	–.25	.04	–.39
Leader Sociometric	.35	–.36	.44
Happiness	–.74**	–.86**	–.66**
Psychological Well-being	.74**	.70*	.76**
Delinquency	.33	.11	.44
A–V–L Economic	.01	.57	–.27
A–V–L Social	–.06	–.55	.18
A–V–L Political	.11	.32	–.02
Depression	.10	.59	–.17

*$p < .05$
**$p < .01$

FINDINGS RELATED TO LEADERSHIP

In the initial planning of the study, large amounts of data were to be collected concerning interactions with and communications directed towards leaders. The previously discussed difficulty in comprehension of helium speech made such systematic observations impossible. As a result, much of the data are circumstantial and more sparse than had been hoped. Nevertheless, a number of tentative conclusions can be reached which should be open to evaluation in subsequent field studies.

Some support for the hypothesis proposed by Helmreich and Collins (1967) that stress increases dependency on leaders can be found for postdive leader choice. Divers chose their own team leader as the most preferred leader to a greater extent than they chose any other aquanaut. The leader of Team I had a sociometric choice score of 31 from his teammates while the next highest choice had a score of 12.[2] For Team II, the corresponding scores for assigned leader and second highest choice were 31 and 10 and for Team III, 24 and 16.

Evidence that the choice of own leader was at least partly a response to fear can be found by dividing each team at the median on reported fear (based on the mood checklist) and comparing sociometric choice of own leader by divers above and below the median on fear. When this is done, it is found that 69% of the aquanauts below the median on fear chose their own leader as most preferred, while 94% of those above the median made this choice. However, the Chi square reaches only the 15% level of significance.

Another approach to the issue of leadership is to look at the characteristics associated with choice as a leader. Leadership choice scores are available for each aquanaut, derived from the post-dive sociometric questionnaire. These scores are the sum of choices weighted for rank. It is possible, then, to consider various hypoth-

[2] As with the peer sociometric scale, scores were weighted with first choice = 5, 2nd = 4, 3rd = 3, 4th = 2, 5th = 1, and unchosen = 0. As a result, individual scores could range from 0 to 45.

esized reasons for choosing or preferring a leader and to see if these are related to actual choice. The intercorrelations of all variables used in the leadership analysis are presented in Table 6-5.

As previously reported, post-dive choice as a leader was correlated only +.35 with the global adjustment criterion, suggesting that factors other than successful adjustment were involved in leader preference.

Two possible criteria influencing choice of a leader are experience and performance. These are certainly criteria which are used by high command in assigning laders to subordinate units. If followers were to apply these criteria, leader choice should show a high positive correlation with years of diving experience and performance on common activities such as diving time and number of sorties from the capsule. The results indicate clearly that these factors were not associated with leader choice. The correlations with leader choice are: years of diving experience (+.22); diving time (−.03); and number of sorties (+.11). Thus, men who did quantitatively more of the common work and had more experience in this area were not preferentially chosen as leaders. Therefore, those men preferred as leaders earned this choice by serving the group in other capacities. What other possibilities exist?

A preferred leader might be one who could provide a lower fear model for his men—the cool, collected, fearless leader. Rabbie's (1961) finding that a person in a state of lower fear was desired for affiliation under stress would support this view. A leader in a state of low fear might provide a source of reassurance and social support. If this motive were operating, one would expect a high negative correlation between leader choice and such a stress index as fear. Again, the data do not support this hypothesis. The correlation of fear with leader choice is only −.25. Thus, divers' preferences for a leader were not significantly related to the chosen leader's level of fear. It must be noted, however, that the measure of fear is subjective (based on self-report) and divers in choosing might base their choice on external manifestations of stress. This point can only be clarified by further research, for example, by

TABLE 6-5
Intercorrelations of Items Related to Leader Choice

	(1)	(2)	(3)	(4)	(5)	(6)	(7)	(8)	(9)	(10)
1. Leader Choice	1.00									
2. Age	.51**	1.00								
3. Diving Experience	.22	.67**	1.00							
4. Maturity	.41*	.26	.11	1.00						
5. Choice as a peer	.24	.28	.14	.09	1.00					
6. Fear	–.25	–.11	.01	.05	–.22	1.00				
7. Psychological Well-being	.21	.20	.17	.10	.47*	–.56**	1.00			
8. *N* performance tests	–.07	.00	–.21	.14	–.02	–.25	.14	1.00		
9. Diving Time	–.03	–.04	.01	.15	.28	–.50**	.52**	.22	1.00	
10. *N* sorties	.11	.13	.14	.10	.33	–.44*	.47*	.09	.89**	1.00

$^{*}p < .05$
$^{**}p < .01$

asking subjects to estimate the levels of fear and arousal of other group members.

The most preferred leader might also be one who greatly emphasizes social relations. That is, he might be a leader who serves as a "social-emotional specialist" (Bales, 1958) concerning himself with the social aspects of the group experience. In this case, leader choice should show high positive correlations with sociometric choice as a peer, gregariousness and an index such as participation in meal preparation. Choice should also show a high negative correlation with communication directed away from the group (outside phone calls), as the "social-emotional specialist" should direct his social concern towards the group. The results do not support this interpretation. Choice as a peer and choice as a leader were *not* significantly correlated ($r = +.24$, n.s.). This finding is similar to that of Hollander and Webb (1955) that chosen leaders were not highly chosen as peers. The correlation between leader choice and gregariousness was $-.13$ while that with participation in meal preparation was $-.15$ and with communication outside the group $-.29$. It thus appears that the social behavior of an aquanaut in the SEALAB setting was not strongly related to his perceived desirability as a potential leader.

The hypothesis of a dependency reaction in the stressful situation was supported by two significant correlations. Choice as a leader was significantly, positively correlated with age ($+.51$, $p < .01$) and with score on the pre-dive maturity scale ($+.41$, $p < .05$).

The picture of a desired leader which emerges is of an older, mature, perhaps aloof man rather than someone more social, fearless and high performing. In relation to other groups which face high stress as a unit, this leadership pattern is reminiscent of senior echelon military leaders rather than front-line officers. That is, this type of leader would appear to be more similar to the battalion commander or ship captain who remains somewhat isolated from his men and exerts indirect authority than to the platoon leader or leading petty officer who works and interacts directly with his subordinates. Of course, in the SEALAB situation, this distance refers to psychological rather than physical separation.

The findings would fit into Fiedler's (1964) contingency model of leader effectiveness. In Fiedler's terminology, the SEALAB environment should fit in Octant I—leader-member relations were good (as measured sociometrically), the task (diving and living in SEALAB) was relatively structured and the leader's position power was strong, as this was a military setting. Fiedler's prediction from the model would be that the most effective leader would be psychologically distant (aloof). What is interesting is that the men apparently shared this belief as they expressed their sociometric preferences for leaders.

One can speculate that in a group retaining direct contact with other units, the immediate leader can fill social and task needs while regressive and dependent needs can be projected on a more remote senior commander who can serve as a "father surrogate". Indeed, too much interaction with the senior leader might impair his effectiveness as someone towards whom dependency and reassurance needs are projected. It might be that too much contact would result in the discovery that the hero has feet of clay. In a group which is irrevocably isolated, however, dependency and reassurance needs can best be satisfied by someone immediately present. Thus, a more aloof and older leader may provide the greatest possible satisfaction of needs.

While this is highly conjectural, it can be subjected to test by comparing preferred leader traits in isolated and nonisolated groups under stress. It does seem apparent, however, that the leader in a group facing stress must serve needs beyond task performance and social interaction.

BIRTH ORDER EFFECTS

The prediction that firstborn and only children would show greater fear and relatively lower performance in SEALAB was strongly supported by the data. Sixteen of the aquanauts were firstborn and only children and 12 laterborn. Means and standard deviations for first and laterborns on relevant variables are summarized in Table 6-6. Correlations with the composite criterion are shown in Table 6-7.

Firstborns reported significantly higher fear and lower well-being while logging less diving time and making fewer sorties from SEALAB. This finding for level of fear clearly replicates

TABLE 6-6
Firstborns versus Laterborns Means

Variable		Firstborn	Laterborn
1. Age		33.94	36.75
2. Diving Experience		9.69	12.67
3. Size of Hometown		3.00	2.83
4. Theoretical	A–V–L Scale of Values	48.56	49.25
5. Economic	A–V–L Scale of Values	41.25	42.50
6. Aesthetic	A–V–L Scale of Values	40.38	33.67
7. Social	A–V–L Scale of Values	33.50	36.79
8. Poltical	A–V–L Scale of Values	44.31	45.29
9. Religious	A–V–L Scale of Values	32.00	32.50
10. Insolence		18.75	18.58
11. Achievement Mot.		14.88	14.58
12. Autonomy		28.00	28.25
13. Succorance Need		21.68	20.50
14. Compulsivity*		21.62	16.08
15. Activity Need		19.06	18.58
16. Harm Avoidance		28.12	38.83
17. Maturity		65.88	65.67
18. Delinquency		109.94	115.75
19. Fear*		0.83	–.98
20. Psychological Well-being*		–1.22	1.79
21. *N* performance Tests		1.27	1.28
22. Diving time**		–5.53	9.24
23. Number of Sorties*		–1.14	0.27
24. Peer Sociometric Choice (Post)		7.06	10.00
25. Leader Sociometric Choice		9.62	13.14

*Difference $p < .05$ (t test)
**Difference $p < .01$ (t test)

TABLE 6-7
Correlations With Composite Criterion for First and Later Borns

	Overall (N = 28)	Firstborn (N = 16)	Laterborn (N = 12)
Age	.31	.30	.34
Fear	–.68**	–.44	–.76**
Psychological Well-being	.74**	.73**	.58*
Happiness	–.74**	–.60*	–.73**
Size of Hometown	–.43*	–.23	–.69*
A–V–L Political	.11	–.27	.51

*$p < .05$
**$p < .01$

laboratory studies of fear (Darley & Aronson, 1966; Helmreich & Collins, 1967; Schachter, 1959; Zimbardo & Formica, 1963). It also strongly replicates Torrance's (1956) findings related to Korean fighter pilot effectiveness (as reanalyzed by Schachter, 1959). In the Torrance study, the investigator found that significantly fewer firstborns achieved "ace" and near ace ratings by shooting down MIGs in combat.

Birth order had the following correlations with the stress indices: fear ($-.49$, $p < .01$), and well-being ($+.57$, $p < .01$). Correlations with the performance variables are of the same magnitude. They are: diving time ($+.52$, $p < .01$), number of sorties ($+.56$, $p < .01$) and number of performance tests ($+.09$, n.s.). The effect is, thus, a strong and highly significant one.

Despite the large differences in emotional response and performance, first and onlyborns differed from laterborns on only *one* of the personality and demographic measures—compulsivity. Firstborns measured lower on the compulsivity scale than laterborns.

Birth order effects represent an extremely confusing phenomenon in psychology. A large number of studies have found significant differences between first and laterborns on a wide range of variables. Recent reviews by Altus (1966) and Warren (1966) summarize portions of this inconsistent mass of data. In particular, however, a few stable patterns emerge. First and onlyborns achieve eminence more than laterborns (as measured by objective indices of accomplishment such as *WHO'S WHO* or rosters of scientists (Schachter, 1963) and are over represented in college populations (Altus, 1966). In addition, firstborns are more likely to volunteer for psychological experiments (Capra & Dittes, 1961) and also for such hazardous undertakings as space flight (Perry, 1966).

Attempts to isolate ordinal position differences in personality have generally resulted in contradictory findings. Altus (1966) sums up the state of current knowledge in a single sentence "Ordinal position at birth has been shown to be related to significant social parameters, though the reasons behind the relations are as yet unknown or at best dimly apprehended".

The replication of Torrance's study showing inferior performance by firstborns under high stress has important implications for authorities selecting men for hazardous occupations. This finding assumes additional importance if it is generally true that firstborns volunteer for such assignments differentially. The apparent paradox of persons volunteering more for tasks at which they will perform worse represents an exciting challenge for research.

Two other aspects of the ordinal position phenomena underscored in this study raise questions relevant to the generality of the birth order findings. One question is whether the performance deficit reported is limited to volunteer populations. Both fighter pilots and aquanauts are members of select, volunteer groups. One can ask whether such differences would be present in a nonselected, nonvolunteer population. One could hypothesize that firstborns volunteering for hazardous tasks represent a deviant subgroup of the universe of first borns and that the obtained results would not generalize to a broader population. Two recent studies by one of the authors (Helmreich, Kuiken & Collins, 1968; Helmreich & Kuiken, 1967) provide some indication that strong birth order effects are present in nonselected, nonvolunteer populations. Both of these studies were conducted with randomly selected groups of Naval recruits undergoing training. The subjects in these studies were nonvolunteers and could be considered as representative of the general male population between 18 and 25. The results indicate that the previous findings of higher fear under stressful conditions replicate in this more heterogeneous group.

A second question relates to the problem of facing stress alone or in groups. It might be proposed that the differential response of first and laterborns to stress could be accentuated or caused by situations where the stress is faced *alone*. It is clear that flying a fighter plane is a solitary activity. Diving, however, can be an equally solitary experience, despite the fact that one customarily dives in the company of at least one other person. The lack of diver-to-diver communications and the dense, dark medium heighten a sense of dissociation and isolation. Stanley Schachter (1959) has suggested that perhaps the inferior performance of firstborns would not be found in stressful situations where the stress is faced by groups. This hypothesis can be derived from the fact that firstborns consistently show greatly increased desires for affiliation under high stress. It could, thus, be possible that being in the presence of a group could reduce the anxiety of firstborns (Wrightsman, 1961) and result in the elimination of differential levels of fear and performance by first and laterborns under high fear. However, Helmreich and Collins (1967) studied subjects both alone and in groups and found similar results for birth order and fear.

HALTING STEPS TOWARDS A THEORY OF BIRTH ORDER EFFECTS

A number of theoretical formulations have been advanced to account for the consistently observed differences between first and laterborns in reactivity to stressful conditions. Schachter's original contention was that differential dependency could account for many of the results. He cited numerous studies (e.g., Sears, Whiting,

Nowlis, & Sears, 1953; Whiting & Child, 1953; Haeberle, 1958; Ehrlich, 1958) examining the relationship between ordinal position and expressions of dependency which generally showed greater dependency on the part of firstborns.

Zimbardo and Formica (1963) offered another explanation for the ordinal position effects observed in stress research. They hypothesized that the greater need for affiliation is caused by lower self-esteem rather than dependency. Zimbardo and Formica feel that the dependency hypothesis is not theoretically tied to needs for emotional comparison which are served by affiliation.

Walters and Parke (1964) favor an integration of developmental and social psychological propositions. They propose that self-esteem is a self-reaction related to the transmission of achievement standards by parents and other authority figures during socialization. They feel that low self-esteem results from a combination of high achievement standards with habits of depending on others. They see low self-esteem as an outcome of child-rearing when the socialization process includes consistent reward for orientation towards authority figures and punishment for self-reliance. They feel that the antecedents of low self-esteem will include the frequent use of parents as symbolic models whom the child cannot hope to emulate successfully. Abelson and Lesser (1959) proposed a similar set of childrearing practices as causal factors in low self-esteem.

In the case of birth order effects, the model works consistently. Research findings typically show parents instilling the highest achievement standards in their firstborn children. In addition, firstborns should be most consistently rewarded for attending to and orienting towards others (i.e., for approach behavior towards parents). Finally, the absence of slightly older peers to serve as behavioral models doubtless forces the firstborn to employ parents and other adult authority figures as social models. The combination of these factors in the socialization of firstborn and only children can encompass the pattern of birth order results showing higher need achievement, lower self-esteem, greater dependency and more uncertainty and need for social support in stressful situations.

Recent research by Miller and Zimbardo (1967) and Helmreich, Kuiken and Collins (1968) casts additional light on ordinal position. Miller and Zimbardo argue that the effects of ordinal position on need for affiliation under stress may result primarily from the fact that firstborn and only children use as models for social and emotional comparison, family members who are widely, discrepant in age and ability. Their argument, in this respect, is completely consonant with the position of Walters and Parke (1964). Miller and Zimbardo go on to postulate that if the inappropriate model effect is the most important, then the size of the age discrepancy between laterborn siblings may be a crucial variable. The laterborn who is considerably younger than his next oldest sibling should find models for social and emotional comparison as inappropriate as does the firstborn. They point out that another characteristic of the firstborn's environment is the absence of other siblings competing for the attention of parents. In this respect, similarity should be greatest between firstborns and lastborns whose siblings are considerably older. One can predict that, in particular, lastborns with a large age gap between themselves and their next older sibling should respond in a manner similar to that of firstborns. This should be true especially if social and emotional modelling are the most important characteristics of ordinal position differences.

Miller and Zimbardo (1967) tested this proposition in a study where firstborns, lastborns less than three years younger than their next oldest sibling and lastborns more than five years younger than their next oldest sibling were offered the opportunity to affiliate while waiting for an extremely painful series of electric shocks and taking of blood samples. A number of personality measures were also collected on all subjects. Birth order was associated with differences in motives for affiliation, fear responses and other reactions on a number of self-report measures. Ordinal position differences between firstborns and *narrow gap* lastborns were consistently in the direction expected from Schachter's (1959) data. However, when the lastborn was much younger than his next older sibling, his behavior on a wide variety of measures was less like a laterborn and more like a firstborn. This pattern was true for measures of fear, certainty of reaction to the anticipated threat, interest and value of the experiment in general, as well as the importance of different motives for affiliation.

The explanation for these data must lie in differing patterns of socialization and reinforcement for the three ordinal position groups, which in turn can be explained by social comparison processes (Festinger, 1954). If social comparison becomes more stable and accurate as the difference between self and model decreases (a direct derivation from Festinger's formulation which has received strong support in a study by Radloff (1966)), then firstborns should have much less accurate comparison information than laterborns and may develop greater needs for social comparison. This effect should be strongest in situations where the individual is uncertain about what he should feel or think or how he should behave.

The models who offer the most accurate comparisons during socialization are slightly older siblings, as they are most similar in physical, social, intellectual and sexual development. As Miller and Zimbardo (1967) put it, "Where one has siblings who are much older, then comparison with them may provide information which is more accurate than comparison with parents, but certainly less so than if the siblings were similar in age. Moreover, these laterborns with much older siblings may continue to use these less appropriate comparison models for a longer period of time than firstborns use their parents. If so, then some of the predictable social comparison effects should be even stronger for them than for firstborns". Miller and Zimbardo found the predicted differences in many instances. The most crucial result was for the motive to affiliate for social comparison ("to see if others are reacting like I am"). This motive for affiliation was most important for large gap lastborns, next most important for firstborns and least important for small gap lastborns. This pattern was stronger when self-esteem was experimentally lowered. Radloff (1961) found that first and onlyborns gave more reasons for affiliation reflecting social comparison needs than did laterborns when needs for social comparison were manipulated experimentally.

Helmreich, Kuiken and Collins (1968) also found significant differences between large gap and narrow gap lastborns, using the 5-year criterion employed by Miller and Zimbardo. This study consisted of presentation of a persuasive communication under conditions of high and low fear caused by an irrelevant, external situation. Subjects were nonvolunteer Navy recruits about to go into a chamber filled with tear gas (in the high fear condition). The data for both fear (as reported on a mood checklist) and susceptibility to persuasion show that large gap lastborns fall between firstborns and all other laterborns and differ significantly from other laterborns but not from firstborns. The study found that firstborns and large gap lastborns were more frightened than laterborns and showed less attitude change under high fear than laterborns (who were more persuasible under high stress). The most parsimonious explanation for the ordinal position phenomena observed in SEALAB and in other research seems to rest with the social comparison needs differentially developed during socialization. This would also seem to be the most fruitful course to follow in subsequent research on ordinal position and stress.

CORRELATES OF PERFORMANCE IN SEALAB

In a preceeding section, we have considered the relationships between various predictors and the general adjustment criterion. The criterion included work performance, the primary component of which was diving time. In this section we expand the consideration of work performance, using three separate criteria—diving time, number of sorties and number of human factors tests performed in the water.

The correlations between reported fear and amount of diving and number of sorties were $-.50$ ($p<.01$) and $-.47$ ($p<.05$)

respectively, confirming the existence of a strong and consistent relationship among these variables. As can be noted in Table 6-8, diving time and number of sorties are highly correlated (+.89). It was originally thought by the authors that these measures might reflect differing reactions to the requirement of working in the water. For example, a man could substitute a number of short dives for one long and strenuous dive which could be more dangerous. This possibility is precluded by the high correlation between the two criteria.

The third performance measure, number of human factors tests completed in the water, was almost orthogonal to diving time and number of sorties; fear and well-being were not significantly correlated with this measure (the r's were $-.25$ and $-.14$). One correlation, however, seems to indicate the nature of this variable. The index of participation in meal preparation was highly correlated with the number of performance tests completed ($r = +.64$, $p < .01$). This implies that completing the performance tests may have been primarily a function of general cooperativeness and helpfulness. In addition, the human factors tests, for the most part, could be performed in the anti-shark cage just outside the entrance hatch and were among the least dangerous activities a diver could undertake in the water.

Birth order was significantly related to diving time and number of sorties. Firstborns logged significantly less diving time and made fewer sorties from SEALAB, while there was no relationship between birth order and number of psychological tests completed. The correlations with the three criteria were: +.52, +.56 and +.09, (p's $<.01$, $<.01$ and n.s. respectively).

The relationships between failure to share in group reactions and activities and the major performance criteria were also highly significant. The following three variables, (*a*) amount of communication directed outside of the group, (*b*) gregariousness and (c) participation in meal preparation and cleanup were all compared with the performance criteria. The data provide strong support for a view that sharing in group responses is related to performance.

TABLE 6-8 Intercorrelations of Items Related to Performance and Mood

	(1)	(2)	(3)	(4)	(5)	(6)	(7)	(8)	(9)	(10)	(11)	(12)	(13)	(14)
1. Age	1.00													
2. Diving Exper.	.67**	1.00												
3. Ordinal Position	.32	.25	1.00											
4. Size of Hometown	.05	.00	-.15	1.00										
5. Fear	-.11	.01	-.49**	.26	1.00									
6. Anger	-.07	-.06	.05	-.22	.34	1.00								
7. Happiness	-.26	-.23	-.53**	.46*	.53**	-.33	1.00							
8. Psychological Well-being	.20	.17	.57**	-.19	-.56**	.22	-.87**	1.00						
9. Communication outside SEALAB	-.39*	-.04	-.39*	.23	.40*	.06	.55**	-.46*	1.00					
10. Gregariousness	-.09	.06	.32	-.48*	-.24	.20	-.55**	.51**	-.18	1.00				
11. Participation in meal preparation	.16	-.01	.00	.36	-.16	-.21	.22	-.13	-.16	-.38*	1.00			
12. *N* performance tests	.00	-.21	.49**	.04	-.25	.08	-.09	.14	-.33	-.07	.64**	1.00		
13. Diving Time	-.04	.01	.52**	-.48**	-.50**	.20	-.52**	.52**	-.50**	.50**	-.10	.22	1.00	
14. *N* Sorties	.13	.14	.56**	-.37	-.44*	.23	-.48**	.47*	-.49**	.46*	-.14	.09	.89**	1.00
15. Choice as a peer	.28	.14	.25	-.21	-.22	.21	-.44*	.47*	-.41*	.14	.19	-.02	.28	.33

$^{*}p < .05$ $^{**}p < .01$

Directing communications away from the group was negatively correlated with diving time ($-.50$, $p < .01$), number of sorties ($-.49$, $p<.01$) and number of human factors tests ($-.33$, $p < .10$). Gregariousness was also associated with performance. Interaction with peers was positively correlated with both diving time ($+.50$, $p<.01$) and number of sorties ($+.46$, $p<.05$).

Participation in meal preparation, as previously mentioned, was significantly related only to number of human factors tests completed. The small size of the galley limited the number of people who could work there, and such an activity probably reflected more a desire to help than to interact with other group members. The high correlation with number of human factors tests also seems to indicate that this measure reflects interest in general cooperation more than in social behavior. The failure of the meal preparation measure to correlate with sociometric choice seems further to indicate that persons were accepted more on the basis of involvement than helpfulness or general interaction. It also gives indirect support to the conclusion that food was not a primary source of gratification in SEALAB. By way of contrast, Gunderson and Nelson (1966) report that cooks are consistent sociometric stars at small Antarctic stations.

Multiple regressions were performed on the three performance criteria using *a priori* demographic and behavioral variables as predictors in an attempt to see how much of the variance in performance could be accounted for. The independent variables used as predictors were fear, well-being, ordinal position, outside phone calls, gregariousness and participation in meal preparation and cleanup. The results of the multiple regressions indicate that half of the variance on each of the performance criteria can be accounted for by the six predictors. The multiple correlation of the six predictors with number of psychological performance tests completed was $+.70$ ($F = 3.43$, $df = 6.21$, $p < .02$). The multiple correlation coefficient for diving time was $+.72$ ($F = 3.77$, $df = 6.21$, $p < .02$). The six predictors gave a multiple correlation coefficient of $+.71$ with number of sorties ($F = 3.49$, $df = 6.21$, $p < .02$). Thus, it appears that a limited number of predictors can successfully explain objective performance under the stressful conditions found in SEALAB.

CORRELATES OF EMOTIONAL STATE

As previously reported, the mood scale of fear was significantly related to the general adjustment criterion and to the specific performance criteria. Relatively unfrightened divers were better adjusted socially and performed significantly better. The obverse of the fear scale, the scale of well-being, was positively correlated with performance and adjustment.

Considering the relations between the other four mood scales and performance and adjustment, one notes that the scale of happiness has a strong relationship to the criteria. Happiness was correlated $-.74$ ($p<.01$) with the adjustment criterion and $-.52$, $-.48$ and $-.09$ with diving time, number of sorties and number of human factors tests. The scales of anger, lethargy and depression showed no significant correlations with performance or adjustment criteria.

Fear and well-being were also strongly related to measures of interpersonal relations. Directing communications away from the group was positively correlated with fear ($+.41$, $p<.05$) and negatively related to psychological well-being ($-.46$, $p < .05$). Gregariousness was not significantly related to fear ($r = -.24$), but was related to well-being. However, this relationship was significantly negative ($r = -.50$, $p < .01$). The implication of this finding is that the divers who felt less alert and vigorous spent more time interacting with peers. It is interesting to note in this respect that gregariousness was not significantly related to sociometric choice ($r = +.14$). Thus, although gregarious divers tended to be better performers, social interaction was not related to being chosen by teammates as a desirable peer for another underwater experience.

The mood scale of happiness shows an unusual pattern of correlations. Self-report of happiness was positively correlated with fear ($+.53$, $p <.01$) and negatively with well-being ($-.87$,

$p < .01$). Happiness also was negatively correlated with diving time ($-.52$), number of sorties ($-.48$), gregariousness ($-.55$) and sociometric choice ($-.44$). It was positively related to number of outside phone calls ($+.55$, $p < .01$).

Thus, it appears that the frightened diver who did not share in the group interaction and directed his attention towards the outer world was rejected by his peers, but reported being happy in his underwater environment. This pattern of results suggests a denial reaction by the frightened and rejected diver. The group clearly sanctioned the admission of fear and much group banter surrounded admissions and discussions of danger and fright. However, the aquanaut who was rejected by the group and unable to share in its emotional life may have denied his unhappiness with the experience as a justification for his presence underwater. Communicating with persons outside SEALAB may have reinforced this tendency to deny unhappiness with the situation.

Dissonance theory (Festinger, 1957) would predict that the frightened and rejected diver could report greater happiness. Dissonance between the incongruent cognitions "I am really frightened and rejected by my peers and I am stuck down here 200 feet underwater" could be resolved by concluding "I am really happy with this great experience". Support for this interpretation can be found in a recent study by Helmreich (In press). In this study, subjects were asked to evaluate a dull and tedious task performed under conditions of high and low fear. Subjects under high fear found the task significantly more enjoyable than those in a low fear state. It was reasoned that individuals resolved their dissonance about being in the threatening situation by concluding that it was really a rewarding and enjoyable experience.

Observing the divers in the capsule, the authors could detect resentment of the diver who directed his attention away from the primary group. Informal observations indicate that the diver who communicated most with the outside world was severely ridiculed by his teammates for his preoccupation with "earth people"—but reported a high level of happiness in his SEALAB experience.

General consideration of the findings related to self-reports of mood reveals several important implications for research workers in psychological stress. The first, and perhaps the most important, is that self-report is always suspect. If the group had not sanctioned admission of fear in the underwater setting it is likely that only random noise would have appeared on the mood checklists. This is strongly suggested by the anomalous findings for happiness. However, if the investigator is aware of the group norms concerning admissions of stress and has other indices against which to evaluate self-report, the mood checklist can provide a useful means of ranking individuals. Nevertheless, our advice to any worker in the area would be to beware of self-report.

Given the recent work on emotion by Stanley Schachter (1964) and others which implies that much of emotion is determined by cognitive influences superimposed on a substrate of physiological arousal, the accurate assessment of physiological arousal state would seem to be one of the most promising means of getting at individual differences in response to stressful situations. A major problem in this area has been the need for bulky electronic equipment to measure GSR or other indices of arousal, but recent work (Harrison & MacKinnon, 1962; Thomson and Sutarman, 1953; Ferreir & Winter, 1963; Johnson & Dabbs, in press) has demonstrated the feasibility of measuring arousal with a simple plastic solution which can be applied to the finger tips and which records palmar sweat (a good index of arousal). Such an approach could easily be applied in field situations and could give a more objective measure of arousal than does self-report.

To close the discussion of emotion on a more positive note, however, it seems certain that, of self-report measures, the mood checklist is the most reliable, most easily administered and the most valid index of individual response to stressful situations. The method of collection (by checking a large number of adjectives) is probably less threatening than any other approach and thus elicits less defensiveness and denial. It would certainly seem warranted to continue to collect mood checklist data in field studies of stress wherever feasible.

OTHER FINDINGS

In this section we consider findings which are of importance in defining reactions to the SEALAB experience and which have not been discussed specifically in earlier sections. These include variables about which we did not make specific *a priori* hypotheses and variables which are of interest independently.

The size of the hometown in which an aquanaut grew up has been mentioned earlier as being strongly related to performance and adjustment. The pattern of correlations is highly consistent and indicates that men from smaller towns reacted more favorably to the stressful conditions present (the breakdown of number of divers from various size towns is given in Table 5-6, p. 000). Size of hometown was classified on a 6-point scale from rural (1) to cities of over 500,000 (6). Divers from small towns were evaluated more favorably by their team leaders ($r = -.34$, $p < .10$), achieved more diving time and made more sorties from the capsule (r's = $-.48$ and $-.37$, respectively). Small town men were more gregarious ($r = -.48$) but reported being less happy ($r = +.46$) and showed less gross activity inside SEALAB ($r = +.43$). These correlations show a clear parallel with the pattern of good adjustment and performance discussed earlier. There were no significant correlations with ordinal position, reported fear, communications with surface personnel or sociometric choice.

We had not made specific predictions as to the effect of this variable on reactions to SEALAB, but a review of the literature on isolated groups under stress indicates that this is a consistent finding in studies where the variable has been measured. Eilbert, Glaser, and Hanes (1957) found that men with rural backgrounds performed better at isolated Arctic stations, while Stunkel, Tye and Yankey (1952) reported that men interested in activities associated with city life adjusted more poorly to Arctic environments.

Wright, Sisler and Chylinski (1963) report that men from small towns perform better at remote telephone company outposts in Canada. Nelson (1962) found a trend for men with rural backgrounds to perform and adjust better at Antarctic stations. Finally, Perry (1965) reports that a high percentage of astronauts and astronaut trainees have small town origins.

These findings, along with the significant findings from SEALAB, indicate that size of hometown is a variable which accounts for considerable variance in the behavior of isolated groups. Rather reminiscent of birth order, size of hometown is not a psychological variable but a demographic factor influencing psychological reactions. Any hypotheses as to the theoretical function of this variable can only be speculation at this stage of stress research. However, several factors do seem plausible as determinants of the differential responses of men with small town backgrounds.

One important factor may be that men from small towns are more accustomed to living in close and intimate contact with a number of other people and may have adjusted to the idea of having little or no real privacy and little chance to lose themselves in the more anonymous environment of a large city. This could account for greater ease in adjusting to the enforced intimacy of an isolated group.

A second factor might be that men from rural and small town environments are more accustomed to having their every move subjected to close scrutiny and intense evaluation. The adage that life in a small town is like life in a goldfish bowl may portend the better adjustment of small town natives through innoculation against anxiety about constant observation. This may have been especially true of the men in SEALAB who were monitored continuously by TV and open microphones.

Whatever the etiology of the effect, it would certainly seem essential to include this variable in studies of reactions to isolation and confinement and to attempt to uncover more about the nature and causes of the effect.

Gregariousness

This variable has been mentioned in conjunction with a number of other criterion and predictor variables, but it represents an important enough aspect of human behavior to merit independent discussion. Laterborns and men from small towns tended to be more gregarious in the SEALAB setting. Men high on gregariousness reported more psychological well-being, but were less happy and less active than their less gregarious peers. Gregariousness was also positively associated with amount of diving time and with the number of sorties made from the capsule. Correlations of gregariousness with other variables are reported in Table 6-9.

The findings for gregariousness clearly support a view that social interaction is strongly related to successful adaptation to a rigorous environment It seems most likely that the social comparison and emotional ventilation gained through interaction are of great value in aiding an individual in adjusting to stress. The importance of the primary group under stress has been emphasized in the clinical literature. The SEALAB findings offer empirical evidence that group influences are a vital factor in successful performance under prolonged stress.

TABLE 6-9
Correlations With Gregariousness

Size of Hometown	–.48**
Delinquency	.40*
Psychological Well-being	0.50**
Fear	–.24
Meal Preparation	–.38**
Number of Sorties	–.49**
Diving Time	–.50**
Number of Performance Tests completed	–.07

*$p < .05$
**$p < .01$

Meal Behavior

As mentioned in Chapter 3, we expected to gain a great deal of valuable information from social behavior connected with eating, particularly since food has been reported to assume great importance in many stressful environments such as the Antarctic. The peculiarities of the SEALAB experience led, however, to a de-emphasis on meals and a consequent degrading of the importance of the concomitant variables. Nevertheless, the variable of number of meals missed provided several correlations of borderline significance which do give some information about the situation underwater. Younger men and firstborns were most likely to skip meals. Missing meals was associated with sociometric rejection after return to the surface. It was also positively correlated with fear and negatively correlated with psychological well-being, although men missing meals reported themselves more happy. Missing meals was also associated with late arising in the morning and with the number of communications directed to topside personnel. Correlations of this variable with other indices are reported in Table 6-10.

Although the effects of this variable are not strong, the pattern of correlations does emphasize the importance of meals as social encounters and supports a view that withdrawal from the interaction

TABLE 6-10
Correlations With Number of Meals Missed

Age	–.35*
Peer Sociometric Choice (Post-dive)	–.40**
Fear	.35*
Psychological Well-being	.34*
Outside Phone-calls	.37**
Meal preparation	–.44**
Number of Sorties	–.26
Diving time	–.24
Number of Performance Tests Completed	–.36*

*$p < .10$
**$p < .05$

accompanying eating is indicative of poorer adjustment. While the men of SEALAB did not "live to eat," regular participation in mealtime activity was related to successful adjustment.

The Ones Which Failed

Discussion of two variables which failed to provide any useful information may serve to emphasize the importance of planning data collection and attempting to devise alternative modes of collecting data on the same variable. We have mentioned earlier that we added the variable of gross motor activity while the study was in progress because it appeared to reflect some kind of systematic behavior inside the capsule. We had no *a priori* theoretical reasons to believe that this was an important indicator of psychological reactions. The results gained from the painstaking collection of these data were essentially meaningless, and probably represent chance significant correlations. Again, it seems the wisest course to decide in advance on variables which offer promise for theoretical reasons and to avoid being attracted to new and obscure bits of data to collect.

With territoriality, we were in a quite different situation. Many reports of behavior in isolation and confinement have emphasized that man is a territorial animal and will seek to stake out an area of his own. We had, accordingly, expected to find strong evidence of territoriality in SEALAB. However, the results were nil. Using our measure of territoriality, there was no evidence that any aquanaut claimed an area of the capsule as his own. There are a number of possible reasons why we failed to find evidence of territoriality. One may have been that under the extreme conditions of crowding present, there was no spot which a man could attempt to occupy consistently. A second reason may have been that our instrument was too crude. We had divided the capsule into sextants and recorded which sextant a man was occupying every thirty minutes. Because of difficulties experienced with TV monitoring and identification, we may have simply been unable to observe the attainment of territorial identification. The variable remains one which seems worthy of continued investigation, hopefully with a more precise measure. The failure to obtain useful data on this measure was not a serious problem in interpreting social behavior *because* we had assumed that we would have difficulty collecting data on some variables and had planned for alternative sources. In the case of social behavior, we had data from measures of interaction, meal behavior, communications with topside and sociometric choice.

We have seen that the three teams of divers became significantly more cohesive during their underwater sojourn. This increased concern for members of one's own team was reflected in changes in sociometric choices of teammates after returning to the surface. Despite a strikingly high overall level of performance, individual differences in achievement and adjustment were measurable. These differences were quantified along the three highly related areas of overall adjustment—task orientation and performance, emotional stability and social compatibility.

The best adjusted divers were highly ranked by leaders, sociometric stars, high performers and strongly oriented towards the peer group. Standard personality tests and indices failed to predict adjustment along these dimensions, but demographic and situational variables were highly successful in accounting for variance in adjustment.

The mood scales of fear and well-being were significant in relating to performance and adjustment. Divers who were frightened and who reported less well-being were poorer performers and less well-adjusted in general. Laterborns and aquanauts from small towns reported less fear and ranked significantly higher on performance and adjustment criteria.

The preference of aquanauts for their team leaders was marked and was highest among the more frightened divers, supporting a view that perceived stress increases dependency on leaders. Analysis of preferences for leader characteristics based on leader sociometric scores for each aquanaut revealed that age and maturity were the only factors significantly related to leader choice.

Emotional state, as measured by self-report on the mood checklist, was a successful predictor of performance and adjustment, but it was stressed that caution must govern reliance on self-report data.

Other variables such as size of home town and number of meals missed add additional information on adjustment in SEALAB. Several variables, originally seen as promising, failed to provide useful data.

CHAPTER 7

New Potentials in Field Research

This book is concerned with the measurement and explanation of individual and group responses to stress. In essence, it is a case study of reactions to an exotic environment containing a multitude of psychological and physical stresses. In studying this unique setting, we developed an orientation which may be applicable to the general study of social phenomena in natural settings. In this concluding chapter we will attempt to demonstrate and illustrate the potential application of this approach to the study of behavior in natural settings—realizing that it is difficult to arrive at a precise definition of naturalistic research.

At present, there is an emerging controversy over the relative merits of divergent orientations towards the goals and conduct of psychological research (Ring, 1967; McGuire, 1967; Trumbull, 1966; Wolfle, 1966). This discussion has been further stimulated by scientists outside the field of psychology (Hornig, 1965). In short, there seems to be a growing concern about our purpose, our methods and our directions. The terms of this dialogue are variously stated—field versus laboratory, artificial versus real, theoretical versus practical, pure science versus "helping people", molecular versus molar. We feel that it would be unfortunate if this introspection should open a schism in psychology with proponents in one camp seeing *their* approach to research as the exclusive path to truth. While much of the following discussion could be interpreted as advocacy of the field over the laboratory approach, this is not our intent, since we are firmly committed to the laboratory as an essential setting for psychological research. Both of us were trained as, have practiced as and will continue to be, experimental social psychologists—committed to laboratory research. Notwithstanding, we feel that the field approach has been sadly neglected and unfairly castigated as sloppy, unscientific and unrewarding. We will attempt to specify some of the causes for this denigration of field research, and hope, through this discussion, to stimulate development of untapped potentials. We cannot provide a handbook or cookbook for field research; our attempt is rather to present a conceptual framework within which a natural setting can be analyzed, techniques formulated and measures specified to examine theoretical propositions.

We feel that the only feasible approach to naturalistic research is to begin with a conceptual analysis of the problem. From this analysis one must work backward to the conceptual criteria and thence to the independent variables and predictors and an operationalization of the specific variables to be measured. We are convinced that this initial conceptual analysis is essential to avoid becoming lost in the overwhelming complexity of the "real world". Beginning with a theoretical analysis of the behavior to be studied is essential to measuring complex behavior precisely.

To illustrate, in the SEALAB project, our conceptual analysis and familiarity with the setting under investigation led us to believe that optimum adjustment to such a total environment could only be achieved through positive reactions in three areas—task performance, social interaction and individual emotional response. From this analysis we were able to arrive at operational definitions of behavior reflecting our conceptual criteria. For example, it followed logically that the amount of diving achieved under the demanding conditions of 205 feet would be a good measure of performance and that sociometric choice on return to the surface would be an excellent indicator of adjustment to the underwater environment.

It should be stressed at this point that multiple criteria are not only desirable but probably essential in understanding complex field behavior. By multiple criteria we mean both multiple measures of a given conceptual variable and the measurement of several conceptual variables. The first follows logically as a means towards greater precision, reliability, and validity of measurement in poorly controlled field settings, while the second refers to the distortions which can occur if only limited segments of multidetermined and highly variable responses are assessed (for example basing all of our conclusions on task performance alone in SEALAB). We feel that a major deficiency in most field research has been the use of a single criterion or of highly similar criteria. We will consider the implications of this point in detail later.

As previously mentioned, a careful, conceptual, specification of the behavioral criteria should lead directly to the identification of relevant independent variables, which, as predictors, should also be multiple in the sense that they can be derived from multiple sources and obtained through diverse methods of data collection. This is important both to give a more representative picture of behavior in the research setting, and to avoid results based more on shared method variance between predictors and criteria than on actual correspondence.

The goal and hopeful result of this approach to naturalistic research should be not only a better understanding of the particular behavior in question, but also the development and refinement of theoretical models of behavior under diverse conditions. It seems unlikely that a "shot gun" or "dust bowl empiricist" approach to field research can achieve either of these goals.

BEHAVIORAL CRITERIA

Let us consider the practical problems of deriving conceptual criteria for the behavior under study. We have conceded that no pat formula can be provided, but we will try to illustrate the processes through which we arrived at our *a priori* hypotheses about reactions in SEALAB, trusting that the general nature of these illustrations will be apparent.

After surveying the literature concerning the behavior of isolated groups under stress, we considered the specific situation of SEALAB. We knew that the group would be irrevocably cut off from physical contact with the surface and would be living under conditions of extreme crowding and physical discomfort while performing work of a highly dangerous nature. Given these factors, we decided that the model developed by Gunderson and Nelson (1966) provided the most adequate conceptual model of performance and adjustment (as outlined in Chapter 6); therefore we decided that the overall criteria of success would have to include performance, social and emotional components. Given this model, we sought to operationalize these nebulous conceptual variables.

In moving from conceptual definitions to variable specification, the researcher is forced to make value judgements concerning whether a given variable will adequately reflect "good" or "poor" adjustment to the situation under investigation. The possibilities of error are great, but the success of an investigation will depend in large measure on the accuracy of these judgements. Therefore, the researcher venturing into the "real world" must recognize that he cannot escape the necessity of making such judgements.

Our analysis led us to select the nine criteria discussed in Chapter 6. Clearly, some choices were more fortuitous than others. Some, such as diving time, proved, as expected, to be excellent indices. Others, such as meal behavior, were chosen hesitantly and with reservations. Despite the anticipated and obtained variability in merit of the criteria, the composite criterion based on such varied facets of behavior provided an excellent picture of responses to SEALAB. This picture differs markedly from the more typical case where a single criterion measure is used to define reactions to a total environment. Examples of this univariate approach would include such things as counting number of planes shot down as the indicator of success in combat (Torrance, 1954) or a pass–fail criterion for military flight training (Curran & Wherry, 1966). We should emphasize that we are not opposed to the use of single criteria *per se.* The single criterion approach is adequate and excellent for many purposes—including the instances cited above. It can be of great practical utility, but we feel that the use of single criteria contributes little to the development of theoretical models of behavior. Theoretical models based on multiple criteria will be not only immediately applicable, but should generate, in addition, basic propositions concerning human behavior. What we wanted in SEALAB was a set of variables yielding the maximum possible information about total responses to the situation. Our goal was not completely achieved, however. For example, we had included physiological variables in our plans, but the difficulties in obtaining these data from men living under water precluded obtaining enough observations for analysis. In summary, a conceptual model attempting to encompass complex field behavior demands multiple criteria.

We cannot stress too strongly the necessity of using heterogenous methods of measurement. A major problem in field research has been the use of subjective self-report measures as the sole criteria for performance and adjustment. In many cases, conclusions are reached on the basis of correlations between subjective psychological tests and equally subjective interviews with participants. The problems of distortion using this technique are enormous. There is normally a marked lack of correspondence between an individual's *reported* behavior and his actual behavior. This unreliability of the subject as a data source is not limited to the field, but also holds true in laboratory research. This problem has been discussed in detail by Aronson and Carlsmith (in press) in their discussion of methodology in social psychology. They conclude, and we are in total agreement, that a behavioral or "behavioroid" measure will be a much more accurate reflection of true response than will a subjective report. In essence, an individual's subjective self-report is only one view of a complex situation—and is highly likely to be a strongly biased view.

Criteria for Criteria

With the orientation outlined above, it is possible to derive specific criteria for judging the merits of behavioral criteria. Four major criteria should determine whether a set of criteria will provide an accurate picture of a social situation. These are: (*a*) the use of objective and quantifiable measures; (*b*) high method variance in criterion variables; (*c*) isomorphism of criterion variables with conceptual variables and (*d*) the use of multiple data points.

To illustrate, let us examine several criteria used in SEALAB in the light of these requirements. It is obvious that all of the measures employed in SEALAB were quantifiable and represented scalable responses. We feel that the use of quantifiable and scalable measures will lead to more accurate conclusions than will the use of seemingly richer clinical evaluations or, at the other extreme, the use of biserial criteria such as "pass–fail". Observations of behavior were recorded objectively with no judgements or interpretations on the part of observers. For example, in measuring gregariousness, observers recorded only the physical locations of all men at a given point in time.

High method variance was achieved through the use of diverse sources of data. Our criteria came from objective observations, official records, evaluations of subjects by peers and leaders and subjective self-report. Such variance in method of collection minimizes the possibility of obtaining false positive results through shared method variance.

Our analysis indicated that the isomorphism of criterion variables with conceptual variables was generally good. Isomorphism was strongest in the task area where we used the variable ofdiving time (the expressed purpose of the mission). We also had the weaker task criteria of time spent in the work area and leader ratings.

In the area of social behavior, our measures also were close to the conceptual variables. Sociometric choices are obviously a good indicator of social adjustment. We felt also that our measures of gregariousness and communication directed away from the group (phone calls) were close to the conceptual variable.

We were least satisfied with emotional criteria, as our strongest criterion measure was subjective self-report of mood reported on the adjective check list. Although reports of mood were highly correlated with behavioral variables, we hoped for additional objective measures of emotion.

The criterion of multiple data points was successfully met. Each variable was assessed repeatedly over the 15 days of the dive. For example, gregariousness was determined on the basis of more than 300 observations of each diver, and mood was based on seven separate reports by each aquanaut. Although there was only a single sociometric score for each man, this score represented the composite judgement of all 27 fellow aquanauts.

It is obvious that strong criteria are the necessary starting point for field research. But the question remains, what do you do with them? Through an understanding of responses to a situation, we should be able to predict and control behavior in similar settings. Perhaps the most obvious utility in being able to predict is in selection—a point we will now pursue at some length. As an example, let us consider the special case of selecting men for hazardous endeavors.

SELECTION FOR HAZARDOUS DUTY

Selection of men for hazardous duty presents an extremely vexatious set of problems for the psychologist. The question of what type of man to send into a hazardous and exotic environment—whether he be an OSS operative, an aquanaut, an astronaut, a pilot, a peace corpsman or a submariner—is one which psychologists are frequently called upon to assist in answering. Extensive work has been done in this area, and a great deal of information is available. Unfortunately, however, there appears to be no general solution to the problems of selection. There remain many unresolved questions concerning assessment methodology in general and in evaluation of the effectiveness of specific predictors. We do not aspire to the final solution of any of these problems. However, since SEALAB was a very unusual situation, it may be useful to indicate some of the salient aspects of selection problems highlighted by our research.

First, it appears that any selection instruments involving subjective self-report are, by their very nature, doomed to failure in such situations. By measures of subjective self-report we mean personality scales and all their numerous variants which rely upon the individual supplying information about his own attitudes, feelings, impressions of experiences, preferences and the like. This is an extreme statement, and it is recognized that it may be highly controversial. With extensive and intensive efforts directed towards increasing the reliability and validity of assessment instruments and guaranteeing nonfakability, it may seem that the development of self-report predictive instruments is essentially a matter of time and effort. However, we feel that, for use in selecting among volunteers for special and hazardous duty, efforts to devise such instruments are essentially futile, basing our statement on a conceptual analysis of the selection process. That the same general difficulty afflicts another similar assessment technique based on self-report is indicated by Perry (1965). In discussing astronaut selection, he states that the psychiatrist can "select out" on the basis of pathology but in "selecting in", "the best selection may be only slightly better than a random one done on the basis of photographs" (p. 823).

There is a good deal of evidence to support the contention that personality inventories do not work well in predicting behavior in stressful environments (Webb, *et al.,* 1966; Peterson, Lane, & Kennedy, 1965; Holtzman & Bitterman, 1952). It is our purpose here to attempt to analyze some of the reasons why they do not work; that is, to try to analyze from our experiences and from an examination of other relevant situations what some of the built-in difficulties are.

Recent discussions of the demand characteristics of the research setting (Orne, 1962); of experimenter biases (Rosenthal, 1966); and of the expectations of subjects (Aronson & Carlsmith, in press) are relevant to the present discussion. The invalidity of measures using subjective self-report in selection for exotic environments derives primarily from the motivations of the candidates. To illustrate, let us assume that a man volunteers for a specific program, and that the program involves a situation containing high costs and high rewards (see Chapter 5). That is, the candidate anticipates that the work will be dangerous and difficult, but challenging, and that he will derive great satisfaction from his participation in the program. In order to volunteer for such a program, the man will obviously have to be highly motivated. The application forms will probably ask him to indicate relevant experiences qualifying him for the program, and his answers to specific questions may demonstrate to him that he should be among the top candidates for consideration. He submits his application and is informed that he has passed a preliminary screening and will have to undergo further evaluation. In this further evaluation, a psychologist administers to him a battery of paper and pencil tests. The responses to the tests may ask him to give his opinions and "true feelings" on a variety of what, to him, may seem very personal, trivial and irrelevant matters. In the best of all possible situations, his attitude towards the testing program may be one of welcome acceptance, based on the feeling that he has the characteristics necessary for participation and that his responses to the psychometric instruments will increase his chances. On the other end of an attitude continuum, he may be extremely hostile towards the entire procedure. This feeling could arise from a variety of causes. He can feel, for instance, that he should be judged on the basis of past performance and not on the basis of responses made to "inappropriate" tests. Hostility can also arise from concern over whether or not he will "measure up", that is, whether his "personality" is acceptable. Such motivation could result in highly defensive reactions.

Whether he is accepting, indifferent or hostile towards the requirement of supplying personality information, however, we can be certain that he will be biased, and the more important his entrance into the program is to him, the more biased he is likely to be. His motivation will be such that he will try to answer the questions put before him in a way that will increase his chances of being accepted. It matters little whether or not his attempts to answer the questions in a manner favorable to acceptance agree with the psychologist's *a priori* conceptions, because the crucial fact is that his answers will be greatly biased by his motivation. Recent attempts to develop more sophisticated instruments to account for such biases will be of little use. One foolproof method to "beat the system", which we have reason to believe was used by some SEALAB subjects, is to respond in an essentially random fashion. While it is true that, in strict mathematical terms, a subject cannot respond randomly, his behavior can be sufficiently random to negate any value which an instrument may have. On a small sample of subjects, only a few men responding randomly can invalidate results for the entire group.

To clarify this point concerning subject motivation, let us consider in contrast the motivations affecting responses to personality tests of persons seeking counseling and/or psychotherapy. A person approaches a counselor or therapist with the goal (manifestly, at least) of being helped to find his niche in life or of being assisted in overcoming personal problems. With such motivations, he has a strong interest in supplying the counselor with the most valid information possible. To be sure, this is not always done, and various deliberate and subconscious biases can result in "irrational" responses; however such biases cannot be directly attributed to the overt motivations of the individual being tested.

Thus, in the personnel selection case, we have strong motivation to give biased responses, while in the counseling/therapy situation, the motivation should produce true answers. In illustration, let us consider a specific test question. Suppose that an applicant for a challenging, high prestige program is faced with the following question: "I very often feel somewhat timid in the presence of my superiors". He may say to himself, "Yes that's true, I do, but if I answer 'strongly agree', they may think I'm not adventurous and self-reliant enough. On the other hand, if I answer strongly disagree, they may think that I am a potential insubordinate.

So I guess I'll answer it right down the middle, 'neither agree nor disagree', which will result in the least trouble."

Now consider a person in a counseling or therapeutic situation encountering the same question. His reasoning might be somewhat as follows: "Yes, that's true I do and I'd better say so or I may wind up in a job that I don't like." Or, "Yes I do and maybe a therapist can help me overcome this. It's something I've worried about for quite some time". To be sure, this is a simplistic analysis of the situation, since many additional factors can operate to influence the validity of self-report in both situations. The intent here is to highlight motivational influences.

Thus, we are skeptical of the value of self-report measures of almost any kind when they are applied to selection of personnel for any position in which motivation for acceptance is very high. The same skepticism would not apply to achievement and aptitude tests, since the motivation to do well should theoretically produce the same results for all applicants. Our pessimism derives not alone from the fact that paper and pencil inventories did not correlate with objective measures in SEALAB nor even from the fact that they have not correlated with performance in other similar environments using much larger and more homogeneous populations, rather it is derived primarily from this analysis of the demand characteristics of testing situations.

What types of information might be used in selecting men for hazardous duty? It is obvious from our criteria that there were enormous individual differences in performance and adjustment in SEALAB, therefore it follows that if similarly precise criteria were generally available, other natural situations should yield performance and adjustment variability of equal or greater magnitude. Also, the fact that the various components of our composite criterion were highly intercorrelated indicates that there is an intra-individual stability determining performance and adjustment in such situations. If the observed behavior is lawful, in the sense that some individuals perform and adjust better than others and that a variety of measures agree upon such performance, then that behavior should be predictable.

Defining the Predictors

In defining predictors, we have suggested working from the criterion behaviors by which a man will be judged in the situation backward to measures which will predict the criteria. To take a specific example, one of the principle criteria of success in SEALAB was diving time. A face-valid predictor of diving time in SEALAB should be the amount of previous diving. That is, a man who has spent much time in the water, in comparison with his peers, is a man who will spend much time in the water in the future. We recognize that such information will be difficult to obtain, far more difficult than responses on paper and pencil tests, but it should be worth the effort.

Another conceptual criterion was social adjustment. A behavior-to-behavior analysis suggests that an individual's previous history of social adjustment will best predict future adjustment. In support of this point, we cite Hollander (1964, p. 91) who has argued and demonstrated that sociometric measures have characteristically been among the most valid predictors of a number of behavioral criteria. "Peer nominations represent a more superior, consistent predictor of performance criteria across situations than any other single variable. The evidence, mainly from military studies, is quite clear on this point. (Jenkins, 1948; Hollander, 1954; Hollander, 1964, 1965)". Again, such information will be quite difficult to secure, but its potential validity justifies acquisition efforts.

The third conceptual area was that of emotional reactions. This was the area which presented the greatest difficulty in both conceptualization and measurement. The initial problem centered around defining optimum, or even adequate, emotional response to a stressful situation. Indeed, recent experimental and theoretical contributions by Schachter (1964) and others have raised fundamental questions about traditional views of the concept of emotion.

Clearly, in SEALAB, we could expect that both flat affect and intense overt emotionality might be indicators of maladjustment. However, a specification this vague is of little utility. Thus, we admittedly had a less than adequate conceptualization of emotion. But even with a satisfactory conceptual definition of emotion, the measurement problems would remain formidable. The low correspondence among physiological, observational, and self-report indices of emotion and the unreliability of these measures has been extensively documented by Lazarus (1966) and many others. It seems almost futile to attempt to predict responses so inadequately defined and so impervious to measurement.

Nonetheless, it is inconceivable that emotional responses, however defined and measured, can be ignored in assessing reactions to physical and psychological stress. Given these considerations, it is obvious that this is an area in need of conceptual and methodological development.

The findings reported in Chapter 6 demonstrate surprisingly high correspondence between the self-report measures of emotion and objective indicators of task and social behavior. These results indicate that conceptually clear and precisely measured task and social indices are potentially invaluable in contributing to the solution of the vexatious problems in the area of emotion.

Let us attempt to clarify this line of reasoning. If it is necessary for an individual to succeed in all three areas (task, social, and emotional) in order to make an optimum adjustment to a stressful environment, it follows that high correlations between emotional measures and more precisely defined, quantitative measures of task and social adjustment are evidence for the validity of both the definition and measurement of emotion.

PREDICTORS

We have discussed some of the characteristics of predictors as they might be used in the selection of personnel. There is, however, no need to limit the use of predictive information to questions of selection. Good predictors have many potential uses other than as criteria for selection. Since behavior is a function of both the person and the environment, adequate prediction of responses may suggest changes in both the physical and social environment. These alterations could include such things as reduction of threat perceptions, stimulus enrichment to decrease monotony, changes in group structure and composition, an increase or decrease in the number of hierarchical levels within a group, leadership style, training programs aimed at such diverse goals as improving mechanical or human relations skills, and many other changes. The important point here is that improved understanding of human behavior through the use of adequate criteria, coupled with effective predictors, will lead to greater precision in evaluation and attempts to improve performance and adjustment in nonstressful as well as in stressful situations.

It should be obvious that the ultimate goal of our approach is the development of concepts and theories within which the interrelationships of these concepts may be understood. Kurt Lewin's dictum that "Nothing is so practical as a good theory" summarizes precisely what we mean. Without an adequate theoretical model, attempts to understand or affect changes in response to any environment are likely to be inchoate and ineffective. The more precise and inclusive the theoretical models available, the greater the variety and effectiveness of controls which can be brought to bear on a particular problem.

Criteria for Predictors

Criteria for predictors are logically similar to the criteria for criteria. Perhaps most important is the necessity that predictors be isomorphic with the conceptual variables. Stated in its simplest form, the point is that the best predictor of future behavior is past behavior. As a practical matter, it will never be possible to have a one to one correlation between past and future behavior, because predictions of any future behavior will, of course, involve unknowns.

Therefore it is never possible to have a sample of behavior completely analogous to the behavior we are trying to predict. However, the goal is to come as close as possible to that ideal. Thus, all other things being equal, a behavioral prediction of a behavioral criterion will be superior to a subjective self-report predictor of a behavioral criterion. In summary, the more similar the predictive behavior to the criterion behavior, the better the prediction.

A study by Plag and Goffman (1966) illustrates this point well. Their problem was the prediction of four year military effectiveness from an examination of the characteristics of Naval recruits at the time they entered the Navy. The criterion was a dichotomous rating of effectiveness–ineffectiveness. Sailors were considered to be effective if they completed their periods of obligated service and were recommended by their commanding officers for reenlistment. Those rated as ineffective were enlistees who required early separation from the service, as well as those who, after completing their obligated service, were not recommended for reenlistment. The following five predictors resulted in the best regression coefficient in terms of predicting the effectiveness criterion: (*a*) education, (*b*) family stability, (*c*) expulsions from school, (*d*) arithmetic score on an entering test battery, and (*e*) mechanical score on an entering test battery. Included among variables which did not predict were: (*a*) religion, (*b*) reasons for enlistment, (*c*) initial clinical rating based upon brief psychiatric screening, (*d*) birthplace, and (e) recruiting area.

If one examines successful and unsuccessful predictors according to their correspondence with the criterion, it becomes clear that past behavior did predict future behavior. The principal job for a Navy enlisted man is to obey orders, fit into the system, to learn a particular skill and to advance within that skill. If he does this he is likely to be recommended for retention, but if he does not, he will be discharged or not recommended for retention. Thus, if a recruit has completed school, is able to pass the arthimetic and mechanical tests, has a stable home background and has shown a previous record of adjusting to another institution, namely high school, it is likely that he will also succeed in the Navy. In essence, those who do well in previous situations demanding the same behaviors which the Navy requires of them will do well in the Navy, while those who do not do well in previous situations demanding behaviors which the Navy requires will not succeed.

It should be noted that this study dealt with thousands of recruits and that it was not possible to gather highly detailed data on a group this large. In addition, the criterion was a rather gross one. Perhaps we will have to be satisfied with relatively gross criteria and predictors and relatively low correlations for large groups; however, for smaller groups such as SEALAB, in which it is possible to specify criteria precisely and to gather detailed information from a variety of sources, prediction coefficients should be much higher than they are in large populations. Precision is probably a matter of how much one is willing to pay for increases in the validity of prediction.

Method Variance

Just as an evaluation of performance and adaptation from several different methodological angles results in a superior criterion, so will utilization of predictor variables obtained from a variety of different methodological approaches result in better prediction. Psychologists too infrequently employ heterogeneous methods of data acquisition, but we will consider this point later in some detail. To illustrate, consider, as an example of method variance in predictors, the wealth of information available to professional football coaches and general managers as they prepare to make their annual selections from the crop of college football prospects for the pro football draft. First, they have a tremendous amount of information from *official records* represented in such statistics as the number of yards gained by backs, the number and percentage of completions of passes by quarterbacks, and the number of tackles and blocks by linemen. Also, they have a great deal of *observational information.* The better college prospects are scouted in all of their senior games, and in many prior games, as they come to the attention of professional football scouts. To supplement such observations, game *films* are often available from which behavior can be studied repeatedly in detail. Reports from coaches supply *supervisor ratings,* also of a very detailed nature. All opponents team selections may provide *information from* a man's *peers.* Sports writers and broadcasters with their All Conference and All America selections provide other information. *Objective information* is available in terms of the height, weight, age, health, and speed of running on most candidates. Attitudes and motivations can be inferred from behavior, and reference is frequently made to such inferences when selections are justified to the public through press releases. Finally, in this process, the coach, scouts and other representatives frequently interview the player, thus obtaining *subjective self-report* information. So far as is known, no research has been conducted to determine the validity of this wealth of predictive information, and furthermore, it is unknown how these variables are combined in a predictive equation.

Objective and Quantitative Predictors

Perhaps the necessity for objective and quantitative predictors is self evident. The case for them has been well made by Meehl (1955) in his analysis of statistical and clinical prediction. However, psychologists do like to make predictions, and clinical assessments will probably be with us for a long time to come, despite frequent demonstrations of their lack of validity.

TYPES OF PREDICTORS

Let us examine predictors from the standpoint of the sources of data and the type of information supplied to see how various predictors fit our requirements of conceptual isomorphism, method variance and objective and quantifiable variables. We divide predictors into four categories according to the source of the information: (*a*) Information supplied by the subject himself; (*b*) evaluation supplied by significant others, including leaders and peers; (*c*) observational data; (*d*) archival or official record data.

Information Supplied by the Subject

Information supplied by the subject is certainly the most commonly used type of information. There are several possible subcategories of subject-supplied information.

Subjective Self-Report. The object of excessive research consideration, in our view, is the category of information which we have called subjective self-report. This type of information has recently been labeled "Tests of Character" by Lovell (1967), and covers all tests of personality, including assessments of character, virtue and psychopathology. Our position regarding the validity of such instruments should be clear to the reader by this point. We feel that such tests have proved to be singularly ineffective in predicting performance and adjustment.[1] This contention is supported by the conclusions of several other studies. Personality tests have also recently come under attack for reasons other than their demonstrated lack of validity (*American Psychologist,* November 1965). Psychologists have been asking themselves whether the use of such questionnaires involves an unwarranted invasion of privacy (*American Psychologist,* May 1966). However, attempts to eliminate "offensive" items from personality tests may well result in destroying what potential validity they have (Butcher & Tellegen, 1966). We feel that such tests have not been effective, cannot be effective, and in the final analysis we agree with Lovell that their use in personnel selection should be greatly restricted, if not eliminated altogether. Before attempting to justify this statement, however, we should like to point out that it is not necessary to accept com-

[1] It is interesting and perhaps instructive to note that while subjective self-report information has been given extensive methodological and theoretical consideration by academic psychologists, current selection procedures utilize information of this type relatively infrequently.

pletely our position to agree with the conclusion that an excessive amount of time and effort has been devoted to attempts to develop and perfect such instruments for use in personnel selection.

It is interesting to speculate why such information is so frequently used if it has been demonstrated, as we contend, to be of such little utility. One reason for the use of subjective self-report is, of course, the ease with which such information can be gathered. Tests of character abound within psychology and their production continues to grow. The psychologist confronted with the bewildering array of tests available has no difficulty in finding many purporting to measure variables with which he is concerned, and it seems to be a very simple matter and little to ask of candidates to spend a few hours filling out subjective tests.

Since reams of reports have appeared on the use of these instruments, it is quite probable that a group norm has developed which dictates their use by psychologists in such situations. It is very difficult not to acquiesce to this norm, despite the mass of information indicating that rejection is the better course.

To be sure, some research results do indicate that predictors based on subjective self-report are useful. Correlations between subjective self-report predictors and "criterion" behaviors have been obtained in a variety of situations, but the vast majority of these correlations are of a rather low level—provocative trends in the .05–.10 significance range. In addition to being relatively low, we suggest that many of these correlations are spurious. To illustrate, we cite the example of correlations observed in SEALAB data. Predictive measures of subjective self-report (personality scales) did correlate with "criterion" measures derived from a questionnaire administered to the aquanauts at the end of their experience. These results seemed to "make sense" until we examined other data. We found that although these subjective self-report predictors correlated with subjective self-report criteria, they did not correlate with *any* objective criterion measures in the "expected" direction. Furthermore, the subjective self-report predictors did not correlate with *any* objective predictors. Finally, there were strong and significant correlations between a number of our objective predictors and objective criteria, as reported in Chapter 6, and among the objective criteria themselves. In summary, the subjective self-report predictor—criteria correlations appear to have occurred because of shared method variance.

Perhaps the most compelling reason for the continued use of and interest in subjective self-report measures is, however, that the understanding of human personality is the business of psychology. That is, psychology is the science of human behavior, and understanding and prediction of individual behavior at the personality level is the essence of the discipline. This philosophy has been dominant since the emergence of psychology as a distinct discipline. In the clinical situation the goal of the therapist is to assist the individual in understanding and altering his behavior. Thus, the following paradigm is suggested: "Understanding personality is necessary to its prediction, and the best way to understand human personality is to measure outputs of the individual." These outputs are usually verbal and are given as responses to questions, projective stimuli, or so-called objective tests. We should emphasize that our criticism here is not directed at the first part of the paradigm, as we agree that the principal goal of psychology *is* to increase the understanding of individual behavior—whether that behavior is determined by internal, external, physical, social, recent or distant stimuli. Our objection is to the method as applied to prediction, selection and evaluation, and we question the assumption that the best way to find out about a person is to ask him. We feel there are many other methods that are far better than asking a person to reveal subjective information about himself.[2]

[2] We do not reject "personality variables" as predictors of behavior. Our objection is specifically to "personality variables" considered as traits which are measured by the use of subjective self-report instruments. Personality, defined as predispositions toward characteristic modes of behavior and determined by the sum total of a person's experiences interacting with his physical characteristics, is a useful concept. A lucid and complete presentation of this point of view may be found in a selection by E. B. Guthrie in J. M. Hunt (Ed.), *Personality and the Behavior Disorders,* Chapter II.

Let us assume for the purposes of discussion that no measures involving subjective self report are permitted in predicting behavior in natural situations.[3]

According to Webb, *et al.* (1966) 90% of all social science research involves the use of questionnaires, most of which are classifiable as subjective self-report measures. The reader may then ask what is left—how can human behavior be measured and predicted if subjective self-report is eliminated? Let us emphasize again that we are not contending that human behavior cannot be predicted. In order for psychology to exist as a science it is necessary to take the position that human behavior is lawful. Certainly there are enduring predispositions to behave in certain ways, and the problem lies in determining the best way of measuring such individual predispositions. Therefore, we will now turn our attention to other types of predictors.

Objective Self-Report. Still in the category of data supplied directly by the subject, there is a definable category of objective self-report. This may be distinguished from subjective self-report by noting that data of this type are relatively insensitive to distortions and biases of the respondent. Within objective self-report there are two discriminable categories; the first being biographical information and the second tests of capacity.

Biographical Information. In our research on SEALAB, biographical information provided our best predictive information, we refer specifically to the variables of birth order, size of home town, and age in predicting the criterion behavior. Other examples of biographical information are work history, education, and history

[3] It should, of course, be clear in this discussion when reference is made to "prediction in natural settings" we do not include the special cases of counseling and psychotherapy. The point has been previously made that in counseling and psychotherapy, client motivations are directed towards self-awareness and personal change. Thus, in the preceding and future discussions when "natural settings" are referred to, these cases are excluded from the reference.

of expulsions from school. In short, we include in biographical information any objective facts dealing with a person's life history. We feel that there are at least two reasons why such data will prove to be superior to subjective self-report. First, such data are relatively objective. In most cases the information which we call biographical is subject to objective verification. Because of this, the possibility of error variance in objective self-report is reduced.

The second reason for potential superiority of such information derives from the fact that people in general do not consider biographical questions so intimate as they do many questions involving subjective self-report. A recent study by Taylor and Altman (1966) dealing with the variable of intimacy indicates that biographical information is not considered intimate and personal in contrast with subjective self-reports dealing with religious beliefs, sexual practices and similar matters. These findings imply that persons will be more willing to answer biographical questions completely and accurately than questions involving subjective self-report. A major drawback in using biographical information, of course, is that there is a paucity of theoretical constructs which would enable us to predict associations with criteria at the individual level. We suggest that a fruitful area of research and theory development will be the determination of "the psychological significance" of this essentially sociological data.

Tests of Capacity. Also included in the category of objective self-report are data which have been called tests of capacity. We refer here to any ability tests, for example intelligence tests, and also include work samples, such as the in-basket techniques (Bray & Grant, 1966) in which the test maker and the subject are in complete agreement as to the desired response. This category includes any instances in which the subject knows that superior performance can maximize potential rewards. Ideally, the test should have high face validity for all concerned, with both experimenter and subject agreeing that the test is a good measure of capacity in a specific area. While this may not always be possible, it is certainly desirable. It may be argued that such a procedure amounts to allowing non-scientists to determine what are good tests of capacity. In response to such an objection we would argue that the demand characteristics of the test situation already dictate that subjects will make such judgments by their responses, regardless of the wishes of the test constructor. The principal consideration in the use of tests of capacity is, of course, isomorphism with conceptual and operational criteria.

Physiological tests are a special type of tests of capacity. We refer here to the possible development of conceptually analogous tests which will produce physiological responses similar to those which may occur in real life situations. Two possible tests of this nature will be discussed in the following section. Upon first consideration, physiological responses may not be seen as measures of capacity, however, we feel that there is no logical reason why they should not be. We should be able to determine what physiological parameters are associated with certain response predispositions, to measure them in analogous test situations and then to predict their occurrence in field settings. We do realize that this has been a long standing goal of psychology, and we do not anticipate an early solution to the problem. We have only outlined a research paradigm in which such variables can be fruitfully examined.

Evaluation by Significant Others

A major category of predictive information is that supplied by others who have observed the subject in the past. Within this major category there are two sub-categories—peer ratings and leader or supervisor ratings.

Peer Ratings. Peer ratings have been discussed in connection with criteria. At that time, a strong case was made for their effectiveness on theoretical–methodological grounds, supported by various impressive findings. Since peer ratings are excellent criteria, they will also be excellent predictors. There are, however, serious problems connected with their use, centering around whom to ask and how to ask the proper questions. It may be quite obvious that peers will be able to make excellent judgments regarding the potential performance of subjects, however, it is quite probable that subjects may come from a variety of locations, and that, accordingly, comparable information may not be available on all of them. Furthermore, it may be very difficult to ask a man's peers to rate him as a subject in comparison to other persons who are not subjects. We know of no published studies dealing with this potential variable. In almost all published reports the peers are rating *each other* with reference to future behavior. An additional question arises over isomorphism of peer ratings with behavior under study. This comes back to specifying first the criterion and then developing questions which will match as closely as possible the expected behavior. Because of the potential utility of peer ratings, we feel that considerable effort is justified in attempting to solve these problems.

Leader and Supervisor Ratings. Leader and supervisor ratings also appear to have great potential. We recognize that they have long been in ill repute among psychologists because of certain problems such as "halo effect". A powerful statement of this problem is contained in a recent article aptly titled "Mine Eyes Have Seen a Host of Angels" (Siskind, 1966). While it is true that leader and supervisor ratings as normally used are probably of limited utility, we do not feel that this necessarily has to be the case. In a later section we will attempt to analyze some of the reasons for their lack of validity and recommended corrective steps to increase validity.

Observations

Another technique, relatively neglected since the OSS assessment studies (1948) has been the systematic observation of subject behavior. As in the case of peer and supervisor ratings, significant problems stand in the way of obtaining good data. If a potential candidate is to be observed, qualified observers must necessarily be on the spot to monitor his behavior. If a large group of subjects is involved this can be very expensive and time consuming. In considering objections based on costs, it is perhaps an interesting commentary on our culture that college students who are potential professional football players are subjected to very stringent observational evaluation, while candidates for graduate or professional schools are not so observed. The amount of money, time and effort spent on these evaluational procedures seems to indicate that it is worth far more to our society to ascertain the caliber of professional football players than it is to ascertain the caliber of graduate students.

In SEALAB, for example, we note that it would be possible to make such observational evaluations during training, but there are major difficulties connected with this procedure. Specifically, if a man has already been selected, there will be economic cost to a program and psychic cost to an individual if he is eliminated as a result of this observational evaluation during training. These costs will have to be weighed against the possibility of having inferior performers in vital positions.

There seem to have been few attempts to validate field-observational methods. One type of observational methodology is involved, of course, in clinical screening interviews. We question clinical interviews because of their lack of isomorphism with criterion behavior. Several recent findings support this skepticism (Perry, 1965; Gunderson, 1966; Plag & Goffman, 1966). Successful use of observational data must, we feel, employ objective and quantifiable variables that involve little or no interpretation by the observer. An example of a satisfactory observational variable would be our gregariousness measure in SEALAB.

Archival Data

The accumulated, quantified records collected for various purposes by survey research centers and government agencies represent a largely ignored but potentially invaluable reservoir of information. Information from such sources has been aptly labelled *archival data* (*cf.* Webb *et al.*, 1966; McGuire, 1967). With the increasing use of computers for storage and retrieval of data, this source should be far more extensively utilized in the future than it has been in the past.

RECAPITULATION

In this section we have attempted to categorize and describe the major types of data which can be used to predict performance and adjustment in exotic environments. Parenthetically, it should be pointed out that there is no reason why these predictors must be restricted to exotic environments, rather they should be generally applicable. We have identified four major categories of data according to their source: subject, significant others, observations, and archival data. Within these categories we have identified seven sub-categories. The vast bulk of theoretical, methodological, basic and applied research has been directed toward the development and utilization of one of these categories—subjective self-report. It is our conviction that this has been an overemphasis, the causes of which we have attempted to analyze. Since one category of information has been overemphasized, there has necessarily been a neglect of research on other categories. Perhaps this research emphasis and the results produced by it have contributed to the general malaise currently noted within psychology. We are proposing as a new direction, a shift in emphasis to the other categories of data which we have identified. This suggestion is not made lightly because we recognize that there are significant problems in research utilizing these types of data, such as the absence of theoretical models and systematic methodological investigation permitting an assessment of the status and value of this orientation. An additional problem is the difficulty of gathering such data. But are these problems and many others which could be mentioned valid reasons for not venturing into the unknown? Rather, do they not present challenges to the field of psychology in general?

It may be that the results obtained from the approach we propose will be no better than those realized from tired and worn variables involving subjective self-report. The results will probably not be available for some time. Our hopes for such data are admittedly based more upon faith than knowledge. However, our faith rests on the promising leads which developed in the SEALAB research. We will conclude by specifying some of the areas in which we feel that research will be most fruitful. The goal of this research should be to integrate various types of knowledge into a theoretical/conceptual framework.

NEEDED RESEARCH AND THEORETICAL DEVELOPMENT

We are convinced that some of the rough conceptualizations which we have developed point to data which it is necessary to collect. At the same time we look for significant improvements in the concepts and in statements linking these concepts (that is theories) which will be developed from data collected with new methodological techniques.

We propose the following canons for naturalistic research. First, that researchers attempting to measure criteria operate under the restriction that they are not permitted to ask their subjects any questions regarding performance and adjustment, as the answers to such questions are subject to biases of a self-defensive or self-glorifying nature. Second, a similar restriction would be that investigators are not permitted to ask their subjects questions regarding their qualifications, the answers to which are not subject to external validity checks. We realize that these are very stringent restrictions under which to conduct research, and that they will be honored in the breach by ourselves and by others. We suggest merely that in imposing such limitations on the data he gathers the researcher will be *forced* to search for alternative means of measurement. After he has exhausted these alternative means of measuring his variables, we have no doubt that he will return to the use of subjective self-report. It is our hope, however, that this return to reliance on measures of subjective self-report will be accompanied by fresh perspectives, and also that measures of subjective self-report will benefit from this search and will be submitted to more stringent validation.

Biographical Information

The SEALAB research, as well as other studies cited, points to the unrealized value of biographical information in predicting behavior in a variety of situations. In particular, there has recently been a great deal of interest in the variable of birth order. A tremendous amount of birth order data has accumulated and several recent attempts to unify this information into a theory have been made (Schachter, 1959; Walters & Parke, 1964; Miller & Zimbardo, 1966; Helmreich & Collins, 1967). It appears that this is a useful variable for many purposes, and that its utility will increase as its dynamic properties are elaborated. Other biographical variables of similar importance seem to be size of home town, family stability, age and situation-specific experience. Again, discovery of the psychological significance of the *objectively specifiable* formative experiences of an individual will add much to our understanding of human behavior. The systematic utilization of biographical information should receive impetus from a recently formed committee which has that goal as its purpose (Henry, 1966).

Emotion

At the present time the definition and conceptual properties of emotion are in a state of ferment. New developments have opened up questions concerning the basis of emotionality, its behavioral manifestations, and its interactions with other behavior. It seems to us that a solution of some of the problems involving emotion will contribute significantly to the understanding of men under stress. At the same time, it should be obvious that the study of men under stress is necessary for an understanding of certain emotional reactions.

In addition to theoretical and conceptual developments regarding emotion in recent years, methodological and technical advances also hold promise for new developments. Included are, for example, new ways of measuring emotional responses on line or *in vivo,* these ranging from highly sophisticated techniques for telemetering physiological data to equally new, but very simple, techniques for assessing emotional reactions under stress such as the Palmar Sweat Index (Johnson & Dabbs, in press). Another recent development is the utilization of video tape recordings.

Mood checklists have been with us for quite some time and have proved extremely valuable in assessing emotional response in a variety of contexts, including SEALAB. However, as Lazarus (1966) observes, the intercorrelations between physiology, observation and self-report in natural settings have been quite low. It seems essential that emotions be studied in natural settings, as only there can the investigator be certain that he is tapping the entire range of emotions. In such studies, a variety of indicators—physiological, observational and self-report must be used, but such measures must also be correlated with other indices of adjustment. This approach will allow one to judge whether a certain emotional reaction is an indicator of good, poor or neutral adjustment.

Just as new indices of emotionality are needed as criteria, so also are new measures of emotionality needed as predictors. In this respect, we see as particularly important the requirement for concepts which link predictors to criteria in meaningful, theoretical terms. A model such as Wherry and Curran's (1966) threat–stress paradigm shows promise for this area. In this model, the subject is exposed in the laboratory to a situation conceptually analogous to the stress he might experience in flying an airplane under combat conditions. The conceptual model proposes that deterioration of performance in the laboratory will predict deterioration of performance in the field, and excellent results have been obtained with large individual differences in performance as a response to the threat of electric shock. It should be pointed out that field correlates of such behavior are necessary before this measure can be utilized in selection.

Another paradigm, pioneered by Lazarus, is the use of films as stressors. This technique also appears promising for the prediction of emotional reactions to stress. Lazarus has used subincision and shop accidents as stimuli to provoke stress reactions. If similar scenarios are developed which use subject matter directly related to the situation which individuals will actually face (for example flying accidents for pilots or diving accidents for divers), this technique should contribute to the prediction of specific *in vivo* emotional responses. This type of measure is another that also needs validation in the field.

For both of these paradigms there remain significant problems such as base-line, response lability, and response range. Despite the remaining methodological problems, however, they represent significant advances in conceptual sophistication over techniques which utilize pre- and post-measurement of physiological parameters with little attention to stimulus control. Obviously considerable methodological and theoretical work is necessary before mood can confidently be used as a predictor. Such research will probably have to include the simultaneous measurement of physiological responses, behavioral manifestations and self-report.

Sociometric Techniques

We have emphasized that sociometric techniques are of great value in providing predictive information, particularly for stressful environments. In most laboratory studies we might observe that such techniques are of limited utility because manipulations frequently are used which depend upon the subjects' unfamiliarity with each other. In the field, the knowledge that group members have of each other is an important consideration. Because of this, most of the methodological work on sociometric techniques will have to be conducted in the field. Studies are needed to determine the meanings of various types of questions. For example, what is the difference between free and a specified number of responses to sociometric questions? Are there any differences in validity between weighted and nonweighted choices? Is there an advantage to using positive choices as opposed to negative or both? Another vital consideration is which of several peer groups should provide evaluation? In most cases sociometric measures are gathered during training or performance. It would be highly useful if sociometric information could be gathered prior to selection.

Leader ratings have also been discussed previously at some length. Again we feel that much work is needed to refine these methods of measurement to realize their full potential. Halo effects exert massive biasing tendencies, reducing the validity of the instruments, and it is toward reduction of these biases that useful effort can be expended. One assumption we might make is that biases in evaluations made by others are easier to reduce than are biases in self-reports. In other words, we are saying that other people will be less biased in evaluating a person than he will be in evaluating himself. Among necessary efforts are attempts to devise scales providing opportunities for finer discriminations, in order to determine the best respondents, the best questions to ask and the best way to treat data collected. What is needed here, it seems to us, is a conceptual framework which puts such instruments in proper perspective.

Based on an analysis of the demand characteristics of leader and supervisor recommendations, it is possible to identify a number of methodological studies which might indicate ways to improve this type of information. One of the principal problems, of course, is the lack of discrimination among subjects when such forms are used, since nearly all applicants are rated in the top categories. This being the case, techniques are needed to overcome this tendency. One proposed strategy would be to force raters to make precise discriminations in the upper range of the scale.

Other questions refer to the persons actually making the ratings. How many supervisors or instructors should be asked to make ratings? Studies are needed to determine the optimum number. What should the relationship of the supervisor to the ratee be? A reasonable hypothesis is that the rater should be the supervisor closest to the ratee. Perhaps one problem encountered in the use of supervisor ratings is that this has not always been done. Does the rater fail to answer candidly because he does not want to assume responsibility for eliminating the candidate? One technique for overcoming such fears has been used by the Peace Corps (Hobbs, 1963). Peace Corps rating forms assure each respondent that multiple ratings will be secured and that no decisions to eliminate or accept candidates will be based upon the recommendations of one person alone. Therefore, the rater can say to himself, "I can be completely candid, and if my opinion is not shared by others, it will not affect the candidate unfairly". Unfortunately, no research has been reported demonstrating the efficacy of this very reasonable sounding procedure. Another question is how far back in an individual's life history to go in asking for evaluations? This is particularly relevant in the case of programs such as SEALAB in which the applicants may have had a great deal of previous experience and may have held many positions. What is the difference between quantitative answers to specific questions and free responses to general questions? Another opportunity for methodological study.

Psychometrics

We have proposed the collection of data from multiple sources and in a variety of forms. This applies to both predictors and criteria. If data of diverse types are gathered, a crucial question is how to combine these data to produce the best indices. Much psychometric work has been done on personality tests and subjective self-report in general. Such instruments have an underlying methodological similarity, thus optimum combinations of data are relatively easy to determine. In contrast, combining heterogeneous measures will present challenging psychometric problems. In analyzing SEALAB data, we recognize that our approach was rather primitive, and we would have welcomed more sophisticated techniques for combining the data than were available. Appropriate statistical models and techniques will, of course, depend upon the types of data which are gathered. At this point we can only say that we feel that new approaches in this area will become necessary.

Objective Observation

In frustratingly complex field settings simple, objective observations and recording of behavior are needed rather than sophisticated observations requiring a great deal of interpretation. To illustrate, many persons asked if we used or considered using the system devised by Bales (1950) for studying discussions in small groups. Our response has been that it was completely impossible to use such a complicated system of recording when one was not able to identify speaker, listener or content of conversation. It was necessary in our circumstances to resort to a much more primitive system for recording behavior—for example, our gregariousness measure. This situation probably prevails in many or most field settings, the point being that simple, objective observations having a conceptually sophisticated underlying rationale are capable of yielding results which enable conceptually complex inferences. The inferences are made by an analysis which takes into account intercorrelations between a variety of measures, some of which are simple behavioral indices. The notion that simple objective data can provide an understanding of complex natural behavior is not original or recent. We recommend a reconsideration of the generally neglected work of Chapple (1941). The development of digital computers renders this type of information much more manageable and useful now than it was during the 1940's when Chapple developed his system. Of course, the utility of such data depends upon the theoretical justification underlying its collection.

Molar Theoretical Models

As has been emphasized, both the data collected and the techniques of their collection must derive from a theoretical model, this being an absolute necessity for field research. A researcher without a theoretical approach will inevitably become lost in the frustrating complexities of the uncontrolled natural environment. The types of models required have been described by theoreticians as molar theoretical models. A molar theory is a theory which relates global behavior to global explanatory principals. An excellent discussion and justification of such models is presented by Rommetviet (1957). This type of theory deals with behavior which is too complex to be studied in the laboratory *alone*. At present, we can expect only very general propositions from such molar theories; however, such general propositions can be expected to guide research which will lead to their refinement, explication and development. We found most useful for understanding the SEALAB situation the cost–reward model developed by Thibaut and Kelley (1959), which holds great promise for extension into field research. The hypothesis of stability of costs and lability of rewards in stressful and exotic environments is an example of the self-refining derivation which we anticipate from the employment of such models.

A number of years ago the position advanced here was elegantly expressed by Harlow in the paper entitled "Mice, Monkeys, Men and Motives." Harlow closed with the following paragraph which summarizes our position. "If we are ever to have a comprehensive theoretical psychology, we must attack the problems whose solution offers hope of insight into human behavior, and it is my belief that if we face our problems honestly and without regard to, or fear of, difficulty, the theoretical psychology of the future will catch up with, and eventually even surpass, common sense." (Harlow, 1953, p. 32.)

Bibliography

Adams, O. S., & Chiles, W. D. *Human performance as a function of the work-rest ratio during prolonged confinement.* ASD Tech. Rep. 61–720, Lockheed-Georgia Company. 1961.

Allport, G. W., Vernon, P. E., & Lindzey, G. *Study of Values.* New York: Houghton Mifflin, 1960.

Altus, W. D. Birth order and its sequelae. *Science,* 1966, **151**, 44-48.

Appley, M., and Trumbull, R. *Psychological Stress.* New York: Appleton-Century-Crofts, 1967.

Aronson, E. & Carlsmith, J. M. The social psychology experiment. In G. Lindzey, & E. Aronson, (Eds.), *Handbook of Social Psychology.* Cambridge, Mass.: Addison-Wesley, in press.

Bales, R. F. *Interaction Process Analysis.* Cambridge, Massachusetts: Addison-Wesley, 1950.

Bales, R. F. Task roles and social roles in problem solving groups. In E. E. Maccoby, T. M. Newcomb, E. L. Hartley, (Eds.), *Readings in Social Pyschology.* New York: Holt, Rinehart and Winston, 1958, pp. 396-413.

Basowitz, H., Persky, H., Korchin, S., & Grinker, R. *Anxiety and Stress.* New York: McGraw-Hill, 1955.

Baumrind, Diana. Some thoughts on ethics of research. *American Psychologist,* 1964, **19**, 421-423.

Berkowitz, L., & Cottingham, D. R. The interest value and relevance of fear arousing communications. *Journal of Abnormal and Social Psychology*, 1960, **60**, 37-43.

Berkun, M. M., Bialek, H. M., Kern, R. P., & Yagi, K. Experimental studies of psychological stress in man. *Psychological Monographs,* 1962, **76**, (15, Whole No. 534).

Bettelheim, B. Individual and mass behavior in extreme situations. *Journal of Abnormal and Social Psychology,* 1943, **38**, 417-452.

Bray, D. W., & Grant, D. L. The assessment center in the measurement of potential for business management. *Psychological* No. 625).

Brehm, J. and Cohen, A. *Explorations in Cognitive Dissonance.* New York: Wiley, 1962.

Broadbent, D. S. Effects of noise on behavior. In C. M. Harris (Ed.), *Handbook of Noise Control.* New York: McGraw-Hill, 1957. Chapter 10.

Broussard, I. G. et al., The influence of noise on the visual contrast threshold. Army Medical Research Laboratory Report #101, 1953.

Butcher, J. & Tellegen, A. Objections to MMPI items. *Journal of Consulting Psychology,* 1966, **30**, 6, 527-534.

Calhoun, J. B. A "behavioral sink". In Bliss, E. (Ed.), *Roots of Behavior,* New York: Harpers, 1963.

Cannon, B. L. Unusual engineering problems in undersea living. In *Man's Extension into the Sea,* Washington: Marine Technology Society, 1966, 211-215.

Capra, P., & Dittes, J. E. Birth order as a selective factor among volunteer subjects. *Journal of Abnormal and Social Psychology,* 1962, **64**, 302.

Chapple, E. D. Measuring human relations: An introduction to the study of the interaction of individuals. *Genetic Psychology Monographs,* 1940, **22**, 1-147.

Chapple, E. D. The interaction chronograph: Its evolution and present application. *Personnel,* 1949, **25**, 295-307.

Chiles, W. D. *Effects of high temperatures on performance of a complex mental task.* U.S.A.F., WADC Technical Report 58-323, 1958.

Collins, B. E., & Guetzkow, H. *A Social Psychology of Group Processes for Decision Making.* New York: John Wiley & Sons, 1964.

Cousteau, J. Y. *World Without Sun.* New York: Harper and Row, 1965.

Cronbach, L. J. Coefficient alpha and the internal structure of tests. *Psychometrika,* 1951, **16**, 297-334.

Curran, P. M., & Wherry, R. J., Jr. Measure of susceptibility to psychological stress. *Aerospace Medicine,* 1965, **36**, 10.

Darley, J., & Aronson, E. Self-evaluation vs. direct anxiety reduction as determinants of the fear–affiliation relationship. *Journal of Experimental Social Psychology,* 1966, Supplement 1, 66-79.

Davidson, W. Z., Andrews, T. G., & Ross, S. Effects of stress and anxiety on continuous high-speed color naming. *Journal of Experimental Psychology,* 1956, **52**, 13-17.

Deese, J., Lazarus, R. A., & Keenan, J. Anxiety, anxiety reduction and stress in learning. *Journal of Experimental Psychology,* 1953, **46**, 55-60.

Disaster Research Group. *Field Studies of Disaster Behavior.* Washington: National Academy of Science–National Research Council, 1961.

Ehrlich, D. Determinants of verbal commonality and influencibility. Unpublished doctoral dissertation, University of Minnesota, 1958.

Eilbert, L. R., Glaser, R., & Hanes, R. M. Research on the feasibility of selection of personnel for duty at isolated stations. AFPTRC-TR-57-4, 1957.

Fenichel, O. *The Psychoanalytic Theory of Neurosis.* New York: W. W. Norton, 1945.

Festinger, L. A theory of social comparison processes. *Human Relations,* 1954, 117-140.

Festinger, L. *A Theory of Cognitive Dissonance.* Stanford: Stanford University Press, 1957.

Festinger, L., & Katz, D. *Research Methods in the Behavioral Sciences.* New York: The Dryden Press, 1953.

Fiedler, F. E. A contingency model of leadership effectiveness. In L. Berkowitz (Ed.), *Advances in Experimental Social Psychology,* Vol. I. New York: Academic Press, 1964. Pp. 150-191.

Fleishman, E. A. A relationship between incentive motivation and ability level in psycho-motor performance. *Journal of Experimental Psychology,* 1958, **56**, 78-81.

Fraser, T. M. The effects of confinement as a factor in manned space flight. NASA Contractor Report #511, Washington, D. C., July, 1966.

Fritz, C., & Marks, E. The NORC studies of human behavior in disaster. *Journal of Social Issues,* 1954, **10**, 26-41.

Funkenstein, D., King, S., & Drolette, M. *Mastery of Stress.* Cambridge: Harvard University Press, 1957.

Glass, A. Problem of stress in the combat zone. *Symposium on Stress,* Washington: National Research Council and Walter Reed Army Medical Center, 1953, 90-102.

Glover, E. Notes on the psychological effects of war conditions on the civil population: Part 3, The Blitz. *International Journal of Psychoanalysis,* 1942, **23**, 17-37.

Goldstein, M. Relationship between coping and avoiding behavior and response to fear arousing propaganda. *Journal of Abnormal and Social Psychology,* 1959, **58**, 247-252.

Grinker, R., & Spiegel, J. *Men Under Stress.* Philadelphia: Blakiston, 1945.

Grossack, M. M. Some effects of co-operation and competition upon small group behavior. *Journal of Abnormal and Social Psychology,* 1954, **49**, 341-348.

Gunderson, E. K. E. Emotional symptoms in extremely isolated groups. *A.M.A. Archives of General Psychiatry,* 1963, **9**, 362-368.

Gunderson, E. K. E. Unpublished research on Operation Deepfreeze, U. S. Navy Antarctic project. U. S. Navy Neuro-psychiatric Research Unit, San Diego, California, 1966.

Gunderson, E. K. E., & Nelson, P. D. Criterion measures for extremely isolated groups. *Personnel Psychology,* 1966, **19**, 67-80.

Haeberle, A. Interaction of sex, birth order, and dependency with behavior problems and symptoms in emotionally disturbed pre-school children. Paper read at Eastern Psychological Association, Philadelphia, 1958.

Harlow, H. F. Mice, monkeys, men, and motives. *Psychological Review,* 1953, **60**, 23-32.

Hardison, J., and Purcell, K. The effects of psychological stress as a function of need and cognitive control. *Journal of Personality,* 1959, **27**, 250-258.

Harman, H. *Modern Factor Analysis.* Chicago: University of Chicago Press, 1960.

Harrison, J., & MacKinnon, P.C.B. Physiological role of the adrenal medulla in the palmar anihidrotic response to stress. *Journal of Applied Psychology,* 1966, **21**, 88-92.

Haythorn, W., & Altman, I. Personality factors in isolated environments. In M. Appley, and R. Trunbull (Eds.), *Psychological Stress,* New York: Appleton-Century-Crofts, 1967. Pp. 363-386.

Helmreich, R. L. Regulation of reproductive rate by intra-uterine mortality. *Science,* 1960, **132**, 417-418.

Helmreich, R. L., and Collins, B. E. Situational determinants of affiliative preference under stress. *Journal of Personality and Social Psychology,* 1967, **6**, 79-84.

Helmreich, R. L., & Kuiken, D. L. Unpublished research. The University of Texas at Austin, 1967.

Helmreich, R. L., Kuiken, D. L., & Collins, B. E. Effects of stress and birth order on attitude change. *Journal of Personality,* 1968, in press.

Helper, M. M. *The effects of noise on work output and physiological activation.* Fort Knox, Ky.: Army Medical Research Laboratory, 1957.

Henry, E. Conference on the use of biographical data in psychology. *American Psychologist,* 1966, **21**, 247-249.

Hobbs, N. A psychologist in the Peace Corps. *American Psychologist,* 1963, **18**, 47-55.

Hollander, E. P. Peer nominations on leadership as a predictor of the pass–fail criterion in Naval Air Training. *Journal of Applied Psychology,* 1954, **38**, 150-153.

Hollander, E. P. *Leaders, Groups and Influence,* New York: Oxford University Press, 1964.

Hollander, E. P. Validity of Peer Nominations. *Journal of Applied Psychology,* 1965, **49**, (6), 434-438.

Hollander, E. P. & Webb, W. B. Leadership, followership, and friendship: an analysis of peer nominations. *Journal of Abnormal and Social Psychology,* 1955, **50**, 163-167.

Holtzman, W. H., and Bitterman, M. E. *Psychiatric screening of flying personnel, VI. Anxiety and reactions to stress.* Randolph A.F.B.,Texas: U.S.A.F. School of Aviation Medicine Project No. 21-37-002. Rep. No. 6, 1952.

Holtzman, W. H., & Bitterman, M. E. A factorial study of adjustment to stress. *Journal of Abnormal and Social Psychology,* 1956, **52**, 179-185.

Hornig, D. F. Challenges before the behavioral sciences. Speech delivered at the dedication of A.P.A. Headquarters Bldg., Oct. 16, 1965.

Janis, I. L. *Air War and Emotional Stress.* New York: McGraw-Hill, 1951.

Janis, I. L. *Psychological Stress,* New York: John Wiley & Sons, 1958.

Janis, I. L. Group identification under conditions of external danger. *British Journal of Medical Psychology,* 1963, **36**, 227-238.

Janis, I. L., & Feshbach, S. Effects of fear arousing communications. *Journal of Abnormal and Social Psychology,* 1953, **48**, 78-92.

Janis, I. L., & Leventhal, H. Human reactions to stress. In E. Borgatta, and W. Lambert (Eds.), *Handbook of Personality Theory and Research.* New York: Rand McNally, in press.

Jenkins, J. G. The nominating technique as a method of evaluating air group morale. *Journal of Aviation Medicine,* 1948, **19**, 12-19.

Johnson, J. F. & Dabbs, J. M., Jr. Enumeration of active sweat glands: A simple physiological indicator of psychological changes. *Nursing Research,* In press.

Lanzetta, J. T., Haefner, D., Langham, P., and Axelrod, H. Some effects of situational threat on group behavior. *Journal of Abnormal Social Psychology,* 1954, **49**, 445-453.

Lanzetta, J. T., & Roby, T. B. Effects of work-group structure and certain task variables on group performance. *Journal of Abnormal and Social Psychology,* 1956, **53**, 307-314.

Lazarus, R. *Psychological Stress and the Coping Process.* New York: McGraw-Hill, 1966.

Lazarus, R. S., Deese, J., & Hamilton, R. Anxiety and stress in learning: the role of intra-serial duplication. *Journal of Experimental Psychology,* 1954, **47**, 111-114.

Lazarus, R. S., & Ericksen, C. W. Psychological stress and personality correlates: effects of failure stress upon performance. *Journal of Abnormal and Social Psychology,* 1952, **43**, 100-105.

Lesser, G. S., & Abelson, R. P. Personality correlates of persuasibility in children. In C. I. Hovland, & I. L. Janis (Eds.), *Personality and Persuasibility.* New Haven: Yale University Press, 1959. Pp. 187-206.

Lester, J. T., Jr. *Behavioral research during the 1963 American Mt. Everest expedition.* ONR Contract Nonr-3930(00), NR171-257. Final report, Sept., 1964.

Leventhal, H., & Singer, R. P. Affect arousal and positioning of recommendations in persuasive communications. *Journal of Personality and Social Psychology,* 1966, **4**, 137-146.

Lindzey, G. (Ed.). *Handbook of Social Psychology.* Vols. I and II. Cambridge: Addison-Wesley, 1954.

Lindzey, G., & Borgata, E. F. Sociometric measurement. In G. Lindzey (Ed.), *Handbook of Social Psychology.* Cambridge: Addison-Welsey Pub. Co., 1954. Pp. 405-448.

Lovell, V. R. The human use of personality tests: a dissenting view. American Psychologist, 1967, **22**, 383-393.

Lucas, J. D. The interactive effects of anxiety, failure and intraserial duplication. *American Journal of Psychology,* 1952, **65**, 59-66.

Mackworth, N. H. *Researches on the measurement of human performance.* Medical Research Council, Special Report Series 268, H. M. Stationary Office, London, 1950.

McGuire, W. Some impending reorientations in social psychology: Some thoughts provoked by Kenneth Ring. *Journal of Experimental Social Psychology,* 1967, **3**, 124-139.

Meehl, P. E. *Clinical and Statistical Prediction.* Minneapolis: University of Minnesota Press, 1955.

Menninger, C. Regulatory devices of the ego under major stress. *International Journal of Psychoanalysis,* 1954, **35**, 412-420.

Milgram, S. Behavioral study of obedience. *Journal of Abnormal and Social Psychology,* 1963, **67**, 371-378.

Miller, N., & Zimbardo, P. G. Motives for fear-induced affiliation: emotional comparison or inter-personal similarity. *Journal of Personality,* 1966, **34**, 481-503.

Murphy, R. E. Effects of threat of shock, distraction and task design on performance. *Journal of Experimental Psychology,* 1959, **58**, 134-141.

Myers, T. Unpublished research. Naval Medical Research Institute, Bethesda, Maryland, 1966.

Naval Research Reviews. ONR Physiological research for man-in-the-sea. August, 1965, 1-8.

Nelson, P. D. *Human adaptation to Antarctic station life.* San Diego: U. S. Naval Medical NPRU, Report No. 62-12, 1962.

Newcomb, T. M. The interdependence of social-psychological theory and methods: a brief overview. In L. Festinger and D. Katz (Eds.), *Research Methods in the Behavioral Sciences.* New York: The Dryden Press, 1953. Pp. 1-12.

Nordhoff, C. B., & Hall, J. N. *The Bounty Trilogy.* Boston: Little Brown, 1934.

Office of Strategic Services Assessment Staff, *Assessment of Men: Selection of Personnel for the O.S.S.*, New York: Rinehart, 1948.

O'Neal, H. A., Bond, G. F., Lanphear, R. E. & Odum, T. *Project SEALAB summary report: An experimental eleven day saturation dive at 193 feet.* ONR Report ACR-108, 1965.

Orne, M. T. On the social psychology of the psychological experiment: With particular reference to demand characteristics and their implications. *American Psychologist,* 1962, **17**, 776-783.

Perry, C. J. G. Psychiatric selection of candidates for space missions. *Journal of the American Medical Association.* 1965, **194**, 841-844.

Perry, C. J. G. A psychiatric "back-up" system for selection of space crews. *The American Journal of Psychiatry,* 1966, **123**, 821-825.

Peterson, F. E., Lane, N. E., & Kennedy, R. S. *The relationship of the Edwards Personal Preference Schedule to Success in Naval Flight Training.* U.S. Naval Aerospace Medical Institute, 1965, Report No. 46.

Pett, S., & Loh, T. *Washington Post,* Dec. 4, 1966, Section E, pp. 1-5.

Plag, J. A. & Goffman, J. M. The prediction of four year military effectiveness from characteristics of Naval Recruits. *Military Medicine,* 1966, **131**, 729-735.

Rabbie, J. M. Factors influencing the magnitude and direction of affiliative tendencies under stress. Unpublished Ph.D. dissertation, Yale University, 1961.

Radloff, R. Social comparison and ability evaluation. *Journal of Experimental Social Psychology,* 1966, Supplement 1, 6-26.

Radloff, R. Opinion evaluation and affiliation. *Journal of Abnormal and Social Psychology,* 1961, **62**, 578-585.

Ring, K. Experimental social psychology: Some sober questions about some frivolous values. *Journal of Experimental Social Psychology,* 1967, **3**, 113-123.

Rohrer, J. H. *Human adjustment to Antarctic isolation,* ONR Report, Contract Nonr1530(07), September, 1960.

Rosenthal, R. *Experimenter Effects in Behavioral Research.* New York: Appleton-Century-Crofts, 1966.

Ross, B. M., Rupel, J. W., & Grant, D. A. Effects of personal, impersonal and physical stress upon cognitive behavior in a card-sorting problem. *Journal of Abnormal and Social Psychology,* 1952, **47**, 546-551.

Rommetveit, R. *Social Norms and Roles.* Minneapolis: University of Minnesota Press, 1955.

Sarnoff, I., & Zimbardo, P. G. Anxiety, fear and social affiliation. *Journal of Abnormal and Social Psychology,* 1961, **62**, 356-363.

Schachter, S. *The Psychology of Affiliation,* Stanford: Stanford University Press, 1959.

Schachter, S. Birth order, eminence and higher education. *American Sociological Review,* 1963, **28**, 757-768.

Schachter, S. The interaction of cognitive and physiological determinants of emotional state. In L. Berkowitz (Ed.), *Advances in Experimental Social Psychology.* Vol. I. New York: Academic Press, 1964. Pp. 49-80.

Schmideberg, M. Some observations on individual reactions to air raids. *International Journal of Psychoanalysis,* 1942, **23**, 146-176.

Schutz, W. C. *FIRO: A three dimensional theory of interpersonal behavior.* New York: Rinehart, 1958.

Scott, J. P. Relative importance of social and hereditary factors in life adjustment during periods of stress in laboratory animals. *Life Stress and Bodily Disease.* Association for Research in Nervous Mental Disease, 1949, 48-60.

Sears, R. R., Whiting, J.W.M., Nowlis, V. & Sears, P. S. Some child-rearing antecedents of aggression and despondency in young children. *Genetic Psychology Monographs,* 1953, **47**, 135-236.

Sells, S. B. *Research report on leadership and organizational factors in effective A.C. & W. sites.* Contract No. AF41(657)-323. Arctic Aeromedical Laboratory. Ft. Worth, Texas: Institute of Behaviorial Research, 1965.

Selye, H. *The Physiology and Pathology of Exposure to Stress.* Montreal: ACTA, 1950.

Shils, E., & Janowitz, M. Cohesion and disintegration in the Wehrmacht in World War II. *Public Opinion Quarterly,* 1948, **12**, 280-315.

Siskind, G. Mine eyes have seen a host of angels. *American Psychologist,* 1966, **21**, 804-806.

Slotkin, R. *Personality Development.* New York: Harper, 1952.

Smith, W. M. Observations over the lifetime of a small isolated group: Structure, danger, boredom, and vision. *Psychological Reports,* 1966, **19**, 475-514.

Sobol, R. Anxiety–depressive reactions after prolonged combat experience: the "old sergeant syndrome". *Bulletin U.S. Army Medical Department,* 1949, **9** (Suppl. No. 1), 137-146.

Spence, K. W., Farber, I. E., & Taylor, J. The relation of electric shock and anxiety to level of performance in eyelid conditioning. *Journal of Experimental Psychology,* 1954, **48**, 404-408.

Stouffer, S., Suchman, E., DeVinney, L., Star, S. & Williams, R. *The American Soldier.* Vols. I and II. Princeton: Princeton University Press, 1949.

Stunkel, E. R., Tye, V. M., & Yankey, D. W. Validation of experimental selection instruments for Antarctic service. Washington: Personnel Research Section, The Adjutant General's Office, Dept. of the Army, Report No. 945, 1952.

Taylor, D. A. & Altman, I. *Intimacy scaled stimuli for use in studies of interpersonal relationships.* Research Report No. 9, NMRI, April, 1966.

Thibaut, J., & Kelley, H. *The Social Psychology of Groups.* New York: John Wiley & Sons, 1959.

Thompson, M. L., & Sutorman, M. The identification and enumeration of active sweat glands from plastic impressions of the skin. *Transactions of the Royal Society of Tropical Medicine and Hygiene,* 1953, **47**, 412-417.

Torrance, E. P. A psychological study of American jet aces. Paper read at Western Psychological Association, Long Beach, California, 1954.

Trumbull, R. Need to Know: Relevance. Presidential address, Division of Military Psychology, American Psychological Association, Sept. 5, 1966.

Walters, R. & Parke, R. Social motivation, dependency and susceptibility to social influence. In L. Berkowitz, (Ed.), *Advances in Experimental Social Psychology.* Vol. I. New York: Academic Press, 1964. Pp. 232-277.

Warren, J. R. Birth order and social behavior. *Psychological Bulletin,* 1966, **65**, 38-49.

Webb, E. J., Campbell, D. T., Schwartz, R. D. & Sechrest, L. *Unobstrusive Measures: Non-reactive Research in the Social Sciences.* Chicago: Rand McNally, 1966.

Weybrew, B. B. *Psychological and psychophysiological effects of long periods of submergence. I. Analysis of data collected during a 265-hour completely submerged habitability cruise of the USS Nautilus (SSN 571).* U.S.N. Medical Research Laboratory Report #281, New London, Connecticut U.S. Navy Submarine Base, 1957.

Weybrew, B. B. Psychological problems of prolonged periods of marine submergence. In N. Burns, R. Chambers, and E. Hendler (Eds.), *Unusual Environments and Human Behavior.* New York: Collier-McMillan, 1963. Pp. 85-125.

Wispé, L. G., & Lloyd, V. E. Some situational and psychological determinants of the desire for structured interpersonal relations. *Journal of Abnormal and Social Psychology,* 1955, **51**, 57-60.

Whiting, J. W. M., & Child, I. L. *Child Training and Personality.* New Haven: Yale University Press, 1953.

Withey, S. Reaction to uncertain threat. Ann Arbor: University of Michigan, 1956. (Mimeographed report.)

Wolfle. D. Social problems and social science. *Science,* 1966, **151,** 1177.

Wolfenstein, M. *Disaster.* Glencoe: Free Press, 1957.

Wright, M., Sisler, G. & Chylinski, J. A. Personality factors in the selection of civilians for isolated northern stations. *Journal of Applied Psychology,* 1963, **47,** 24-29.

Wrightsman, L. The effect of small group membership on level of concern. Unpublished doctoral dissertation, University of Minnesota, 1959.

Zimbardo, P. G., & Formica, L. Emotional comparison and self-esteem as determinants of affiliation. *Journal of Personality,* 1963, **31**, 141-162.

Zimney, G. H. Effect of various motivational techniques upon learning and performance tasks. *Journal of Experimental Psychology,* 1956, **52,** 251-257.

Additional References

Guthrie, E. R. Personality in terms of associative learning. In J. McV. Hunt (Ed.) *Personality and the Behavior Disorder* (Vol. I), New York: Ronald Press, 1944. Pp. 49-68.

Helmreich, R. L. Attitudinal effects of stress and justification. *Journal of Experimental Social Psychology,* 1968, in press.

Appendices

A. Pre-dive Questionnaires

- I. Personal History Booklet
- II. Opinion Survey—Personality Scales
- III. Adjective Checklist

B. Leader and Peer Ratings

- I. Choices of Leader and Team Mates
- II. Choices of Leader and Team Mates
- III. Leader-Rating Forms

C. During Dive Measures

- I. Checklist of Feelings
- II. Checklist Scales
- III. Checklist of Activities and Feelings
- IV. Order of Arising Form
- V. Meal Recording Form and Instructions
- VI. Location Recording Form and Instructions
- VII. In-Capsule Activity Count
- VIII. Night Watch Recording Form and Instructions

Appendix A
I. PERSONAL HISTORY BOOKLET

NAME (Print) ______________________ DATE __________

RATING/RANK/OCCUPATION ______________ AGE __________

SERVICE NUMBER __________ YEARS ACTIVE DUTY OR IN PRESENT OCCUPATION ______

FOR THE FOLLOWING QUESTIONS CIRCLE *ONE* NUMBER OR FILL IN APPROPRIATE SPACE

1. How many years of SCUBA or deep sea diving experience have you had? ________

2. What is the highest grade you completed in school?
   1. 9th grade
   2. 10th grade
   3. 11th grade
   4. Graduated high school
   5. 1 to 2 years college
   6. 3 to 4 years college
   7. Graduated college
   8. Master's degree
   9. Ph.D. or M.D. degree

3. What is your marital status?
   1. Single
   2. Married, no children
   3. Married, with children
   4. Divorced, remarried
   5. Separated
   6. Divorced

4. If ever married, what was your age at marriage?
   1. 17 years or less
   2. 18 years
   3. 19 years
   4. 20 years
   5. 21 years
   6. 22 years
   7. 23 years
   8. 24 years
   9. 25 years or older

5. What is your religious preference?
   1. Catholic
   2. Jewish
   3. Episcopalian
   4. Baptist
   5. Presbyterian
   6. Methodist
   7. Lutheran
   8. Other
   9. None

6. How often do you participate in organized worship?
   1. Weekly
   2. Once or twice a month
   3. Two or three times a year
   4. Not at all

7. Which of the following applies to your parents?
   1. Living together
   2. Separated
   3. Divorced
   4. Father deceased, mother living
   5. Mother deceased, father living
   6. Both deceased

8. If you have been without one or both of your parents, how old were you when you lost your first parent through either separation, divorce, or death?

1. 4 years old or less
2. 5 or 6 years old
3. 7 or 8 years old
4. 9 or 10 years old
5. 11 or 12 years old
6. 13 to 16 years old
7. 17 years or older

9. How many brothers do you have?_____

10. How many sisters do you have? ______

11. If you were not an only child, which of the following applied to you?
    1. Oldest child 2. Youngest child 3. Neither oldest nor youngest

12. Were you an adopted child? Yes_____ No_____

13. About how many times did your family move to new neighborhoods or towns while you were growing up?
    1. Never 2. Once 3. Twice 4. Three times 5. Four times 6. More than four times

14. In what size community did you spend most of your boyhood?
    1. Farm/ranch in country 2. Village under 5,000 3. Town 5,000 to 50,000 4. City 50,000 to 500,000 5. Large city over 500,000

15. How many times do you recall running away from home as a teenager (for more than a day)?
    1. Never 2. Once or twice 3. Three or four times 4. More than four times

16. How many times do you recall playing hookey from school as a teenager?
    1. Never 2. Once or twice 3. Three or four times 4. More than four times

17. Were you ever expelled from school? Yes_____ No_____

18. As a teenager, were you ever in trouble with juvenile authorities (not counting truant officer)?
    1. Never 2. Yes, once or twice 3. Yes, several times

19. As a teenager or an adult, have you ever received a traffic ticket for a moving vehicle violation?
    1. No. 2. Yes, once or twice 3. Yes, several times

20. As a teenager or an adult, have you ever been arrested for something other than a traffic violation?
    1. No 2. Yes, only once 3. Yes, more than once

20a. If you answered "yes" to Question 20, what was the nature of the offense or offenses and how long ago did they happen?

21. What was your father's (stepfather's) education?
    1. Less than 8th grade
    2. 8th or 9th grade completed
    3. 10th or 11th grade completed
    4. High school graduate
    5. Some college, non-graduate
    6. College graduate
    7. Postgraduate training

22. What was your mother's (stepmother's) education?
    1. Less than 8th grade
    2. 8th or 9th grade completed
    3. 10th or 11th grade completed
    4. High school graduate
    5. Some college, non-graduate
    6. College graduate
    7. Postgraduate training

23. What type of occupation was your father (stepfather) engaged in most of the time while you were growing up?
    1. A profession (law, medicine, teaching, etc.)
    2. Business management
    3. Clerical or sales
    4. Skilled trade
    5. Unskilled trade
    6. Farming or forestry
    7. Military service
    8. Unemployed
    9. Don't know
    10. Other____________

FOR THE FOLLOWING TWO QUESTIONS, *WRITE THE CODE NUMBER OF THE REGION*

24. In which region have you lived most of your life? ________________

25. In which region would you like most to live? ________________

REGION	*STATES*
1	Maine, New Hampshire, Vermont, Rhode Island, Connecticut, Massachusetts
2	New York, Pennsylvania, New Jersey, Delaware, Maryland, District of Columbia
3	Virginia, North Carolina, South Carolina, Florida, Georgia, Alabama, Mississippi, Louisiana
4	West Virginia, Kentucky, Tennessee, Arkansas, Missouri
5	Ohio, Michigan, Indiana, Illinois, Wisconsin
6	Iowa, Minnesota, North Dakota, South Dakota, Nebraska, Kansas
7	Texas, Oklahoma, New Mexico, Arizona
8	Colorado, Idaho, Montana, Nevada, Utah, Wyoming
9	California, Oregon, Washington, Alaska, Hawaii
10	Other

FOR THE NEXT TWENTY ITEMS, PLACE A (+) MARK NEXT TO THOSE WHICH *YOU LIKE TO DO VERY MUCH* AND PLACE A (-) MARK NEXT TO THOSE *YOU DISLIKE VERY MUCH*

___ 26. Building models
___27. Working on radio gear
___28. Listening to classical music
___29. Riding motorcycles
___30. Going to dramas, plays
___31. Listening to popular music
___32. Painting, drawing
___33. Participating in individual sports
___34. Reading magazines
___35. Listening to hillbilly music
___36. Collecting stamps
___37. Hunting and fishing
___38. Participating in team sports
___39. Repairing things
___40. Reading books
___41. Hiking and camping
___42. Going to movies
___43. Working on hot-rods
___44. Photography
___45. Playing cards

(IF YOU NEITHER STRONGLY LIKE NOR STRONGLY DISLIKE ANY OF THE ABOVE ITEMS, MAKE *NO* MARK NEXT TO THOSE ITEMS.)

46a.(CIVILIAN) Have you ever served in the Armed Forces? __________ Branch_____ Years_____

46b.(MILITARY) Have you ever left the service for 90 days or more to take other employment?
1. No 2. Yes, once 3. Yes, more than once

47. Do you consider your speed of advancement in your occupation to be:
1. Above average 2. Average 3. Below average

48. In general, how do you feel about your present occupation?
1. I am strongly dedicated to a career in my present field.
2. I enjoy my present job, but am not sure about a career in it.
3. I don't really enjoy my job, but it's about as good as any other.
4. I look forward to getting into another occupational field soon.

49. Why did you volunteer for the Sealab project? ______________

____

50. Have you ever applied for underwater demolition training, the submarine service, Antarctic duty, or other special programs? Specify program and the year you applied:

____

51. What was your last assignment before you joined Sealab? (Where did you work and what did you do?)

____

____

52. Briefly describe your special role in the Sealab project. (What particular tasks will you have during the submersion period?)

____

____

53. What are the most critical problems you expect to face during the period of submersion in Sealab II?

____

____

54. Briefly describe yourself as a person and some of your major goals in life:

____

____

____

II. OPINION SURVEY–PERSONALITY SCALES

Instructions

Place the *number* that indicates how much you agree with each statement in the appropriate space on the answer sheet. For example, if you "agree moderately" with the first statement in the booklet, you would place a *2* in the space for Item 1 below. If you "disagree slightly" with the second statement, you would place a *4* on the answer sheet after Item 2, and so on.

1. Agree strongly	4. Disagree slightly
2. Agree moderately	5. Disagree moderately
3. Agree slightly	6. Disagree strongly

The items were scored so that a *low* score represents agreement with the scale items.

Scale I
Achievement Motivation

1. I like to assume total responsibility for things.
2. I like to stick to a job when everyone else has given up on it.
3. When I fail in a task, I usually double my efforts and try again.
4. I like to keep working on a problem until it is completely solved.
5. The harder the job, the better I like it.
6. The type of problem I like best is that which is almost impossible to do.

Scale II
Autonomy

1. I like to do things my own way, even though they turn out badly.
2. I like to criticize people who are in a position of authority.
3. It bothers me when someone tries to tell me what to do.
4. Once I have made up my mind, no one can change it for me.
5. I prefer to do things my own way without regard to what others may think.
6. I like to be able to come and go as I please.
7. I like to feel free to do what I want to do.
8. I like to disregard rules that I consider to be unjust.

Scale III
Succorance

1. I like people who try to cheer you up when you're feeling depressed.
2. I like people to show concern for how I'm getting along.
3. I like other people to tell me how well I've done a difficult job.
4. I like for people to offer help when I'm having difficulty.
5. I enjoy being with the type of person who always tries to be sympathetic.
6. I enjoy being with people who go out of their way to do things for you.
7. I like people to express their sympathy when I am sick.

Scale IV
Compulsivity

1. Any written work that I do I like to have precise, neat, and well-organized.
2. I like to keep records of continuous routine details or events.
3. I like to keep an accurate and up to date record of my personal expenses.
4. I often recopy notes or records in order to make them neater.
5. I like to maintain a filing system for my personal papers.
6. I can't stand leaving something only half done.

Scale V
Need for Activity

1. I usually need more work to keep me busy.
2. I am often very bored.
3. I usually find myself in need of something to do in my spare time.
4. Time passed too slowly to suit me in my last job.
5. I often wish for more excitement.

Scale VI
Harm Avoidance

1. At times I have been somewhat afraid of the dark.
2. I would probably be apprehensive if I were alone in an empty house at night.
3. I have avoided passing through certain city districts for fear of being assaulted.
4. Sometimes I fear that I may be injured in an accident.
5. I would be a little afraid if challenged to a fight.
6. I fear certain things such as lightning, high places, rough water, horseback riding, flying, etc.
7. I am sometimes conscious of a vague fear of death.
8. I am afraid of physical pain.
9. Sometimes I have experienced a fear that I might be attacked by someone.

Scale VII
Maturity Scale

(A high score on this scale represents maturity)

1. I get a kick out of keeping people in the dark as to my next move.
2. Since I can't do anything about public affairs, I am not very interested in them.
3.* I dislike guys who are always breaking the rules.
4. I wouldn't mind being feared by other people, if I thought that they respected me.
5.* I enjoy influencing people.
6. I take a lot of chances in driving.
7. I think if given a fair chance I would make a good leader.
8.* At times I have felt I would be a good commissioned officer.
9.* I like to give orders and get things moving.
10. Compromising with others with a different religion or ideals is the same as lowering your own standards.
11. There is a good type and a bad type that almost all people can be separated into.
12.* In most groups that I am in, I usually handle some of the leadership responsibility.
13. If someone does something nice for me, I usually wonder if there is a hidden reason.

*Scoring reversed.

14. A man who leaves himself open for it deserves to be taken advantage of.
15. One person is just as likely to get into trouble as another because it is the breaks that count.

Scale VIII
Delinquency Scale

1.* I think I am stricter about right and wrong than most people.
2.* I often think about how I look and what impression I am making upon others.
3. I never cared much for school.
4. When I meet a stranger, I often think that he is better than I am.
5.* I have never done any heavy drinking.
6.* My table manners are not quite as good at home as when I am in company.
7. I have used alcohol excessively.
8. I often act on the spur of the moment without stopping to think.
9. I often feel that I made the wrong choice in my occupation.
10.* Most of the time I feel happy.
11. Life usually hands me a raw deal.
12. Sometimes I used to feel that I would like to leave home.
13. A person is better off if he doesn't trust anyone.
14. My parents never really understood me.
15. I never worry about my looks.
16.* I hardly ever get excited or thrilled.
17.* I have never been in trouble with the law.
18.* I keep out of trouble at all costs.
19. When I was going to school, I played hookey quite often.
20.* I get pretty discouraged with the law when a smart lawyer gets a criminal free.
21. With things going as they are, it's pretty hard to keep up hope of amounting to something.
22.* The members of my family were always very close to each other.
23. As a youngster in school I used to give the teachers lots of trouble.
24. I sometimes wanted to run away from home.
25. I have had more than my share of things to worry about.
26. I used to steal sometimes when I was a youngster.

---

*Scoring reversed.

III. ADJECTIVE CHECKLIST

Name:______________________________Date: _______________

Listed below are some personal characteristics which you might or might not like in the type of man you would choose as a close friend. Place a number from the scale below next to each characteristic to indicate approximately how much you would like to have that characteristic apply to a close friend.

Not At All			Somewhat			Very Much	
1	2	3	4	5	6	7	8

Example 1: _7_ CALM
Example 2: _2_ SARCASTIC

Example 1 indicates that CALM is a characteristic very much preferred in a close friend while Example 2 indicates that SARCASTIC is not at all liked as a characteristic. Choose the number on the scale that best represents your feeling toward each characteristic.

1. ___INDUSTRIOUS
2. ___TACTFUL
3. ___CONSERVATIVE
4. ___PUNCTUAL
5. ___SOCIABLE
6. ___THEORETICAL
7. ___AMBITIOUS
8. ___ORDERLY
9. ___THRIFTY
10. ___DIGNIFIED
11. ___ATHLETIC
12. ___ALERT
13. ___COMMONPLACE
14. ___SENTIMENTAL
15. ___CONFIDING
16. ___APOLOGETIC
17. ___CAUTIOUS
18. ___PRACTICAL
19. ___ADVENTUROUS
20. ___UNINHIBITED
21. ___OPTIMISTIC
22. ___TOUGH
23. ___CHANGEABLE
24. ___STUDIOUS
25. ___REBELLIOUS
26. ___PERSERVERING
27. ___WARM
28. ___MORALISTIC
29. ___TIDY
30. ___SELF-CONFIDENT
31. ___FLEXIBLE
32. ___SYMPATHETIC
33. ___HUMOROUS
34. ___TALKATIVE
35. ___CURIOUS
36. ___ASSERTIVE
37. ___IDEALISTIC
38. ___ARTISTIC
39. ___SHREWD
40. ___FRANK
41. ___EFFICIENT
42. ___ARGUMENTATIVE
43. ___EDUCATED
44. ___HOSTILE
45. ___CONFORMING
46. ___PRAISING
47. ___COMPETITIVE
48. ___FORMAL
49. ___SHY
50. ___GENEROUS

Appendix B
I. CHOICES OF LEADER AND TEAM MATES

Name ______________________________

Suppose you were allowed to choose the *leader* for your SeaLab II crew. Please list below, in order, the five men you would choose as most desirable as a leader. (You may include among your choices any of the men trained and qualified for participation in SeaLab II. Do not restrict your choices to the ten men in your team if you would prefer to have someone else.)

1. ______________________________
2. ______________________________
3. ______________________________
4. ______________________________
5. ______________________________

Again, suppose you were allowed to choose the other members of the SeaLab II crew. Please list below, in order, the five men that you would most like to have along. (Again, you may include men not on your team. Also, you may repeat all, any, or none of the men already listed above as your choice for leader.)

1. ______________________________
2. ______________________________
3. ______________________________
4. ______________________________
5. ______________________________

II. CHOICES OF LEADER AND TEAM MATES

Name ______________________________

Suppose you were taking part in another undersea experiment. Please list below the five men, in order, whom you would choose as most desirable as crew leader for that experiment. (You may include among your choices any of the men trained and qualified for participation in SeaLab II. Do not restrict your choice to the ten men in your team if you would prefer to have someone else.)

1. ________________ 4. ________________
2. ________________ 5. ________________
3. ________________

Now please list, in order, the five crew men you would most like to have along in another undersea experiment. (Again, you may include men not on your team. Also, you may repeat all, any, or none of the men already listed above as your choice for leader.)

1. ____________________ 4. ____________________
2. ____________________ 5. ____________________
3. ____________________

III. LEADER-RATING FORMS

SEALAB II TEAM______

Rating as a Diver

____________________'s overall competence and performance as a diver were:

/__________/__________/__________/
Fair Good Very Good Excellent

(The above sentence and scale were repeated nine times on a form with the name of each of the nine divers on each leader's team being inserted in the blanks.)

SEALAB II TEAM______

Rating on Common Work

____________________'s willingness to do his share or more of the common work was:

/__________/__________/__________/
Fair Good Very Good Excellent

(The above sentence and scale were repeated nine times on a form with the name of each of the nine divers on each leader's team being inserted in the blanks.)

Appendix C
I. CHECKLIST OF FEELINGS

Name____

Below is a list of words describing different kinds of moods and feelings. Indicate how each word applies to how you feel NORMALLY, by placing a number in the blank next to the word. If a word describes a feeling *not at all* characteristic of you normally, place a *1* in the blank. If the word describes a feeling *somewhat or slightly* characteristic of you normally, place a *2* in the blank. Finally if the word describes a feeling *mostly or generally* characteristic of you normally, place a *3* in the blank. Remember for each word place a 1, 2, or 3 in the blank, according to whether the feeling described is (1) not at all, (2) somewhat or slightly, or (3) mostly or generally characteristic of you normally. Please work rapidly, but do not leave any spaces blank.

1 = NOT AT ALL   2 = SOMEWHAT OR SLIGHTLY   3 = MOSTLY OR GENERALLY

___ 1. Low
___ 2. Lively
___ 3. Irritated
___ 4. Grief stricken
___ 5. Restless
___ 6. Contented
___ 7. Active
___ 8. Leisurely
___ 9. Wonderful
___10. Impatient
___11. Lighthearted
___12. Mean
___13. Weary
___14. Apprehensive
___15. Mad
___16. Calm
___17. Blue
___18. Panicky
___19. Terrified
___20. Burned up
___21. Sorrowful
___22. Boiling mad
___23. Steady
___24. Overjoyed
___25. Sarcastic
___26. Afraid
___27. Happy
___28. Miserable
___29. Alarmed
___30. Hostile
___31. Quiet
___32. Lazy
___33. Drowsy
___34. Downcast
___35. Pleased
___36. Satisfied
___37. Depressed
___38. Solemn
___39. Energetic
___40. Cheerful
___41. Uneasy
___42. Lonely
___43. Grouchy
___44. Sluggish
___45. Vigorous
___46. Hopping mad
___47. Desperate
___48. Joyful
___49. Indignant
___50. Alert
___51. Angry
___52. Timid
___53. Raging
___54. Scared Stiff
___55. Annoyed
___56. Fearful
___57. Despairing
___58. Top of the world
___59. Sad
___60. Refreshed
___61. Fine
___62. Hopeless
___63. Insecure
___64. Jittery
___65. Indifferent
___66. Inactive
___67. Good

II. MOOD CHECKLIST SCALES

Instructions

Below is a list of words describing different kinds of moods and feelings. Indicate how characteristic each word is of how you feel TODAY by placing a 1, 2 or 3 in the blank before each word.

1 = NOT AT ALL 2 = SOMEWHAT OR SLIGHTLY 3 = MOSTLY OR GENERALLY

Mood Scales

I - *Anger*

1. Raging
2. Boiling Mad
3. Angry
4. Mad
5. Grouchy
6. Irritated
7. Impatient
8. Hopping mad
9. Burned up
10. Hostile
11. Mean
12. Indignant
13. Sarcastic
14. Annoyed

II - *Happiness*

1. On top of the world
2. Wonderful
3. Joyful
4. Fine
5. Good
6. Pleased
7. Calm
8. Overjoyed
9. Cheerful
10. Happy
11. Lighthearted
12. Satisfied
13. Contented
14. Quiet

III - *Fear*

1. Terrified
2. Desperate
3. Fearful
4. Alarmed
5. Jittery
6. Apprehensive
7. Indifferent
8. Scared Stiff
9. Panicky
10. Afraid
11. Insecure
12. Uneasy
13. Timid

IV - *Depression*

1. Grief-stricken
2. Miserable
3. Sorrowful
4. Lonely
5. Blue
6. Sad
7. Solemn
8. Hopeless
9. Depressed
10. Despairing
11. Downcast
12. Low

V - *Psychological Well-being*

1. Energetic
2. Lively
3. Refreshed
4. Vigorous
5. Alert
6. Steady
7. Restless
8. Active

VI - *Lethargy*

1. Leisurely
2. Drowsy
3. Lazy
4. Weary
5. Sluggish
6. Inactive

III. CHECKLIST OF ACTIVITIES AND FEELINGS

NAME________________________________DATE________________

A. *Sleep*

1. I went to bed at ______hrs. last night.
2. I got up at ______hrs. this morning.
3. How well did you sleep? (Check one)

___Very restlessly ___Somewhat restlessly ___So So ___Quite well ___Very well

4. I was up during the night ______times.

B. *Eating*

5. Did you eat breakfast? _____Yes _____No
6. (If yes) How well did you enjoy your breakfast? Did you feel it was: (Check one)

   _____Excellent _____Good _____Fair _____Poor _____Terrible

7. Did you eat lunch? ______Yes ______No
8. (If Yes) How well did you enjoy your lunch? Did you feel it was: (Check one)

   _____Excellent _____Good _____Fair _____Poor _____Terrible

9. Did you eat dinner? ______Yes ______No
10. (If Yes) How well did you enjoy your dinner? Did you feel it was: (Check one)

    _____Excellent _____Good _____Fair _____Poor _____Terrible

C. *Free time activities*

How much time today did you spend on each of the following activities?

11. Reading ______________
12. Conversation ______________
13. Watching TV ______________
14. Looking out portholes ______
15. Writing letters ______________
16. Playing cards, games, etc. ______
17. Drawing ______________
18. Studying ______________
19. Other ______________
(Please specify)
20. Other ______________
(Please specify)
21. How many hours of free time did you have today? ______________

IV. ORDER OF ARISING FORM

Instructions

Try to determine the order in which the men come through the door from the bunk area. Record this information below. Under "Comments," indicate whether the man is enthusiastic or lackadaisical about starting the day's activities. Try to describe the first thing he does when he comes into view.

Day __________ Time __________ Recorder's name ______________________

Numbers of men on watch ______ ______

Other men up 30 minutes or more before reveille ____ ____ ____ ____

Order	*Man No.*	*Time*	*Comments*
1	____	____	______________________
2	____	____	______________________
3	____	____	______________________
4	____	____	______________________
5	____	____	______________________
6	____	____	______________________
7	____	____	______________________
8	____	____	______________________
9	____	____	______________________
10	____	____	______________________

V. MEAL RECORDING FORM

1. Day__________ 2. Name of Recorder________________

3. Meal ______________
4. Time preparation began ______________
5. Men scheduled to prepare _____ _____
6. Men who did main preparation _____ _____
7. Others who assisted_____ _____ _____ _____ _____
8. Time serving began ______________
9. Order of serving____ ____ ____ ____ ____ ____ ____
____ ____ ____ ____

10. Comments on order of serving____________________
____

11. Location of men while eating (See Location Recording Form)
____

Disposition ot the group in general while eating?

12. Activity ____ 13. Tension ____ 14. Mood ____ 15. Appetite ____

Men who react markedly different from the group.

16. No. _____ 17. Variable _____ 18. Reaction _____
No. _____ Variable _____ Reaction _____
No. _____ Variable _____ Reaction _____
No. _____ Variable _____ Reaction _____
No. _____ Variable _____ Reaction _____
No. _____ Variable _____ Reaction _____
No. _____ Variable _____ Reaction _____
No. _____ Variable _____ Reaction _____
No. _____ Variable _____ Reaction _____
No. _____ Variable _____ Reaction _____
No. _____ Variable _____ Reaction _____
No. _____ Variable _____ Reaction _____

19. Man who did main clean-up _____ _____
20. Others who assisted _____ _____ _____ _____
21. Time clean-up completed ______________
22. Comments on clean-up ____________________
____

23. Did any of the men begin eating after most of the others were finished or nearly finished? _____Yes _____No

24. (If Yes) Indicate the numbers of such men and possible reasons for their eating late below:

Man	*Comment*
______	________________________________
______	________________________________
______	________________________________
______	________________________________

Instructions - Meal Recording Form

Numbers below refer to numbers on *Meal Recording Form.*

3. Use letters in recording: B = Breakfast; L = Lunch; D = Dinner.

4. At what time did you notice the first signs of meal preparation? Could be putting on a chef's hat, putting on water to boil, going to refrigerator, etc.

5., 6., 7. Men on watch are scheduled to prepare the meal. You should know who they are. Put their numbers in blanks following 5. It may be relatively easy or difficult to determine who actually does the main preparation if many men participate. Be prepared to discuss this problem after observing a few meals.

8., 9., 10. There may not be a regular chow line but there should be some sort of announcement indicating that "Soup's on." Watch for it. Get at least first few and last few men in line if order becomes confused. Indicate in response to 10. how orderly the chow line was.

11. Wait until all men have been served or serve themselves. Then record the position of each man within the capsule while he is eating. In case all men do not come to chow, or if they eat in shifts, record the data on location after about a five-minute break in serving, i.e., a period of five minutes during which no one has been served and most of the men are eating. You will probably have to exercise judgment on this. The notion is to record position during eating after the meal has begun for as many men as it "reasonably" appears will be eating that meal. Record "late" eaters under 23. and 24.

12. - 18. The idea here is to try to characterize the group atmosphere during the meal and to pick up any notable deviations from it. Observe as much of the group as possible during the meal. About the time the first man is finished, these recordings should be made. Items 12 - 15 are a series of 7-point judgmental scales. In each blank you will record a number from 1 to 7. The numbers applying are indicated below:

12. Activity: During this meal the group was:

1	2	3	4	5	6	7
Lively						Subdued

13. Tension: During this meal the group appeared:

1	2	3	4	5	6	7
Tense						Relaxed

14. Mood: During this meal the group appeared:

1	2	3	4	5	6	7
Happy						Sad

15. Appetite: The meal was eaten:

1	2	3	4	5	6	7
Listlessly						Heartily

On items 16. - 18., record information on any of the men who seem to depart from a fairly distinct group norm. For example, if most of the group is laughing and happy during the meal but one or two men are sitting glumly in a corner, indicate this as follows: In the blanks following 16, indicate the number(s) of the deviate(s); in the blanks following 17, write "14", indicating that they deviated in mood; and in blanks following 18, write "6" or "7", indicating that they appeared unhappy. In general, if a man appears to deviate four or more points from the group norm on any of these variables, record the information under items 16 - 18.

19. - 21. Comments for 6. - 8.

22. Try to assess whether clean-up was conducted with dispatch and business like manner or in a sloppy and haphazard way. Was the galley left shipshape for the next crew, etc.?

23. If men eat late, is this because they were out of the capsule at the time the meal started? Were there other logical reasons? Or why did they eat late?

VI. LOCATION RECORDING FORM

Day__________Time__________Observer____________________

F	
L	R

B	
L	R

Comments

Man	Out	In O. C.	Activity	Tension	Mood	What's he doing?

Location Recording Form Instructions

When: Every half hour, five minutes after the half hour beginning at 0805 and continuing through until taps at 2200. Delete comments at meal times but do make recordings of locations at meal times on this form.

Procedure: Immediately after writing the day, time, and your name on the top of the page, make a record of the location of each man in the capsule and in view of the camera (s). Do this as quickly as possible. Record this information in the two boxes labelled F (front) and B (back). Make a circle for each man with the man's number in the circle. "Front" is the part of the capsule nearest the exit hatch. "Back" is nearest the bunking area. Left and right orientations are taken from a view from the exit hatch area. Thus, if you are viewing a picture from the camera looking toward the exit area, right and left will be reversed. If a man is moving from one area to another at the time you make the record, try to indicate where he was when you began. If this is not possible, indicate where he was when you finished recording this part of the data.

Fill out the spaces below, beginning with the man's number. Next, the status of men not recorded above, either a check mark for men out of the capsule or a mark for a man in the capsule who is off camera. For the Off cameras, use these symbols: B = Bunk area, E = Exit area, or D.K. = Don't know where the man was. For Activity, Tension, and Mood, use the 1 to 7 scales in the Meal Recording Form Instructions. Use the number 8 if your view of the man is so poor that you cannot determine his activity, tension, or mood.

Under "What's he doing?", be brief but ingeniously creative. Notations in this category may range from the very general to the specific. Try to be as specific as possible. Following are some possible comments. "21 (man no.) taking blood pressure on 5 (man no.). " "13 on watch talking to topside." The above are not meant to be exhaustive but illustrative only. We'll have to see what we can come up with here as we go along.

VII. FORM 019 *** IN-CAPSULE ACTIVITY COUNT

Time: Eight times per day at the following times for one-half hour per measurement.

Record the number of times each man moves on and off camera two.

S # Team ____________ DTG ____________

	ON Camera	OFF Camera	Total
0	______	______	____
1	______	______	____
2	______	______	____
3	______	______	____
4	______	______	____
5	______	______	____
6	______	______	____
7	______	______	____
8	______	______	____
9	______	______	____

Note: If a man is in the capsule throughout the recording period but makes no change of position enter zeroes. If a man is out of the capsule for any portion of the period, leave the spaces blank.

VIII. NIGHT WATCH RECORDING FORM

Time	*Man*	*Comments*
2215		
2230		
2245		
2300		
2315		
2350		
2345		
2400		
0015		
0030		
0045		
0100		
0115		
0130		
0145		
0200		
0215		
0230		
0245		
0300		
0315		
0330		
0345		
0400		
0415		
0430		
0445		
0500		
0515		
0530		
0545		

0600 ______ ______________________________

0615 ______ ______________________________

____

0630 ______ ______________________________

____

0645 ______ ______________________________

____

0700 ______ ______________________________

____

Night Watch Form Instructions

This is a simple log to be kept throughout the night watch hours. Taps are scheduled at 2200 and Reveille at 0700. Thus, the only man up between 2200 and 0700 should be the man on watch. However, some men may retire late or get up early. Therefore, you have two lines on which to make comments between 2200 and 2300 and 0600 and 0700.

Comments should apply to activity during the previous 15 minutes. If other men do stay up beyond 2200, note who they are and when they go to bed. Do they appear to stay up to keep watch stander company or not? Record watch stander's level of activity. Does he pace the floor or sit in one chair? Does he read, write, or just sit? Does he communicate with topside only on business or for social reasons in addition? Does any one get up at any time? Does the relief come on duty on time? Note any conversation between relief and man going off duty. In general, be alert for and record differences between behavior of various watch men.

INDEX